THE

THE

An interdisciplinary series edited by
faculty at the University of Illinois

BOOKS IN THE SERIES

Wildlife and People: The Human Dimensions of Wildlife Ecology
Gary G. Gray

Sustainable Agriculture in the American Midwest: Lessons from the Past, Prospects for the Future
Edited by Gregory McIsaac and William R. Edwards

Green Nature/Human Nature: The Meaning of Plants in Our Lives
Charles A. Lewis

Justice and the Earth: Images for Our Planetary Survival
Eric T. Freyfogle

Agricultural Biotechnology and the Environment: Science, Policy, and Social Issues
Sheldon Krimsky and Roger P. Wrubel

A Wider View of the Universe: Henry Thoreau's Study of Nature
Robert Kuhn McGregor

A Wider View of the Universe

A Wider View

UNIVERSITY OF ILLINOIS PRESS · URBANA AND CHICAGO

HENRY THOREAU'S
STUDY OF NATURE

A Wider View of the Universe

ROBERT KUHN McGREGOR

The photograph "Fog from Nawshawtuct, Concord, Massachusetts, August 23, 1900" appears on pp. iv–v courtesy of the Herbert W. Gleason Collection.

Manufactured in the United States of America

1 2 3 4 5 C P 5 4 3 2 1

This book is printed on acid-free paper.

Library of Congress Cataloging-in-Publication Data
McGregor, Robert Kuhn, 1952–
A wider view of the universe : Henry Thoreau's study of nature / Robert Kuhn McGregor.
p. cm. — (The environment and the human condition)
Includes bibliographical references and index.
ISBN 0-252-02318-8 (alk. paper). — ISBN 0-252-06620-0 (pbk. : alk. paper)
1. Thoreau, Henry David, 1817–1862—Knowledge—Natural history.
2. Nature in literature. 3. Natural history—United States—History—19th century. 4. Ecology in literature. I. Title. II. Series.
PS3057.N3M28 1997
818'.309—dc21 96-45799
CIP

To Deborah Elizabeth Kuhn McGregor,
who consistently demonstrates the union
of the material and the spirit.

The poet says the proper study
of mankind is man—
I say study to forget all that—
take wider views of the universe.

—HENRY DAVID THOREAU
Journal, April 2, 1852

Contents

Acknowledgments

RESEARCH INTO THE LIFE and work of Henry David Thoreau is both a difficult and an arresting task. Little known or appreciated in his time, Thoreau inspired few contemporary remembrances. Apart from the vast corpus of his own work, very little of which was truly autobiographical, he left few traces for later biographers and analysts. Several scholars have had to dig very hard for the information on Thoreau's daily existence currently available. I would especially like to acknowledge the labors of Walter Harding, J. Lyndon Shanley, Linck Johnson, and Robert Sattelmeyer, who have done so much to restore Thoreau's world to our sight. Without their work, this book would have been very nearly impossible to contemplate, much less complete.

I wish to thank Dr. Harding and the anonymous readers chosen by the University of Illinois Press for their thoughtful critiques of this manuscript. George Hendrick and John Tallmadge also provided incisive and heartwarming readings of this work, just when I needed them most.

So much of my interpretation rests on the content of Thoreau's *Journals.* I salute the extraordinary effort of Bradford Torrey and Francis H. Allen to produce a true facsimile of the *Journal* in 1906, when strict adherence to original documents was not regarded as a virtue. The more recent efforts of Elizabeth H. Witherell, Leonard N. Neufeldt, Nancy Craig Simmons, Joseph Moldenhauer, William Howarth, and the remaining editors of the Princeton Edition have nevertheless produced a gold mine of further material, especially for the years 1837–49. There is a special joy in reading the original Walden journals.

By editing Thoreau's "Dispersion of Seeds" manuscript and seeing it through publication as *Faith in a Seed,* Bradley P. Dean probably saved my eyesight. Anyone wishing to understand Thoreau's work after 1850 (including *Walden*) must read this work.

At a more personal level, I received help from all sides in committing my ideas about Thoreau to paper. Money for research was critical, of course. A grant from the American Council of Learned Societies sustained several days of profitable archival work back east, while grant programs at the University of Illinois at Springfield supported both travel and long bouts of reading and writing.

Early motivation for this work came from Carolyn Merchant, who included my initial thoughts on Thoreau in her text, *Major Problems in Environmental History.* Thomas Blanding, regarded by many in Concord as the greatest of the current Thoreau scholars, read early versions of manuscript chapters and offered perceptive encouragement.

In the gathering of materials, especially the unusual and out-of-the-way, Mrs. Marcia Moss, curator at the Concord Free Library, was extremely supportive and helpful. Edmund Schofield, Director of the Thoreau Country Conservation Alliance, brought me up to date on recent efforts to save Walden woods. David Wood of the Concord Antiquarian Society went to extra trouble to provide access to Thoreau's own copies of Oriental scriptural works (willed to Emerson and still a part of his library).

Among the UIS community, several people lent moral and material support. Larry Shiner, Norman Hinton, and Deborah McGregor read early portions of the manuscript; Ethan Lewis taught me much about literary point of view; William Bloemer and Suzy Langellier guided me through the bureacratic maze; Mary Brancado and Julie Atwell exhibited extraordinary secretarial patience. Three graduate students, Brenda Griffin, Barbara Peebles, and Stacy McDermott, assisted with tracking down references and computer analysis of census materials.

At home, my family kept life from ever becoming dull. Deborah, Molly, Leaf, Blue, Janna, and Bran all know what I mean. Very occasionally, something resembling an academic life broke out.

Finally, there is my editor, Karen Hewitt, who used to think there was no such thing as a stupid question, and my copy editor, Louis Simon, whose careful editing was always sensitive to the life of the original work.

I truly thank you all.

A Wider View of the Universe

I had no idea that there was so much going on in Heywood's Meadow.

—*Journal,* May 1850

INTRODUCTION

BY JUNE OF EACH YEAR, nature in Concord, Massachusetts, had largely spent the turbulent energies of springtime. Rivers and meadows resumed the placid aspect that had inspired the Algonkian name for the valley: "Musketaquid." Quiet water. Dead water.

The violent agitation that disturbed the small pool in Heywood's Meadow in the spring of 1850 was strange, then. In this small, marshy tributary to the Sudbury River, there came a repeated commotion of writhing life, roiling the surface and setting off ripples that rebounded from the edges of the pool. All else was quiet. The cattails, the false pimpernel, the swamp candles surrounding the basin stood motionless in the sunshine. The pipes rooted in the muddy bottom swayed gently with the ripples. One after another, three muskrats swam past, seemingly attracted to the commotion. The splashing abruptly ceased.

Henry Thoreau, thirty-two-year-old poet, writer, and transcendentalist, was exploring the swampy meadowlands lying between Walden Pond and Fair Haven Bay that May afternoon. Attracted by the tumult, Thoreau followed the lead of the muskrats, covertly investigating "that insignificant pool." After a prolonged period of quiet observation, he removed shoes and socks, waded into the pool, and with a sudden effort heaved a large mud turtle up onto the shore. The thrash had been the death struggle of a large horned pout, caught unawares from beneath and still held by the turtle.

Recording the incident as an undated entry in his journal, Thoreau fashioned a minor moral tale—the fish so unaware of the monstrous dangers lurking in the mud below. Yet, he was careful to record the natural history of the event in exacting detail, noting the vegetation, the lay of the land, the activities of pout and turtle. Mud turtles live almost wholly in the water. This one had buried itself to its eyes in the bottom mud to await unsuspecting prey. The pout was a likely candidate. A bottom scavenger, horned pouts preferred weedy waters such as the Heywood Pool. As the fish swam overhead, seeking its own food, the turtle suddenly attacked. Emerging from a cloud of mud, ironlike turtle jaws clamped onto the pale underside. In less than a minute, the pout was dead and partially consumed.[1]

A Concord spring bore witness to countless such small dramas of survival, as myriad species of life began new patterns of activity. The turtle was not long from hibernation; the pout was perhaps preparing to nest. The horned pout's own intended prey—bottom-dwelling insect larvae and mollusks—were beginning new cycles of life as well. A freshly sprouted generation of plants provided the backdrop for the incident. The semi-aquatic pipes and the edge-dwelling cattails and swamp candles were perennials, growing new stems and leaves after surviving the winter living in the damp soil. The annual false pimpernel was starting fresh, growing from seeds manufactured by the flowers of 1849. And the pool itself was newly remade, a product of climatic and hydrological forces renewed each spring.[2]

Turtle, fish, insect, mollusk, plants, the pool; one small predatory incident encapsulated so much of the history of the Concord meadows. Each had followed its own peculiar path to arrive at the condition particular to that day in late spring. Each played an indispensable part in the drama. And on this particular day, there was one thing more, a critical ingredient that transformed this tiny example of natural selection into a page of history. Henry Thoreau was there to observe, to investigate, to try to find the meaning in a mud turtle's lunch.

Thoreau himself was at a critical juncture in that spring of 1850. He was in the process, perhaps consciously, of shedding a multiplicity of roles, of focusing his thoughts and researches on the themes that would enable him, in ten years' time, to develop a unique vision of the natural world. Through 1849, he had been a struggling writer dividing his time among subjects as diverse as domestic economy, civil politics, literary criticism, and historical biography. By 1860, he was applying himself almost exclusively to nature study, and was in the process of laying down the fundamental principles describing the interactions that govern the natural whole. Discovering that every aspect of nature had a value completely independent of human notions of worth, he had determined to deny humanity its traditional place as the pinnacle of creation. Thoreau by then firmly understood that people were nothing more than component parts, equals of all the other parts in a large and complex natural community. Almost by himself, Henry Thoreau was inventing what we now call the principle of biocentrism and the science of ecology.

The years 1849 and 1850 were a critical watershed in Henry Thoreau's life. Ringed with disappointments, haunted by disillusion, he in these years undertook a painful process of reevaluation. In the end he would discard much. The biographies, the literary and classical studies, the poetry that had consumed so much of his time in the previous decade would diminish in importance. Yet the creative energies that had sustained him would, if anything, increase in intensity. More importantly, Thoreau now concentrated those energies far more exclusively on a single topic: the study of nature. In five years' time, Henry Thoreau became an expert botanist, a skillful and observant zoologist, and a keen student of the geological, hydrological, and meteorological forces that shaped the face of nature in Concord. Further, he honed the craft of writing to communicate as fully as possible the vision of nature that his explorations inspired. Before 1850, Thoreau had written in praise of nature, but only after that date did he truly begin to understand it.

For environmentalists, the attraction of Henry Thoreau is due in large measure to the voice, at once analytical and poetic, which he breathed into the description of nature. Reading his journal, his later essays, and *Walden,* the reader senses the confidence of the artist speaking from a radical environmental perspective and drawing from a broad and deep fund of exacting ecological knowledge. That very effect raises a series of fundamental questions about the author. Just what was Thoreau's ecological vision of nature? What were the intellectual elements of this vision, and how did he derive them? And why did he set out to do this?

Henry David Thoreau's literary legacy has done much to obscure the answers to these questions. The man himself is in part responsible. Many of our impressions of Thoreau's life in the 1840s come from his description of himself living in that cabin near the pond. Yet large portions of *Walden* were written after 1850, written in the period in which he began to devote his attention far more fully to nature's behavior. In *Walden,* Thoreau essentially reinvented himself, creating a character far more familiar with nature's ways than the historical Thoreau who actually lived in the woods for two years, two months, and two days. This drastic self-reinterpretation clouded the genius of his transformation in the later period. He conveyed the notion that he had always known and understood nature far more thoroughly than most human beings. This simply was not true.

Equally unclear to most casual readers is the depth of his ecological vision. A reading of *Walden, The Maine Woods,* his later nature essays, and portions of his journals reveals an author who studied nature avidly, learned an incredible array of minutia, and got it down on paper exceedingly well. Yet, excepting the minor glimpse provided in his essay "On the Succession of Forest Trees," the impression is that Thoreau's nature study was essentially for descriptive purposes. Observation and analysis seem to be in the service of a writer, rather than a naturalist. This impression, also false, is the product of Thoreau's untimely death and the maltreatment of his last unedited manuscripts by his literary executors.

By the late 1850s, Thoreau was hard at work on a series of phenological charts and long essays drawing together an analysis of much of the "undigested" nature observations recorded in his journals during the previous ten years. The works included a wider ranging study of forest succession, a consideration of the behavior of wild fruits, and an investigation into the role of wind, weather, and animals in the dispersion of wild seeds. In effect, Thoreau was attempting in these studies to discover the interrelationships among species, the mutual dependencies that made nature work. These books, if completed, would be currently recognized as pioneering works in the field of ecology.[3]

The work was never finished. Thoreau in fact caught the cold that plunged him into his final bout with tuberculosis while doing field research on his forest succession project (he was counting tree rings in the dead of winter). After his death, his finished essays and books all found publication. As America slowly caught up with his genius, his journals too came into print. Not so with the ecological material. Divided, scattered across the landscape, partially lost, his work on forest succession, wild fruits, and seed dispersion came to rest in a variety of public archives and private collections, unread by all but a few truly devoted researchers.

The combined result of Thoreau's own reinterpretation of his early life and the fate of his last manuscripts has been to produce a curiously truncated view of his life and work. We are left with a kind of "standardized" Thoreau, neither the neophyte naturalist of the 1840s nor the advanced ecologist of the late 1850s. To fully comprehend the character of Thoreau's achievement, it is necessary to undertake two projects. The first is to draw an honest picture of Henry Thoreau's skills as a naturalist in the 1840s and to place this aspect of his character in the context of his overall endeavors during the period. Thoreau was not born a naturalist; he became one, in a society that did not privilege the undertaking.

The second task is to determine the nature of the revolution that occurred in Thoreau's own mind after 1849. Why did the change take place, what did he set out to do, with what intellectual tools did he prepare himself, and what methods did he employ? In tracing Thoreau's personal revolution, we begin to achieve an understanding of his ecological vision.

This is a book about transformation. What is it that makes a classically and staidly trained transcendentalist into a radical naturalist? Determining the answer to the question will result in neither a full-length biography of Henry David Thoreau nor a full academic analysis of his complete works. The Concord naturalist was a many-sided man. In a writing career of twenty-five years, he addressed a broad range of political and economic topics; much of his work had nothing to do with nature. His opposition to slavery, his suspicion of industrial capitalism, his demand for a life of moral principle have become commonplace to generations of literary biographers.

Yet another familiar theme is Thoreau's interest in nature. Any reader of *Walden* will testify to Henry's love of the natural world; the vivid images of Canada Geese circling the pond, the war of the ants, the autumnal game of tag with a Common Loon speak of his devotion.

Where did that devotion come from? Thoreau lived in a society built on principles of Christianity and progress; his neighbors in no way shared his love of birds and animals, nor the face of the natural world itself. Despite the influences of a lower middle-class upbringing and a Harvard education, Thoreau did not "keep pace with his companions" when it came to the apprehension of nature. Essentially on his own, he outgrew the wearied and insensitive comprehensions of his neighbors, developing a view of the natural whole uniquely his own.

Why?

Where did the impetus for such a radical transformation come from? How, in the end, did Thoreau shape the tenets of his understanding? Just what was nature, to Henry Thoreau?

That is all this book is attempting to discover.

Concord is the oldest inland town in New England, perhaps in the States. There are square miles in my vicinity which have no inhabitant.— First along by the river & then the brook & then the meadow & the woodside— Such solitude from a hundred hills I can see civilization & abodes of men afar. These farmers & their works are scarcely more obvious than woodchucks.

—*Journal,* August 1850

1 CONCORD

HE WAS BORN ON JULY 12, 1817, in Concord, Massachusetts, and christened David Henry Thoreau. Forty-four years and ten months later, he died of consumption in the same town, in a bed of his own devising.[1]

The mention of the hometown of Concord emerges from this obligatory biographical gloss to assume fundamental importance. For Henry, Concord would stand always as the center and foundation, the anchor of his life. Very few historical figures possessed so strong a sense of place, nor did they remain so specifically tied to a single location throughout a lifetime. Thoreau lived on this earth for almost forty-five years; for all but seven of them he maintained his home in Concord.[2]

The thought of leaving his native town forever was more than he could bear. During his teenage years, Henry once asked his mother what he should do with his life. When she innocently replied that he could shoulder a pack and "roam abroad" in search of fortune, tears began to roll down the boy's cheeks. His older sister Helen came to the rescue, reassuring him, "No, Henry, you shall not go: you shall stay at home and live with us."[3]

The years lived beyond the bounds of Concord are easily chronicled. When he was fifteen months old, the family moved from the town to nearby Chelmsford, as his father sought profitable employment. Over the next twenty-nine months, the family moved twice more, ending up residing once again in Concord in March 1823. Henry (as he was known to family and friends) lived out his boyhood in the town and did not leave again until September 1833, to attend Harvard University. The greater part of the next four years he spent in Cambridge, Massachusetts, leaving only for visits to his family and a winter teaching assignment in Canton, Massachusetts, under the aegis of Orestes Brownson. Graduation from Harvard in August 1837 brought him back home, where he began a brief and checkered career teaching school. He left town once more in May 1843, to become the private tutor of William Emerson's children on Staten Island, New York. After ten months he quit and returned to Concord for good.[4]

Throughout his adult life, Henry Thoreau enjoyed the occasional excursion, especially to places in New England. He climbed practically every mountain of importance in the region, occasionally rode the train to Boston to borrow books, made four separate trips to Maine, and journeyed four times also to Cape Cod. In 1850 he traveled to Canada. Beginning in 1848 he also undertook speaking engagements in several New England towns, and twice made more extended speaking tours, going as far as Philadelphia in 1854 and New Jersey in 1856. Finally, in 1861 he made a two-month journey to Minnesota seeking futilely to repair his ravaged health. All these travels possessed certain elements in common. They were brief, they were purposeful, and they disrupted the normal beat of his Concord life as little as possible.[5]

In his adult years, Thoreau's friends and associates often expressed concern over his devotion to life in Concord. Warning against the stagnation of the intellect, they advised longer journeys to the American West, to Europe. Exposure to new ideas, new cultures, new modes of living could only serve to "rub off some rust," inspire Thoreau's pen, they argued. Too much of Concord could lead only to mundanity.[6]

Henry Thoreau listened carefully to the well-meaning advice of his friends, and toyed occasionally with the idea of leaving. In October 1847, as he saw Ralph Waldo Emerson off to Europe, he admitted to the attractions of a move to Oregon Territory. Nothing came of the idea, nor of the numerous other projects and job applications that might have pried Thoreau loose from his native soil. Thinking of California in 1852, he concluded, "It is only 3000 miles nearer to Hell." When British acquaintance Thomas Cholmondeley offered to pay all expenses if Henry would join him in a trip to the West, he could only reply, "I think I had better stay in Concord."[7]

In the last analysis, Thoreau invariably dismissed the idea of leaving. There was too much work to be done right there. Even as he made his momentary reach for fame and acclamation with a speaking tour supporting *Walden* in 1854, he worried about the potential effects on his work at home.

> I have given myself up to nature; I have lived so many springs and summers and autumns and winters as if I had nothing else to do but *live* them, and imbibe whatever nutriment they had for me; I have spent a couple of years, for instance, with the flowers chiefly, having none other so binding engagement as to observe when they opened; I could have afforded to spend a whole fall observing the changing tints of the foliage. Ah, how I have thriven on solitude and poverty! I cannot overstate this advantage. I do not see how I could have enjoyed it, if the public had been expecting as much of me as there is danger now that they will. If I go abroad lecturing, how shall I recover the lost winter?
>
> It has been my vacation, my season of growth and expansion, a prolonged youth.[8]

Three years later, contemplating a travel essay on a stormy evening, he decided that "If a man is rich and strong anywhere it must be on his native soil. Here I have been these forty years learning the language of these fields that I may the better express myself. . . . We only need travel enough to give our intellects an airing." As one of his neighbors observed, "Henry talks about Nature just as if she'd been born and brought up in Concord."[9]

Subsequent generations of readers, scholars, and critics have tended to sustain the opinion of Thoreau's well-meaning friends. The great nature writer John Muir scoffed at the idea that Thoreau could know nature through studying the little woods and streams of Concord. Sherman Paul, perhaps the most meticulous analyst of Thoreau's works, argued that his art diminished in the years following the completion of *Walden*. He became, Paul contended, too provincial. While more recent critics have denied this supposed diminution of Thoreau's talents, they too have lamented the extent to which he perversely tied himself to the Town of Concord, a genius rusticating in a sleepy farming village. Why did Henry not go out and get some wider views of his universe?[10]

This criticism rests, of course, entirely on the point of view of the critic. Researchers have generally dismissed Thoreau's own arguments for staying as self-serving and self-deluding. Only since the 1970s have new schools of thought arisen; intellectual frameworks that not only echo Thoreau's belief in geographical attachment and sense of place, but put these ideas into practice as well. Arguing for a "bioregional" approach to life, emphasizing the importance of personal devotion to the welfare of a decentralized ecological region, advocates maintain that "there is a connection—even a necessary unity—between the natural world and the human mind." To comprehend this connection, the bioregionalists contend, it is necessary to form a deep and abiding attachment with a specific part of the earth that one can call home.[11]

In stubbornly calling Concord home all his life, Henry Thoreau anticipated the bioregionalists by a century and a quarter. Any study of the development of Thoreau's ecological thought must begin with a consideration of the Town of Concord. Two questions are especially imperative. How did the physical and social geography of Thoreau's home influence his environmental thought? And, to what extent was the Concord community cognizant of their natural surroundings? Each question will be considered in turn.

Concord lies in the County of Middlesex, Massachusetts, nineteen miles west of Boston. In the middle of the nineteenth century, those nineteen miles represented a very large gulf between the residents of the growing metropolitan port city and the quiet agricultural community of the interior. The Fitchburg Railroad, constructed in 1844, drew the two entities somewhat closer together, but Concord would retain much of its provincial isolation throughout Henry Thoreau's lifetime.[12]

Town and village were set in a small, river-drained intervale located in the inland portion of what geographers have labeled the "New England Seaboard Lowland." The gentle foldings of the earth's crust that took place in geologically ancient times provided the skeletal outlines of the region's physiography, but repeated glaciations scoured and molded the essential landscape. The Wisconsinian, the latest of the ice sheets, relaxed its grip some ten thousand years before, leaving behind scrapes and depositions that obscured the activities of glacial predecessors. The Wisconsinian rearranged the topography to some extent, sculpting new hills and moving large boulders, millions of rocks, and tons of surface soils. Most of the material did not move more than a few miles. When the climate warmed again, the glacier did not so much retreat as melt away, at the rate of about two miles a year.

The melt was irregular. Large blocks of ice broke off from the main sheet, impeding the drainage of melt waters and contributing to the formation of vast but temporary lakes. One such glacial lake inundated much of Concord for a brief time. When the water finally drained away, the geologic deposits left behind formed a quiltlike mantle of soils and gravel roughly ten feet thick. Occasionally, large ice blocks became imbedded in kame terrace deposits, slowly melting to form kettle ponds and sphagnum bogs. In Concord, White Pond, Walden Pond, Goose Pond, and Fair Haven Bay formed in this fashion, as did Ledum Bog and the smaller Andromeda Ponds.

As the ice and meltwater receded, the essential topography of Thoreau's Concord emerged—a valley drained by two rivers, the Sudbury and the Assabet, which joined to form the northward flowing Concord River. The valley, about one hundred feet above sea level, was flanked by slightly higher uplands and occasional rounded, nobby hills rising more than one hundred feet above the rivers.[13]

In Thoreau's time, the vast glacial prehistory lying beneath the current topography was little known or understood. Louis Agassiz, the Swiss-born naturalist and fossil expert, was the first to recognize the effects of glaciation on New England's landscape. He had emigrated to the United States in the early 1840s, and eventually took a post as Professor of Comparative Zoology at Harvard. Although Thoreau met and corresponded with the scientist, the glacial origins of Concord's hills and ponds seemingly held little attraction. He makes almost no mention of the subject in his journals.[14]

More intriguing was the pattern of flora and fauna that grew and developed in the wake of the glacier's departure. The majority of the species occupying the town in the 1850s became established over a period of roughly five thousand years following the melt. An Oak-Hickory forest association became dominant in much of the region, with varieties of oak establishing themselves as the most common trees. Stands of different conifers interspersed locally, along with large numbers of hickories, red maples, and some black birch, dogwoods, and tulip trees. Another eight hundred to a thousand smaller plant species came to live in Concord as well, along with more than one hundred different kinds of birds and a generous variety of fish, reptiles, amphibians, and mammals, to say nothing of innumerable species of insects. Together, the plants and the animals created a patchwork system of interrelated habitats; the nature Thoreau loved and came to know so well.[15]

The first people probably entered the region some 9,500 years before Thoreau's time. Described now as "Paleo-Indians," these omnivorous hunters of big game and gatherers of plant foods came on the heels of the retreating glaciers, pursuing rapidly disappearing prehistoric fauna, including the mastodont. Eventually they developed tools defining the Archaic-Lauerentian culture, which lasted more than two thousand years.

Algonkian woodland groups displaced them roughly 1,800 years prior to the nineteenth century. Also hunter-gatherers, these peoples considerably influenced the plant and animal ecologies of the region through hunting, forest burning, and selective plant consumption. Essentially, they managed the forests to create a more open, parklike, "edge habitat," conducive to the growth of a larger deer population. They also began to practice some shifting crop agriculture, although they kept no domestic animals. At their peak during the sixteenth century, they numbered perhaps 13,000. Living in small bands, these peoples moved with each season, following the cyclical life patterns of the plants and animals upon which they depended. They visited the Concord region frequently, establishing summer fishing villages or late autumn hunting communities. Most died in a series of epidemics brought to America by the Europeans early in the 1600s.[16]

Thoreau was well aware of the former presence of Native American inhabitants in Concord. Occasionally, a sad and bewildered survivor of the Algonkian bands still visited the town, endeavoring to sell crafts or find work in a world made over by the English invaders. More often, the reminders came in the form of artifacts found in the earth: projectile points and other stone and flint echoes of an obliterated culture.

Henry was especially adept at finding arrowheads. Fresh from his Harvard graduation in 1837, he and his older brother John spent considerable time walking in the woods, "searching for Indian relics." Abundant success seized their imaginations, and they began to address one another as brother sachems. Between 1838 and 1841, while running the Concord Academy, the brothers made ample use of their knowledge of local Indian sites to challenge and excite their pupils. This prosaic use of the knowledge lasted only a short while, but the talent for finding the relics lasted all of Henry's life.[17]

In his earliest musings, Thoreau tended to view Native Americans as symbols of a lost and lamented American wildness, rather than as actual human beings. He made some effort to study Indians at Harvard, primarily to contrast their philosophy of life with the views of Asian religious adepts. His early essays contain occasional allusions to the "dark ages"—Thoreau's image for the European destruction of Indian life during the colonial era. He began a concerted effort to expand on these ideas in the years after 1845, when he came to see the violent removal of the Indians from New England as the central tragedy of American history: the loss of a pastoral ideal. The results of this research would become a central theme of his first major work, *A Week on the Concord and Merrimack Rivers.* Yet even in this sensitive interpretation (so at odds with the general opinions of his time), Thoreau portrayed the Algonkians more as elusive figures fading into an indistinct past, rather than as people with a distinct, viable, and instructive culture. It was not until the decade drew to a close, and he began to cast about for new intellectual materials upon which to build a view of life, that his Indian research and the arrowheads he uncovered in his walks would become a doorway for one of the most rigorous, ambitious, and relatively unbiased studies of Native Americans undertaken in the antebellum era. The knowledge of the Indian presence in Concord became in the 1850s a tool for the development of Thoreau's ecological ideas.[18]

The microparasites that destroyed the preponderance of New England's Native American population accompanied the European groups who began to appear on North American shores during the sixteenth century. Initially they came seasonally to fish and to trade, but in the 1620s they began to colonize and stay. The Europeans carried with them a commitment to settled agriculture, animal domestication, land alienation, and a belief that the New England "wilderness" they encountered was inherently evil. While shattering the remnant Indian populations in a series of wars lasting into the eighteenth century, these English newcomers set about removing the forest and introducing new plants and animals. Cattle, swine, wheat, rye, and other familiar agricultural species were brought purposefully; the black rat, the house mouse, the dandelion, and the English plantain came uninvited. ("Wherever you see an old house, there look for an old rat's nest," Thoreau advised.) In all, European colonists had imported roughly one plant species of every ten found in Concord in the 1850s, and a handful of birds and animals as well.[19]

The English claimed the Concord region in 1635. The broad, flat meadows flanking the rivers and their tributaries offered a resource the colonists eagerly sought: forage for their domestic animals. William Wood, a Puritan traveler, passed through the area in 1633. He described "great broad meadows, wherein grow neither shrub nor tree, lying low, in which plains grows as much grass as may be cut with a scythe, . . . so that a good mower may cut three loads in a day." Wood's observations both described the condition of the Concord meadows in the seventeenth century and revealed the essential attitudes of the colonists toward this "new world." The wild grasses were a commodity to be exploited for personal gain.[20]

The Massachusetts General Court awarded a six-mile tract encompassing the meadows to a group of settlers headed by a Kentish soldier and a Puritan minister. These settlers then purchased rights to the land from the local sachem, a woman named Tahattawau, for a parcel of wampum, some cotton cloth, and several metal knives, hatchets, and hoes. By 1679, 120 males over the age of sixteen lived in Concord, despite the loss of one-sixth of the population in a war with the Algonkian tribes three years before.[21]

The European occupation of the region quickly wrought a great change in the landscape, as religious belief and economic determination combined to destroy the parklike forests of the Indians. Thoreau understood the mindset perfectly well: "The race that settles & clears the land has got to deal with every tree in the forest in succession— It must be resolute & industrious-and even the stumps must be got out or are— It is a thorough process-this war with the wilderness— breaking nature taming the soil-feeding it on oats The civilized man regards the pine tree as his enemy. He will fell it & let in the light-grub it up & raise wheat or rye there. It is no better than a fungus to him."[22]

Concord quickly became a patchwork of fields and woodlots. The settlers established a central village along a ridge overlooking the Concord River and set about removing the forests covering the uplands. Mainly they wished to employ the forested land for crops and grazing, but the timber also had some value as fuel and construction material. Between 1635 and 1850, the fireplaces of Concord burned enough wood to consume all the trees in the town three times over. Houses, farm buildings, places of commerce, politics, and worship, fences, and bridges consumed lumber as well. Woodland was at a premium by the middle years of the nineteenth century, and only the ongoing need for fuel prevented the total disappearance of the forests. With the introduction of railroads at mid-century, the value of timber (especially chestnut) grew so temptingly that many a farmer's woodlot was resurveyed and given over to the woodman's axe. As a hired surveyor, Henry Thoreau played a reluctant but necessary role in this deforestation.[23]

When the original forest cover disappeared, forest dwelling bird and animal species also disappeared. The settlers actively extirpated most of the larger predators (bears, wolves, cougars, bobcats) in an effort to protect their domestic stock, trapped out such fur-bearers as beaver, otter, and marten to obtain the value of their pelts, and hunted down deer and other ungulates for food and to prevent their competing with sheep and cattle for grazing forage. The plants and animals surviving this onslaught were those able to adapt to living in the interstices of this European-style occupation. Waterfowl grew wary but continued to occupy the ponds and streams at their appointed seasons of the year. Mice, both native and imported, flourished under the new conditions, taking up residence in barns and in grain fields. Owls, hawks, and foxes—hunted, driven into hiding, but never extirpated—fed on the mice (and the occasional chicken).[24]

From the time of establishment, the Town of Concord encapsulated the typical history of the township system of colonization and settlement in New England. The first occupants lived in neighboring lots in close proximity to the Puritan Meeting House and owned as many as three or four separate surrounding fields. Although lots and fields were allotted unequally (the richest got the most), all the members of this initial generation possessed room and to spare, as did their children. By the third generation, division and subdivision of the original holdings among all the male descendants began to create problems. Farmers could not further divide their lands without creating farms too small to be economically viable. Some young people began to move away from Concord, while others accepted lower-class occupations as wage laborers. The social structure became more rigidly stratified.

Along with stratification came dispersion. Farm families consolidated their holdings, so that they owned one distinct plot of land in a specific part of the town, rather than several separate fields spread across the landscape. By the eighteenth century, most farm families had removed from the central village, taking up residence on the actual farmstead. The village, now a center of commerce and artisan production, migrated westward to its current location near "the Milldam." Agricultural homes farthest removed from the Meeting House successfully petitioned the Massachusetts government to separate from Concord and organize new towns. The old Town of Concord, with reduced boundaries, a commercialized village, and a scattered population still largely committed to agriculture, assumed the contours familiar to Henry Thoreau. Between 1765 and 1840, the population did not vary by more than 225 persons, a stability marking an agricultural society operating at near capacity.[25]

After 1840, the population began to climb significantly. The census taker in 1850 found 465 more people than in 1840. The change reflected two important and related developments: the construction of the Fitchburg Railroad in 1843, which gave Concord quick and ready access to large markets, and the concurrent establishment of larger industrial operations in the town. The traditional array of blacksmiths, wheelwrights, carpenters, coopers, and shoemakers that had carried on the essential handicrafts of the town almost from the beginning were now joined by representatives of New England's burgeoning factory system. The Assabet River, which flowed more swiftly than its neighboring streams, provided the power for three larger entrants in the industrial revolution. The most important of these was Edward Carver Damon's cloth mill, constructed in the 1830s, and employing between twenty and sixty persons. A pail and tub company built by George Loring employed thirteen men in 1850; ten years later, the factory, now called P. Warner and Company, occupied thirty. A complex of Powder Mills in nearby Acton blew up in 1853, killing three. Lesser manufactories within the confines of Concord village included an assembly line shoe shop, a tailor's establishment that employed three men and four women, and the Thoreau Pencil Company, owned and operated by John Thoreau—Henry's father. The pencil business engaged six.[26]

The rise of these larger manufacturing establishments subtly changed the character of Concord. Drawn more fully into the market economy of New England and the Atlantic world, the town acquired more "bustle." Thoreau complained he was "awakened every night by the panting of the steam-engine. . . . It would be glorious to see mankind at leisure for once."[27]

Newly emigrated Irish people, refugees from the potato famine, accounted for much of the rise in the town's population. A few families settled in shanties near the railroad and on other marginal properties. More often, single men gravitated to the area, taking jobs in the factories or as wage laborers on the larger farms. Thoreau's journals track his reaction to this immigration, registering initial dismay, which gave way to sympathy and respect for the industry of the newcomers. In 1851, he noted with interest the introduction of Irish agricultural techniques, including the construction of sod walls and the use of woven straw ropes to support young plants. By that time, Henry was taking delight in the lighthearted but productive approach to manual labor demonstrated by the Irish laborers, comparing it favorably to the meanness of the Yankee farmer. "The Yankee keeps an account," he observed. "The simple honesty of the Irish pleases me." Thoreau also became increasingly disgusted with the manner in which the wealthier residents of the town exploited these poor immigrants. One of his townsmen, "notorious for meanness," tried to claim a four-dollar prize one of his Irish workers had earned spading at the Agricultural Fair. Another, a dairyman from the northern portion of the town, employed a single Irish girl to do all the cooking and washing for a household of twenty-two. The final version of *Walden* was shaped in part by the growth of this awareness.[28]

Even in a small town such as Concord, village and countryside were separate, distinct entities. Those living at the edge of the village felt uncomfortable with woodlands so close to their homes. To emphasize their status as residents of the village, these homeowners generally removed all the trees from their properties. Woods encircled Concord village, but at a distance.[29]

Other behaviors reenforced the sense of separation. Concord village was a busy place, full of the actions of professionals, business people, farmers on commercial errands. They gathered to talk in offices and shops, or came together for conversation at the town square. Thoreau could distinguish the farmers from the merchants by "how differently they walk in the streets." All seemed to share in common a comfortable faith in developments such as the railroad and the telegraph, which had further separated them from nature. The village treated "the shallow and transitory as if they were profound and enduring," as Thoreau put it.[30]

There is a danger in making too much of the separation between farm and village. For all the bustle of the factories and the railroad, Concord retained the essential mien of the small agricultural community. As in all rural areas, people knew exactly the sources of the foods they ate. "In the midst of our village," Thoreau recorded, "as in most villages, there is a slaughter-house, and throughout the summer months, day and night, to the distance of half a mile . . . the air [is] filled with such scents as we instinctively avoid in a woodland walk." In August of 1859, villagers were disturbed in their slumbers by the bellowings of an animal unskillfully butchered.[31]

Such knowledge of "nature's economy" as existed in Concord derived from its identity as an agricultural community. In 1850, the Federal Census marshall listed one hundred eight farms within the town's boundaries, indicating that agricultural pursuits still occupied far more people than any other economic pursuit. Concord's farmers practiced the manner of mixed agriculture common in Southern New England, devoting a few acres to grains, a few to hay, and one or two to potatoes while maintaining one or more pastures, perhaps an orchard, and a woodlot to provide fuel. Cattle and chickens were the chief domestic animals, eggs and butter the most common commodities sold to obtain liquid capital on a regular basis. Farms ranged in size from the six acres of Asa Hayden to the four hundred acres of Richard Barrett.[32]

The orientation and role of the individual farms in the region's economy varied with their size. Thirty-six farms encompassed less than fifty acres. Many of these were close to the village, including Asa Hayden's insufficiently profitable six acres and Simon Brown's twenty-one acres. Undoubtedly many of the owners of these tiny farms held other occupations, maintaining the orchards and fields essentially to supply food resources for themselves and their families. The census indicates that these small farms devoted greater percentages of their land to the production of such staples as corn, peas, and potatoes than did their larger counterparts. More than half these farms produced enough butter to fulfill the needs of home consumption, suggesting the basic importance of this commodity.[33]

The thirty-five largest farm landowners held an average of roughly one hundred sixty acres apiece. These farms, more or less surrounding the village, defined Concord's rural atmosphere. The people owning these lands farmed full time for their living; agonizing over the rise and fall of market prices, tracking the latest in scientific agricultural developments, worrying over the competition from more wide open and fertile regions to the west. Gleaning from the occasional comments found in Thoreau's journals, the letters written to the editors of farmers' almanacs and journals, and the general demographic trends of New England, it seems that these farmers were not a happy lot. Older farmers found it necessary to exhort the younger generation to do their duty by the family plot, at times drawing angry replies from the young. More than one young farmer abandoned his landed inheritance because he felt the demands of the agricultural life unfair to his bride: he did not want to turn her into a drudge. "Our young Concord farmers & their young wives," Thoreau observed, "hearing this bustle about them-seeing the world all going by as it were . . . -plainly cannot make up their minds to live the quiet retired old-fashioned country-farmer's life."[34]

While an element of subsistence remained in the work of the larger farms, the owners were oriented to production for the market. It was in the planning for market production that a rudimentary knowledge of the local ecology played a part. The selectman had divided the town into seven sections for assessment and administrative purposes; a careful analysis of the Census of the Products of Agriculture for 1850 by section demonstrates that practice differed with location.

Two and a quarter centuries of residence and experiment in Concord had taught the farmers what they could grow most profitably, and where. Henry sometimes encountered "well-preserved walls running straight through the midst of high and old woods"—the evidence of failed agricultural experiments. In *Walden,* he spoke of the abandoned relics of former settlements near the pond, each a testament of economic failure. Records showed that in the seventeenth century, people had tried to farm the area. By the eighteenth century, the lands had returned to woodlot. The reason: Walden woods was a piney sand barren, completely unsuitable for crops. By the nineteenth century, successful farmers knew to avoid such unproductive lands, along with tracts near the old Marlboro Road south of the village and the "Easterbrooks Country," near the town's northern border. "We walk in a deserted country," Thoreau concluded.[35]

The best farm lands lay in a ring around the village, mainly in the lower lands with some proximity to the rivers. The river meadows that had originally drawn settlers to the region remained important; several substantial farmers owned meadow portions, harvesting the long meadow grasses for animal fodder each August.

Even in the best farm lands there was room for fine distinctions. Although virtually all of the town's farmers practiced mixed agriculture, they tended to concentrate on different aspects of the potential agricultural array, depending on their location. Soil types appear to have dictated these differences in concentration. For example, roughly one half of Concord's farms possessed orchards, in locations spread throughout the town's seven sections. All of the largest orchards however, lay south of the village, in sections one, three, and four. In similar fashion, the vast majority of the town's rye fields, and especially those producing the largest yields, stood close to the village or to the south.

At the northern end of the town (sections six and seven), farmers tended to give over more of their land to the raising of animals. Poorer soils would not support extensive cropping, dictating a concentration on pasturage. Although every farmer in town owned at least one milk cow, only three owned dairy herds with more than twenty head—all in the northern sections. The four farmers managing more than sixteen head of beef cattle also lived north of the village. Thoreau referred to the rocky pastures of the Easterbrooks country north of the village in his 1858 essay "Wild Apples."[36]

In response to economic pressure from the more productive farms of the trans-Appalachian west, a few New England farmers had turned to specialty crops such as asparagus. Demand for such produce in eastern urban markets was growing, and such vegetables were far too perishable to be successfully shipped from the Ohio country. Construction of the Fitchburg Railroad provided Concord farmers ready access to the markets of Boston, but as of 1850 only ten of them had chosen to grow produce. Location again seems to have played a role in the decision. All ten lived north of the village, in close proximity to the Concord River, perhaps the only place in town where enough muck and peat soil existed to make the experiment worthwhile.[37]

Concord's farmers were very sensitive to the potentials of their landscape. Although much of their practice represented the received wisdom of their ancestors, they were by no means ignorant rubes. The Concord Farmers Club, active between 1852 and 1855, boasted more than forty members who attended monthly lectures on subjects ranging from fertilizers to tree grafting to new methods of livestock management. Much of the new information was incorporated into Concord farm management. *The New England Farmer,* the region's most widely read agricultural journal, originated in Concord over a portion of its existence, and numbered several leading Concord residents among its editorial board. The Middlesex County Agricultural Fair, held in Concord each fall, awarded prizes for the best efforts in a wide range of categories.[38]

Better than anyone, the town's farmers knew the land, knew what it could produce, and where. In the game of calculating nature's economy for human profit, no one could excel their collective expertise.

In June 1853, Henry Thoreau undertook to describe the wild tracts of Concord, listing open lands along the Carlisle Road, a three-mile stretch surrounding the old Marlboro Road, the Walden woods, and the river meadows. These tracts existed in Thoreau's time not because of any unsurpassing love of nature expressed by Concord's residents, but ironically because the accumulation of two hundred years of geographic knowledge dictated that these lands were economically unviable. Thoreau could study nature in Concord because there were portions of the town that farmers had learned to ignore.[39]

With the residents' practical understanding of Concord's geography came a panoply of beliefs and perceptions regarding natural behavior and its relation to human concerns. These included folk beliefs, written expositions, and formal lectures. Collectively, these sources suggest an appreciation of nature in Concord more broad than profound, and an attitude more utilitarian than benevolent.

Most folk beliefs made sense of a sort. The townspeople tended to note the arrival of snow buntings from the north each year, perceiving that an early migration was often the harbinger of a harsh winter. Conversely, the arrival of the bluebirds each April promised the advent of spring. Farmers were well attuned to the rhythm of nature, fully comprehending the signs that promised the end of spring frost or dictated the times of harvest.

Yet not all folk wisdom was so empirical, or sustainable. Townspeople also believed that a large crop of acorns portended a cold winter, that a warm, open winter was unhealthy, and that a woodpecker on a dead tree was a sign of rain. A hooting owl warned of approaching death, as did the cry of the whippoorwill. They tended to anthropomorphize the behavior of animals. Foxes were cunning, otters playful, eagles cowardly—all in the human senses of the words. Drooping willow trees wept, "the emblem of despairing love."[40]

As Henry Thoreau so perfectly expressed it, the farmer knew nature "but as a robber." The farmers understood much, but the point of possessing the knowledge was not to derive a better understanding of nature's ways, but to profit from particular phenomena. While the residents of Concord discerned that the lands to the north of the village were best employed to raise cattle, this in no way implied that they understood the species of wild nature that shared the region in their own time, nor the wilder ecosystems they had displaced. Any knowledge of nature's way was attractive only in so much as it was applicable to the business of making a living.[41]

Nothing made this pragmatic relationship with nature more plain than the behavior of a farmer with a gun in his hand. They shot just about everything that moved. Thoreau's journals are peppered with references to a wide range of shooting incidents, which occurred for several reasons. Farmers sought to protect their livestock, especially chickens, from predators. To that end, they killed foxes, owls, and at least ten varieties of hawks—including a Cooper's Hawk, Marsh Hawks, and Goshawks, three species that had little interest in barnyards. To protect crops, farmers killed mice (employing both cats and dogs in the hunt), skunks, woodchucks, and above all, gray and red squirrels. In the fall of 1853, more than 150 gray squirrels fell to the gun within a mile radius. As Thoreau explained, they "regard them as vermin, and annually shoot and destroy them in great numbers, because—if we have any excuse—they sometimes devour a little of our Indian corn, while, perhaps, they are planting the nobler oak-corn (acorn) in its place."[42]

Residents also killed to supplement their diets. Squirrels and rabbits helped to feed many families, as did a variety of birds. Waterfowl were favored, particularly during the spring and fall migrations. Concord farmers shot two kinds of teal, at least five separate species of ducks, two varieties of dippers, geese, and rails. Away from the water they hunted quail, and played their part in the extinction of the passenger pigeon. Already in Thoreau's time, the numbers of this last species were noticeably diminishing.

The killing did not end with such utilitarian purposes as diet and predator control. Townspeople also killed for the fun of it. There is no other way to explain the avian deaths that in no way benefitted humans at all. Among the victims were Common and Red-throated Loons, Great Blue Herons, swallows, and Lesser Redpolls. By the mid-1850s, shooters were bringing dead songbirds to Thoreau's door for identification, a practice he must have viewed with mixed emotions.[43]

Perhaps the custom that best illustrated the strained association between people and nature was the election day birds contest. The origins and duration of this annual event are obscure, but the election day contest definitely occurred during Henry Thoreau's youth. The rules were simple. On election day in late May, all of the schoolboys owning guns (just about all of them) assembled in the school yard, where they were sent off into the woods to shoot as many birds as possible before sunset. Songbirds, game birds, water birds, predators, all were fair prey. School leaders were on hand to tally each boy's count at sundown; the one who killed the most won. Officials then divided the victims into piles according to species and computed the final number of each. Apparently a growing controversy over the role of various birds in nature eventually discouraged the election day birds contest, as it was not held in later years. Still, for May 25, 1853, Thoreau's journal had this to say: "Election day.—Rain yesterday afternoon and to-day. Heard the popping of guns last night and this morning, nevertheless." The custom died slowly.[44]

In the 1840s, the Massachusetts Legislature began to pass laws for the protection of various species of songbirds, reflecting a growing awareness that many birds profited human enterprise, especially by eating crop-chomping insects and mosquitoes. The legislation did not meet with universal acclaim. In 1851, "some thoughtless & cruel sportsman . . . killed 22 young partridges not much bigger than robins, against the laws of Massachusetts & humanity."[45] A letter written in April 1858 by a Concord farmer bearing the initials "J.B.R." appeared in *The New England Farmer,* protesting legislation to protect a songbird he maintained was nothing more than a fruit eating pest. The identity of this marauding denizen of the orchard? The American Robin.

J.B.R. concluded his observations by arguing that "It is pleasing to see the sprightly redbreast hopping along the ground or skipping among the branches, and it is still more pleasing to hear him at daybreak pouring forth his rich notes with so much animation, but if we are to have these gratifications only at the expense of our cherries, peaches and strawberries, it may be well to inquire whether we are giving more than we are receiving?"[46]

The farmer's opinions were quite characteristic of his time. While living at Walden Pond in the winter of 1847, Thoreau noted that in each autumn, flocks of robins were "at the mercy of every sportsman." In 1859, a neighbor related to him how he had stopped at the home of Concord farmer Stedman Buttrick, and "found him sitting under a cherry tree ringing a bell, in order to keep the birds off!"[47]

A typical Concord farmer had what was in many ways an intimate relationship with nature, but the knowledge he gleaned from over two centuries of practice was overwhelmingly utilitarian. The depth of that knowledge is very much open to question. The farmers knew their soils, the signs of the seasons, the general habits of wild species that threatened their livelihood. Judging from entries in Thoreau's journals, a few of them had a curiosity about nature's ways extending beyond these essentials. (One speculation held that the eels found in the Concord River copulated with clams to produce offspring.) Still, evidence of curiosity is very different from evidence of actual awareness of nature's habits.[48]

The population of nineteenth-century New England enjoyed something of a reputation for its interest in natural history, an interest unique among the business and mechanically oriented majority of America's citizens of the period. As one of Henry's contemporaries observed, "It is a great mistake to suppose that Thoreau was a solitary student of natural history in Concord and vicinity at that time." While this popular fascination took the form of a pastime rather than a proper economic pursuit on a footing with agriculture, commerce, and manufacturing, American environmental consciousness may be rooted in this early attention to nature subjects. A more profound appreciation of the natural world arguably grew from the New Englanders' study of the flora and fauna of their surroundings.[49]

Perhaps. But how penetrating was the typical New Englander's understanding of natural history? It is difficult to judge. Awareness of nature rises through several levels of consciousness.

The natural world is variegated and complex, and human acquaintance with any of its parts may range from the nodding to the astute. Take for example a knowledge of trees. The most painful novice should at least distinguish between an evergreen conifer and a deciduous broadleaf, although awareness may extend no further. A slightly more cognizant individual could separate the pines and hardwood into broad genus categories: pine, spruce, hemlock; maple, oak, chestnut. For the person viewing trees as a set of economically exploitable natural resources, this much knowledge would be enough—the timber-producing species are distinguished; the trees bearing the edible nuts identified. Beyond this level, an observer would begin to recognize individual species: white oak, red oak, scrub oak, swamp white oak. As knowledge grew, a person would not merely identify types of trees, but could describe their habitats, growth habits, and relations to other species. Even the person rising to this level knows only a small portion of the natural whole. The study of herbaceous plants, birds, animals, insects, fish, and much else still awaits.

The average New Englander's awareness of natural history apparently extended beyond the level of simple gross identification, but not very far. Several lines of evidence suggest a relative lack of sophistication.

In 1839, the Massachusetts Legislature, in conjunction with Boston's Society of Natural History, attempted to facilitate nature study by sponsoring the publication of a series of zoological studies cataloging the species of birds, fish, reptiles, plants, insects, quadrupeds, and invertebrates of the state. Uneven in quality, the volumes nonetheless reflected the essential purpose of their sponsors: to inventory the natural resources of Massachusetts. Each book was to serve primarily as an aid to distinguish among species, with the preponderance devoted to discussion of the minute but essential differentiating traits characteristic of each plant or animal. The legislature stipulated that the work was to be completed in one year's time. Given such constraints, the authors not surprisingly committed most of their time to those species considered to have economic significance (in a positive or negative sense). The informants they relied upon knew a great deal more about economically important species, as well as having a greater interest in them. The works therefore assumed a pragmatic cast. The work on insects was by its very title limited to those "injurious to vegetation."[50]

For example, in his *Report on the Fishes of Massachusetts,* D. Humphreys Storer noted that much of the previously published information on his subject was virtual fiction. Lack of time forced him to rely on field informants to construct an entirely new report. Many of these informants were naturally fishermen, and the resulting bias was obvious. In his report, Storer provided less than a page of data on a tiny fish called the Smooth Chironctes. The material was purely descriptive of the fish, and did not even mention where it might be found. His discussion of the common Pickerel ran twice as long, and included information stating that the fish was very tasty, readily saleable in Boston, and that its oil was a good treatment for earache. The balance of the book read in much the same fashion, a genuine attempt to catalog all the species in the region, but with much greater emphasis on the large and edible varieties.

The *Report on the Fishes of Massachusetts* was one of the best of the zoological series, and well illustrates the standing of natural history in New England: broad-based, shallow, and utilitarian. The other reports read in much the same fashion. Although there is considerable evidence that this effort by the Massachusetts Legislature reflected a strong general interest in the subject, there is little reason to believe that the average New Englander's comprehension of the natural world ran much beyond simple identification and description.[51]

The Town of Concord was no different. In the early years of the nineteenth century, various writers and lecturers sought to reflect their town's interest in the subject of natural history, but their efforts were sketchy at best. "A Topographical Description of the Town of Concord," written by Harvard College student William Jones in 1792, briefly describes the rivers, ponds, hills, and woods of the region, mentioning such generic species as "pine, oak, walnut, birch, and maple." Jones mentions no animal life save for ten varieties of fish.[52]

Thirty-eight years later, the first town historian, Lemuel Shattuck, saw fit to include a chapter on natural history in his *History of Concord.* A specific consideration of flora and fauna was rare in the local histories of the era, suggesting that the subject did hold some interest for Concord residents (or for Shattuck, at least). The chapter is eight pages long and includes sections on geology, botany, topography, and zoology. Shattuck consulted several local enthusiasts in preparing these sections, and made ample use of the information they provided. Doctor Edward Jarvis provided him a list of several plant families living in the area, drawing special attention to such comparatively rare or striking plants as the swamp hornbeam and the cardinal flower. Yet, the plant list is very far from exhaustive, and neither Shattuck nor his consultants made any attempt to define plant communities or associate given specimens with their habitats. It was simply a list.

Even more illustrative of Shattuck's approach to natural history is his section on the birds of Concord.

> The *Birds* have no peculiar locality in this town. Those most troublesome to the inhabitants have been the black bird, which frequent the low meadows in great numbers, the crow, and the jay. Rewards were being paid for the heads of the two latter kinds. As late as 1792, the town voted to give for destroying "those pests to cornfields, called crows," the following rates; "for each old crow 1*s.*, for each young crow 6*d.*, and for each crow's egg, that is found in said town and taken out of the nest, 3*d.*"

So much for the birds. In Shattuck's *History*, as in so much of the natural history produced in the first half of the nineteenth century, there are the familiar attributes: utilitarian orientation and superficial description.[53]

Concord's reputation for devotion to nature rests in some measure not on written works, but on the history of the spoken word in the community. The Concord Lyceum, established in 1829, provided residents the opportunity to exchange information and views on a wealth of subjects, and to hear prominent speakers from throughout the New England states. In the first season, no fewer than nine speakers lectured on subjects ranging from "The Natural History of Man" through botany, astronomy, and geography to "The Affinity of Man with the Brute Creation." Several gave multiple lectures; some delivered more than once. A similar emphasis on natural history persisted through each season to 1833, the year Thoreau left to study at Harvard.

These records convey the impression that nature was subject to frequent and profound study on the part of Concord's citizens. Again, this is almost certainly a false impression. Not one of the texts of these early Lyceum lectures is extant; any description of their content is sheer guesswork. Lacking any evidence to the contrary, the logical conclusion is that these lectures were consistent with the superficial natural histories written during the period. The titles suggest a focus on the familiar theme of nature's effects on the human economy. If anyone speaking before the Concord Lyceum did impart an understanding of nature beyond the superficially descriptive, no record of the performance exists.[54]

Henry Thoreau was unaware of any profound expression of awareness of nature's ways. In the 1850s, after his own knowledge began to rise above the cursory, Thoreau noted on several occasions the appalling ignorance of his neighbors. He identified the sources of bird and amphibian cries that had long mystified the townspeople by the simple expedient of going out to look. Many did not even notice the song of the toads each spring, much less identify the source.[55] In January of 1851, he concluded, "It is apparent enough to me that only one or two of my townsmen or acquaintances (not more than one in many thousand men in deed-) feel or at least obey any strong attraction drawing them toward the forest or to nature, but all almost without exception gravitate exclusively toward men or society."[56]

In a slightly convoluted journal entry for May 10, 1857, he further observed: "When I consider how many species of willow have been planted along the railroad causeway in the past ten years, of which no one knows the history, and not one in Concord beside myself can tell the name of one, . . . I am reminded how much is going on that man wots not of."[57]

After giving a lecture on "Autumnal Tints" in 1859, Henry was thoroughly convinced "that there are very few persons who do see much of nature." The problem he identified is by now familiar: his neighbors may have known the generic willow tree by name, but they could not distinguish among the various species, nor could they describe the growth history. Their perceptions were desultory, and related exclusively to the pursuit of factual knowledge promising monetary profit. One neighbor asked Henry "What is a shrub oak made for?" The assumptions underlying that question sum up the general attitude toward nature in Concord.[58]

One last line of evidence clinches the matter. Among the large number of nature enthusiasts living in Concord one family stood out especially: the Thoreaus. Several witnesses, including Waldo Emerson, Nathaniel Hawthorne, and Samuel Hoar, testified to the unusual attention to nature paid by Henry's entire family. Biographers invariably maintain that his family was unusually devoted to nature study. Little is genuinely known of Henry Thoreau's childhood and youth, but enough indications have emerged to sustain the basic notion. Henry's mother, Cynthia Dunbar Thoreau, was primarily responsible for the family interest in the natural world, encouraging her four children to listen to the calls of wild songbirds, follow the flights of raptors across the sky, collect wildflowers. Suggestive incidents illustrate the dedication. The entire family often took long walks over the hills and in the woods and meadows of Concord, even building makeshift stoves to cook outside and make the most of a day's excursion. Henry's mother was so reluctant to abandon these outings that she almost gave birth to one of his sisters on Lee's Hill.[59]

When Henry and his brother John operated the Concord Academy (1838–41), they made ample use of the nature appreciation they had gleaned in childhood, developing a highly atypical curriculum that often took their pupils outdoors for study. John Thoreau took the lead in offering this nature study, although Henry taught their charges the names of the region's leading flowers and the months of their blooming.[60]

In 1836, John Thoreau and his sister Sophia became especially avid in the study of nature. Sophia Thoreau began a botanical collection, while she and John in 1837 took to keeping an ornithological notebook and a list of the birds they encountered in walks through the woods and fields. Entitled "Nature and Bird Notes," the book contained descriptions copied from such experts as Nuttall and Audubon, together with a calendar listing by month the habits of migratory birds due to reappear in Concord. The back pages listed actual sightings.[61] By the standards of the time and place, brother and sister were unusually devoted to the study; each gained the respect of the community. When John Thoreau died in January 1842, Barzillai Frost, the pastor of Concord's First Parish Church, found in the young man's nature study a theme for his eulogy: "He had a love of nature, even from childhood amounting to enthusiasm. He spent many of his leisure hours in straying over these hills and along the banks of the streams. There is not a hill, nor a tree, nor a bird, nor a flower of marked beauty in all this neighborhood that he was not familiar with, and any new bird or flower he discovered gave him the most unfeigned delight, and he would dwell with it and seem to commune with it for hours."[62] By comparison, Henry's own interest in nature was, at this stage of his life, tepid.

Because of their reputations in the early 1840s, the efforts of John and Sophia become a kind of gauge by which to measure Concord's degree of sophistication in nature study. Again, the evidence suggests far more smoke than fire. Sophia's botanical collection did indeed become extensive and included three rare species that Henry never found in Concord. She pressed and mounted her plants, arranging them not with a view to Linnaian organization but rather with an eye to aesthetic impact. (In September 1853, Sophia and Henry engaged in a long discussion that resulted in the ranking of the twelve species of aster found in Concord according to beauty.) Sophia apparently collected the plants for wholly aesthetic purposes and completely eschewed science, not even bothering to record where or when she found each specimen. The purpose was not so much natural history, but art.[63]

And what of the siblings' ornithological list? At the time of John's death in 1842, he and Sophia had personally spotted specimens of forty-eight separate species of birds in Concord. Henry reported two more species to his sister. Friends and neighbors reported sightings of six additional species (and occasionally contributed the dead body as well). Fifty-six local sightings in all. While this was probably a more comprehensive effort than most of their contemporaries could manage, it fell pathetically short of completeness. Species commonly associated with the rivers were most markedly absent. John and Sophia saw no larks, no kingfishers, plovers, herons, curlews, sandpipers, woodcocks; not even any geese. The sole record of another common Concord River bird, the bank swallow, was one John saw in Scituate. Almost unbelievably, in six years of record keeping, neither John nor Sophia ever noted seeing a swift. Either the ornithological notebook was a sporadic and often-neglected enterprise, or the two were enormously careless.

What is worse, when Henry took up the notebook in the spring of 1842, he could manage to find only six additional species. Years later, when he undertook a serious study of Concord's bird life, he came to identify well over one hundred species within the town's boundaries. In all, it would appear that John and Sophia Thoreau may have paid more extensive attention to the natural world than their neighbors, but still they stood on the barest threshold of real knowledge.[64]

For the Town of Concord as a whole, an interest in nature subjects existed. The inclusion of the subject in geographic descriptions, the town history, lyceum lectures, and school curricula supports this. But there is a fundamental difference between interest in a subject and a profound knowledge of that same subject. The existing evidence overwhelmingly suggests that Concord's comprehension of nature was largely superficial.

By the end of his life, Henry Thoreau had woven himself deep into the fabric of life in the rural and rustic Town of Concord, in a manner unprecedented in American history. Eschewing, ignoring, or openly attacking most of the social conventions of mid-nineteenth century America,

Thoreau undertook to understand a small part of New England not as a political or economic entity, but as a small and recognizable bit of the natural universe. The condition of the landscape in his time materially influenced the development of his ideas. Concord had been much altered from the wild state, by nine thousand years of aboriginal occupation, and by two hundred years of intensive European possession. But the land had not been completely made over. Open spaces remained, economically unprofitable tracts where foxes, otters, songbirds, hawks, and countless other species yet roamed free. More or less intact habitats would eventually attract Thoreau's eye, providing the basis for careful study that would produce in him a startlingly modern ecological mindset. Henry Thoreau loved Concord, and willed himself to learn as much of nature's way as possible in this small corner of the universe.

The extent to which human attitudes toward nature in nineteenth-century Concord inspired or assisted Henry Thoreau's studies is another question. In the 1840s, Thoreau's attitude toward nature was somewhat out of step with his companions: he did not view nature with a wholly utilitarian eye. Yet, as the following chapter will explore, Henry's knowledge of the natural world was not vastly different from that of his neighbors. He could name some birds, point out some plants, find some arrowheads; enough to convey the impression that he knew nature's economy. In reality, the awareness was painfully superficial, and not vastly different from that of other natural history enthusiasts in his community. If Henry's talent or luck had been a little different, his understanding of nature might never have developed beyond that level. The mere fact that Concord had a nodding interest in natural history was not alone enough of an impetus to inspire Henry Thoreau to discover ecological modes of thought.

Rural farming community, home of nature enthusiasts; these aspects of Concord life shaped Thoreau in small but important ways. And there was one thing more about Concord that would influence his thinking far more crucially. During a brief period coincident with Henry Thoreau's adult life, Concord, Massachusetts, was the creative center of American intellectual endeavor. For the town was also the home of Waldo Emerson.

Emerson has special talents unequalled—
The divine in man has had no more easy,
methodically distinct expression.
His personal influence upon young persons
greater than any man's
In his world every man would be a poet—
Love would reign— Beauty would take
place— Man & nature would harmonize—

— *Journal,* Winter 1845–46

2 WALDO AND HENRY

NEWLY GRADUATED FROM Harvard University, Henry Thoreau returned home to Concord late in the summer of 1837, seeking work. Over the next five years, he found time for a great many rambles through the woods and fields of Concord, for boating on the Concord River, for sauntering the shores of Walden Pond. He often sought intellectual inspiration out of doors, although the natural world held little real interest for him. Nature simply was not his subject. Filled with "a noble madness,"[1] he pursued other themes, other matters, and referred to plants and animals generally as symbols, if at all. For more than nine years, Henry saw himself as a transcendental poet and writer, focused on universal themes.

Initially intrigued by the promise of transcendental ideas while attending Harvard, Thoreau quickly became acquainted with Waldo Emerson, author of the fundamental transcendentalist proclamation, *Nature.* Entranced by the older man's genius, Henry lived a long and almost fruitless intellectual apprenticeship as Waldo's friend, intellectual conversant, and fellow townsman. Henry's ideas and aspirations became so entangled with those of his good friend that it is now impossible to comprehend the character of Thoreau's intellectual growth during these years without reference to Emerson's beliefs. For better or worse, Waldo almost wholly shaped the views of the natural world that informed Thoreau's writing at the outset of his literary career.

Were it not for Emerson, the twentieth century might never have known Henry David Thoreau. As so much of what must be said in this chapter has to bear inevitably sad and negative connotations, it would do to keep this essential truth in mind. Whatever else may be observed about Waldo, he encouraged and inspired some of America's greatest writers to bring pen to paper.[2]

At the beginning of the year 1831, six years before he met Henry Thoreau, Waldo was a reasonably successful but undistinguished Unitarian minister, the junior pastor of the Second Church of Boston. He had trod a familiar road, graduating from Harvard in 1821, taking teaching assignments at various private schools before beginning to preach in 1826. The Second Church called him to the pulpit in January 1829, a month after his engagement to Ellen Tucker, a young woman of beauty and wealth. The sole cloud on Emerson's horizon was the health of his fiancée: Ellen was an active consumptive. They took the terrible chance, marrying on September 30, 1830. Their happiness lasted little more than five months. Early in the following February, Ellen Tucker Emerson, age nineteen, died at their home in Boston. For Waldo Emerson, the secure road of orthodox respectability had brought him to nothing but crushing loneliness and gnawing spiritual disquiet. How could a loving God provide him such happiness, only to wrench it away so soon?[3]

The gentle platitudes of Unitarian Protestantism held no solace. He hung on to his pastorate for a while, quarreling with the church governing board and finally resigning in September 1832. In miserably poor health, he sailed for Europe, landing first in Malta and slowly traveling northward through Italy and into France seeking both physical and mental healing. In Paris, he became so enamored of the vast botanical panorama of the Jardin des Plantes that he momentarily decided to forsake the ministry and become a naturalist. (This is about the most stunning fact in the entire Emerson biography.) Moving on to England in better spirits, he managed visits with Samuel Taylor Coleridge and William Wordsworth. The tour finished in Scotland, where Waldo struck up a friendship with Thomas Carlyle that would last to the end of his days.[4]

Emerson returned to Boston in November 1833, a profoundly ambivalent man. Reasonably convinced that Unitarianism did not hold the right answers, he still continued to preach from different New England pulpits until 1839. In the same period, he embarked on a marginally separate career as a public lecturer. His first effort, "The Uses of Natural History," was delivered in Boston and met with reasonable success. He followed this with more natural history lectures, and in 1835 began a series on the lives of great men. Intellectual Boston listened with skeptical interest, perhaps valuing the magic of the speaker as much or more than the words he spoke.[5]

Emerson was at this point feeling his way, shedding the tenets of his formal religious training, exploring new means of examining life and the world. He was not a rigorous philosopher, as he repeatedly pointed out, but simply a man searching for ideas to make sense of the world he knew. His sources of inspiration were varied, and included the English romantic poets, the German idealists, and something of the newly translated Asian religious works. Above all the others in his intellectual pantheon stood Plato, although ironically his understanding of Platonic thought owed more to the neo-Platonists, who translated (and subtly altered the meaning of) Plato's great works.[6]

He was not alone in his quest. Many well-educated teachers and ministers were entering into the comparatively free-spirited questioning that characterized the Jackson Age. In 1836, Emerson joined with several of these scholars to form the Hedge Club, dedicated to the discussion of moral, political, and literary ideas. Other members included Bronson Alcott, George Ripley, Orestes Brownson, Theodore Parker, and Margaret Fuller. Over the next seven years the group met irregularly, gathering at the home of one or another of the group. In time the membership changed the name of their society to reflect the tenor of their views, becoming the Transcendental Club.[7]

No one among the transcendentalists was a systematic thinker in the classic philosophic sense. What the membership shared was a faith, an essential belief in the power of intuitive thought. Maintaining that the senses were unreliable allies in the personal search for absolute truth, they believed that insight into the universal reality of God came directly to each individual human mind. Rational scientific investigation, the transcendentalists argued, uncovered knowledge only of the inferior material world. To know God, each individual must set aside reason and fall back on intuitive perception. Doing so, the individual would discover within a knowledge of genuine beauty, morality, and justice. Having transcended the meanness of the material, the individual would then begin behaving in a manner curiously reminiscent of seventeenth-century Puritan moralists.[8]

Concord became a favored meeting place for the Transcendental Club after Emerson established a home in the town. His choice of residence was as much the result of geographic accident as anything else. Waldo's genealogical roots lay in the town; his grandfather, pastor of Concord's First Church in 1775, had been one of the first heroes of the Revolution. When Ellen Tucker died, Emerson sought out the security of the traditional family homestead, living off and on with his relations in the "Old Manse" near the North Bridge for the next four years. After giving the principal oration for the town's two hundredth anniversary, he decided to live in Concord permanently. He proposed marriage again (to thirty-three year old Lydia Jackson of Plymouth), and in preparation for housekeeping purchased the Coolidge house on the Cambridge Pike at the eastern edge of the village. Waldo and "Lidian" took up residence in September 1835.[9]

The house, renamed "Bush" by the Emersons, quickly became a meeting place for the exchange of transcendental ideas. The Hedge Club met there periodically, and several leading lights of the movement came for sustained visits, particularly Bronson Alcott and Margaret Fuller. Alcott eventually established his own residence in Concord, as did promising young authors Ellery Channing and Nathaniel Hawthorne. Waldo Emerson had rapidly become a sort of intellectual magnet.[10]

From the perspective of the twentieth century, we look upon Emerson as the father and guiding light of the Transcendental movement, a force in American intellectual history who rose from triumph to triumph in his crusade to overthrow the forces imprisoning American thought. Certainly his fellow Transcendentalists did not fully see him in this light, and the general public even less so. Fame came to Emerson slowly, a fact critical to understanding his relationship with Henry Thoreau.

Two of the sources of Emerson's supposed notoriety were in fact received tepidly when they originated. The first of these was the book *Nature,* which Emerson published anonymously at his own expense in 1836. Now considered a virtual manifesto of Transcendentalism, the book at publication was overshadowed by the more fully mature works of Orestes Brownson and George Ripley, brought out at the same time. Emerson gave away about half the original printing of one thousand copies, defeating the point of the anonymity and underscoring the feeble impact of the book.[11]

The second supposed source of fame was Emerson's Harvard Phi Beta Kappa address of 1837, "The American Scholar." Now called "America's Declaration of Intellectual Independence," the address was not originally received as such. The topic was not novel—an oration on the American scholar was an annual tradition at Harvard—and Emerson was not even the first choice for speaker that year. Much of the speech was the standard stuff appropriate to the occasion, and although his plea for American students to free themselves from the stranglehold of European tradition was quite eloquent, the idea was far from new.[12]

Emerson made more of an impact a year later with his Harvard Divinity School address, in which he boldly set forth the sources of his disagreement with orthodox Unitarianism. Two centuries earlier, Emerson would have been banished from Massachusetts as a heretic. In 1838, the Harvard Divines were outraged, but they dismissed him as a crank, and transcendentalism generally as a humbug.[13]

So, at the time Waldo Emerson forged his close friendship with Henry Thoreau in 1837–38, he had achieved a certain notoriety in New England, but of a dubious kind. His lectures were popular and well-attended, but very few took his transcendental ideas very seriously. Emerson had moved some important minds, and had laid the groundwork for the creation of a powerful moral vision that would have an essential impact on the great social issues of the day. But in 1838, when Emerson wrote his now-famous letter protesting the Cherokee removal from Georgia, President Martin Van Buren had not heard of him, and probably never read the condemning phrases. Genuine national and international recognition did not come until the 1840s.[14]

If Emerson had been truly famous in 1837, his first contacts with Henry Thoreau necessarily would have been on a different, very unequal plane. The actual circumstances—Emerson, the mildly successful lecturer and preacher, still searching for a meaningful way to express the ideas bursting within him; Thoreau, the new Harvard graduate commencing the same search—enabled the two to form a friendship comparable to that of brothers with a fourteen-year gap in age. They were not equals, but they had much in common. In the next five years, personal tragedies would bind them more fully. The two became very close friends.

Thoreau knew of Emerson's ideas before he knew the man. Away at Harvard when the Emersons moved into Bush, he first became acquainted with transcendental ideas during a teaching stint at Canton, Massachusetts, when he stayed at the home of Orestes Brownson. Thoreau's first awareness of Emerson's ideas came by reading *Nature,* which he twice checked out from the Harvard Library in the spring of 1837. The book worked an immediate and powerful influence. Henry began incorporating transcendental ideas into his college papers, and worked at writing poems. Still, he apparently did not attend Emerson's "American Scholar" address, delivered to his own graduating class. When he read the essay soon after, this too had a forceful impact on his intellect. Emerson sounded the bugle; Thoreau heeded the call.[15]

The two met sometime in the summer of 1837 and had become good friends by the fall. Thoreau was invited to Emerson's home to hear private readings of his lectures, and to join in the discussions with Alcott, Ripley, Fuller, and the others—an intoxicating opportunity for a young graduate, and Thoreau was fully prepared to seize the moment.[16] Modeling himself on Emerson, he began keeping a journal, almost certainly at the older man's behest:

> Oct 22nd 1837
>
> "What are you doing now?" he asked, "Do you keep a journal?" —So I make my first entry to-day.[17]

The modeling did not end there. More than one witness reported a marked change in Henry's very demeanor. In Emerson's company, Thoreau so fully adopted the man's manners, gestures, and speech patterns that "he had become the counterpart of Mr. Emerson. . . . It was a notable instance of unconscious imitation."[18]

Emerson, for his part, was much taken with "My good Henry," Thoreau's "simplicity and clear perception." In his first journal entry regarding Thoreau, written on February 17, 1838, he continued: "How comic is simplicity in this double-dealing, quacking world. Everything that boy says makes merry with society, though nothing can be graver than his meaning. I told him he should write out the history of his college life, as Carlyle has his tutoring."[19] Here was both the unequal nature of the relationship between Waldo and "that boy" and the beginnings of Emerson's efforts to channel and direct Thoreau's efforts as a scholar.

Henry's most immediate problem was finding work. A Harvard education raised one's status in the world, but also severely limited the range of career options. Essentially, the choices were the ministry, medicine, law, or teaching. In Thoreau's case, all but the last were laughable, and he expended several years attempting to establish himself in preparatory school teaching. The two years he spent operating the Concord Academy with his brother were the most successful, and that venture collapsed when John became too consumptive to continue. Henry applied and was rejected for jobs as far away as Virginia and Maine, and he spent a miserable six months as a private tutor for Emerson's brother's children on Staten Island in 1843. It was his last teaching job. Between 1837 and 1845, Henry was more successful at making pencils in his father's shop than anything else.[20]

In the meanwhile, the writings of Ralph Waldo Emerson gave Thoreau a great deal to think about. Three aspects of Emerson's philosophy were critical to Henry Thoreau's intellectual development: his "compound" view of the universe, his definition of Nature, and his clarion call for a uniquely American poetry and scholarship. Much of Thoreau's intellectual direction in the 1840s hinged on these three elements.

Waldo Emerson was primarily, essentially, fundamentally interested in understanding the relationship between the human individual and the mind of God. What was proper human behavior in God's eyes? How was the individual to recognize those activities that brought him or her closer to the genuine spirit of the universe? Emerson sought to intuit the answers to these questions, denying the competence of sensate, rational inquiry to resolve any problem worth considering. By 1836, he had developed a subtle and careful mental image of the universe, drawing heavily on the Platonic reinterpretations of Plotinus and the romantic visions of Goethe, Coleridge, and Wordsworth. Emerson could hardly claim originality in the fundamental basics of his ideas. His importance lay in the beauty of his prose and the manner in which he imparted a peculiarly American twist to the concepts.[21]

He began by positing a separation between his spiritual self (his soul) and "all that is NOT ME," which he labeled "NATURE." He thus enlarged the garden definition of nature to include everything that could be detected by the senses of his own body—or anybody else's, for that matter. This raised the usual philosophical problem: How did one know that nature even exists, as it is impossible to rely on any information provided by your body, so separate from the soul? Emerson replied that this problem really made no difference to the soul, since the relation of the whole and the parts remained the same. What was important was to understand that sensate knowledge was relative, while idealistic knowledge, that which was revealed directly by the soul, was absolute. "Whilst we behold unveiled the nature of Justice and Truth," he wrote, "we learn the difference between the absolute and the conditional. . . . As it were, for the first time, *we exist.*"[22]

To examine Nature was to examine the material world. Emerson recognized some value in this, but only in a subordinate sense. What was truly important was the world of the spirit, where love, beauty, and power all were one, and where humanity could gain "access to the entire mind of the Creator." The point of existence, in Emerson's view, was to open one's individual self to the greatest possible extent to the world of the spirit, a world where all "is one and not compound," to fully comprehend that this spirit is not outside but within each individual. The senses told the mind that we are part of a material world, but this was a lie. For Emerson, humanity was part of a universal soul, and separate from a Nature that might not even exist. By reducing Nature to the point of possible nonexistence, and posing an essential indifference to the whole question, he in effect denied the possibility of a dual creation. More importantly, by denying Nature any significant role in his universe, he denied death. He and Ellen Tucker were still at one in the universal spirit. By 1838, Emerson had given a name to the world of the spirit, calling it the "Over-soul."[23]

Having defined the essential problem and determined the goal to be reached, his mind turned then to methods. It is one thing to state that real truth lies in freeing oneself from the senses and getting in closer touch with the Over-soul, quite another to genuinely achieve the ambition. His duty was to discern a proper path, one that he could follow, and one he could describe for others. He could not lead; each individual had to discover his or her own way to the spirit. He did recognize that "It is essential to a true theory of nature and of man, that it should contain somewhat progressive." Some material things pointed the way to the truth far better than others. Emerson therefore spent much time over the next quarter century lecturing and writing on such proper virtues as prudence, love, friendship, heroism, and reform—all discussed on a spiritual plane. He also acknowledged the importance of history, identifying figures from the past who exemplified the behaviors best calculated to bring the individual closer to the Over-soul. And most importantly (at least for a consideration of Henry Thoreau), he carefully examined the role of the natural world.[24]

Probably Emerson's brief flirtation with the idea of becoming a scientific naturalist inspired him both to entitle his first book *Nature,* and to devote so much of the essay to the human relationship with our natural surroundings. Just as he recognized that certain human activities drew humanity closer to the creator than others, he realized that some portions of Nature ("NOT ME") were more helpful in leading to the Over-soul than others. Human constructs, human institutions—especially those dedicated to the pursuit of commerce and industry—were the least inspiring parts of Nature. The bucolic scenery of the countryside on the other hand—forests, rivers, the sublime view from mountaintops—could lend assistance as "settings" for proper thought. "In the woods we return to reason and faith," he observed. Emerson specifically cited the Concord River as one such proper setting, but warned that the specifics of location and appearance did not really matter. Each varying aspect created just a single impression on the mind engaged in the proper search for the substance of the Over-soul. All forms "make an analogous impression on the mind," he wrote. "The world thus exists to the soul to satisfy the desire for beauty."[25]

The woods, and everything within, existed, so far as Emerson was concerned, to serve as symbols for the higher, unified world of which the human soul was a part. Each part and portion of the natural world represented this greater spiritual unity with equal perfection. A single leaf was reflective of the universal spirit. ("The world is emblematic.")[26]

If all of the natural world was merely a symbol, Emerson theorized, then all the information collected by the scientific naturalists had little value. "Nor has science sufficient humanity, so long as the naturalist overlooks that wonderful congruity which subsists between man and the natural world," Emerson warned. "He cannot be a naturalist until he satisfies all the demands of the spirit."[27]

Although the wonders and beauties of wild nature intrigued Emerson, he made little attempt to study the subject in any systematic way. A reading of his journals leaves the impression that he did not possess the scientific turn of mind in any sense; he was virtually a pure abstract thinker. Between 1850 and 1860, probably influenced by Thoreau, he did keep a specific journal on natural themes. The "Notebook Naturalist" (176 pages; 76 completely blank; several others sparsely filled) bore quotations from a considerable number of scientists, including Linneaus, Cuvier, LaPlace, Humboldt, and Agassiz, organized under subject headings such as "Botany," Zoology," "Geography," "Astronomy," and several more. Most of the quotations were very general in type (for example, "There are 250[,]000 species of animals known, says Agassiz"). Interspersed with these were Emerson's own sporadic nature observations, ranging from such unedifying comments as "England is a shower bath," to a few fairly specific notes:

> Feb 13 1853 in driving snow storm a dense flock of snowbirds on & under the pigweed in the garden—lesser redpoll linnet, Linarea minor.
> black legs, crimson crown or frontlet on the male. H.D.T.[28]

The initials H.D.T. occur after the preponderance of the specific personal observations, indicating that Emerson obtained his information secondhand, from Thoreau. In the main, this journal—Emerson's one effort to apply himself seriously to nature study—reads as an ill-organized and eclectic collection of odd information. There is no evidence that Emerson ever employed any of this material to any purpose; lectures, essays, or even conversation, save perhaps with Henry. It is difficult to escape the impression that Emerson would have had problems distinguishing a finch from a flycatcher, although he did once triumph over Henry by bringing back from Yarmouth, Massachusetts, two berry-yielding plants his friend had never seen. Emerson's regular journals contain almost nothing of the natural world. In all his long years of writing and study, he seems largely to have adhered to the maxim set forth so starkly in *Nature:* "All the facts in natural history taken by themselves, have no value, but are barren like a single sex."[29]

So what was the proper occupation for a man or woman of intellect? Waldo Emerson provided direct answers to this conundrum, initially in his "American Scholar" address at Harvard, and later in an essay entitled "The Poet," published in 1844 but conceived at least three years earlier.

In the "American Scholar," Emerson applied the lessons advanced in his book *Nature,* emphasizing that there existed only one universal "MAN," who had been metamorphosed by society into many: farmers, professors, engineers (and laborers and farm wives, although he did not mention them). To Emerson, by far the most important of these many was the thinking man—the scholar, who attempts to bring order out of the chaos of things, thereby perceiving the spiritual oneness of all humanity. Taught "by nature, by books, and by action," the scholar was the world's heart and eye, a selfless thinker whose sole quest was to reveal the law of nature operating in each individual. "Men in history, men in the world of today, are bugs," Emerson reported bluntly, "are spawn, and are called 'the mass' and 'the herd.'" The highest possible calling was that of the thinking scholar, who would lead this mass of bugs to the light of spiritual truth. "The world is nothing," he advised, "the man is all; in yourself is the law of all nature."[30]

A half century after the address, when writers had begun calling it "America's intellectual Declaration of Independence," they pointed especially to Emerson's admonition, "We have listened too long to the courtly muses of Europe." It was time, he believed (as did many others), for the growth of a uniquely American voice, a voice of scholars and literary spokesmen who would declare the spiritual oneness of the universe to all the American people. Especially, Waldo envisioned a voice of American poetry.[31]

He enlarged on this theme in "The Poet," an essay based on ideas developed between 1841 and 1843. Here he further divided the thinking scholar into three kinds, "the knower, the doer, and the sayer." Of the three, the sayer he considered the most valuable, as this kind of scholar showed that "Beauty is the Creator of the Universe." The sayer was, of course, the poet. For Emerson, the poet's role was absolutely essential, for he must declare—in language that all can hear, comprehend, and love—the truth hidden from humankind, that all of creation is "intrinsically ideal and beautiful." This poet must first comprehend that all of material Nature was a series of symbols for the inner beauty to be found on the spiritual plane, and then be prepared to use those symbols to deliver the true message.[32]

Who would be this uniquely American poet? "I look in vain for the poet whom I describe," Emerson admitted. For the one who succeeded, the rewards were without measure: "O poet! a new nobility is conferred in groves and pastures, and not in castles, or by the sword-blade, any longer. The conditions are hard, but equal. Thou shalt leave the world, and know the muse only. . . . And this is the reward: that the ideal shall be real to thee, and the impressions of the actual world shall fall like summer rain, copious, but not troublesome, to thy invulnerable essence."[33]

Thoreau read Emerson closely. A compound universe, a Nature symbolic of the higher spiritual plane of existence, a clear call for the rise of an American thinker, and especially an American poet. All in all, a heady dose for a young man freshly graduated from Harvard.

Early entries in Henry Thoreau's journals demonstrate that he had heard and understood the essential messages of Waldo Emerson. In his second entry, dated October 24, 1837, he wrote, "Every part of nature teaches that the passing away of one life is the making room for another." Nature, in effect, was the same in all of its parts, a reflection of Emerson's belief in its emblematic quality. Two months later, Thoreau was deeply at work enlarging this theme, stating "How indispensable to a correct study of nature is a perception of her true meaning—The fact will one day flower into a truth."[34]

Thoreau never wrote a sustained piece on transcendental ideas, either for publication or for private entry into his journals. Still, he understood the points perfectly well, and was willing (at least in the early 1840s) to adopt Emerson's view of the universe. On September 28, 1840, he confided to his journal,

> The world thinks it knows only what it comes in contact with, and whose repelling points give it a configuration to the senses—a hard crust aids its distinct knowledge. But what we truly know has no points of repulsion, and consquently no objective form—being surveyed from within. We are acquainted with the soul and its phenomena, as a bird with the air in which it floats. Distinctness is superficial and formal merely.
>
> We touch objects—as the earth we stand on—but the soul—as the air we breathe. We know the world superficially—the soul centrally.—In one case our surfaces meet, in the other our centres coincide.[35]

This basic transcendental idea—the compound form of the universe—informed nearly all of Thoreau's writing through the year 1846.

Still, Emerson's view of the natural world posed some difficulty for Thoreau. By devaluing the importance of the facts of natural history, Emerson reduced to mere symbol a portion of the world where Henry possessed some real knowledge. For nine years, Henry bowed to Waldo's interpretation. In doing so, he betrayed his superficial command of natural history. Thoreau could accept the notion of nature as mere symbol because he did not know enough to argue differently.

What was the extent of Thoreau's natural history knowledge during the 1840s?

As a member of the Thoreau family, Henry of course shared in the bird watching and the country excursions actively encouraged by his parents, especially his mother. Too, he was exposed to his village's general interest in natural history, attending the lectures of the Concord Lyceum, which began when he was twelve years old. As a youth he apparently spent many enjoyable days walking in the woods and fields, becoming generally familiar (along with his brother and sisters) with the names of the more outstanding birds, flowers, and animals of his native town.[36]

What little was recollected by classmates of his days at Harvard suggests that he spent the vast majority of his time there indoors, either in his room or at the library. He did take the college's one offering in natural history (curriculum unknown), but apparently read just one book in connection with the course, *An Introduction to Physiological and Systematical Botany,* the first American edition, by Sir James Edward Smith. It seems unlikely that Henry Thoreau graduated from college with a knowledge of nature any more discerning than that shared by many of his contemporaries.[37]

Essentially, the belief that Thoreau possessed a reputation as an expert naturalist in the 1830s derives from two kinds of sources: the recollections of children he taught at the Concord Academy and the testimony of friends and acquaintances. Typical of the former are the memories of George F. Hoar, who attended the Thoreaus' Academy (1838–41) while in his early teens: "He [Henry] knew the rare forest birds and wild animals. . . . We used to say that if anything happened in the deep woods which only came about once in a hundred years, Henry Thoreau would be sure to be on the spot at the time and know the whole story."[38]

This might seem conclusive but for two problems. First, Hoar was a lifelong resident of Concord, who knew Thoreau not only as a student in the early 1840s, but as an adult in the 1850s, when Thoreau's naturalist expertise had indeed become formidable. Second, Hoar wrote this memoir when he was seventy, thirty-four years after Thoreau's death. It is impossible to rule out a conflation of memory on Hoar's part; the knowledge of "the rare forest birds and wild animals" he attributed to Henry may well have developed much later than 1841.[39]

Two other school students recalled Thoreau's awareness of the wild flora and fauna, but the same basic criticisms again apply—the witnesses looked back from the closing years of the nineteenth century, attempting to recall fifty- and sixty-year-old memories of a man who had become famous for his woodsy lore. Of these sources, a memory of student Henry Warren most rings true: Thoreau "had become so well acquainted with the flowers, large and small, of Concord, Acton, and Lincoln, that without looking in the almanac, he could tell by the blooming of the flowers what month it was." But the knowledge was not perfect. In a journal entry dated September 12, 1842, Thoreau noted the presence of several flowers growing along the banks of the Concord River, including a "kind of coreopsis or sun flower. . . . And a tall dull red flower like milkweed." Henry did not know their names.[40]

Memories of other young people award brief and at times dubious glimpses of Thoreau later in the 1840s. Consider this example:

> He was talking to Mr. Alcott of the wild flowers in Walden woods when, suddenly stopping, he said: "Keep very still and I will show you my family." Stepping quickly outside the cabin door, he gave a low and curious whistle; immediately a woodchuck came running towards him from a nearby burrow. With varying note, yet still low and strange, a pair of gray squirrels were summoned and approached him fearlessly. With still another note several birds, including two crows, flew towards him, one of the crows resting on his shoulder.[41]

Here the author, a boy of seventeen, crossed the borders into sheer fantasy. The only time Thoreau may have whistled at a woodchuck would have been to scare him out of the beanfield. In this case, the exaggeration is painfully obvious. The problem is, there is no way to determine the extent of any possible exaggeration in similar sources. Stories range wildly, and corroboration is almost wholly absent. The memories of Thoreau's students are not to be relied upon.

Perhaps gentlemen of literary standing are more to be trusted on this question. Two such individuals wrote down their impressions of Henry Thoreau as a naturalist *during the 1840s.* One was Emerson, the other Nathaniel Hawthorne.

When Nathanial Hawthorne moved to Concord in 1842 he became acquainted with Thoreau through Emerson. The two friends paid a most awkward call when Hawthorne first arrived, and afterwards he and Thoreau spent some time walking together and boating on the river. (Thoreau sold Hawthorne his boat.)[42] Based on these few contacts, Hawthorne confided to his notebook that

> Mr. Thorow is a keen and delicate observer of nature—a genuine observer, which, I suspect, is almost as rare a character as even an original poet; and Nature, in return for his love, seems to adopt him as her especial child, and show him secrets which few others are allowed to witness. He is familiar with beast, fish, fowl, and reptile, and has strange stories to tell of adventures, and friendly passages with these lower brethern of mortality. Herb and flower, likewise, wherever they grow, whether in garden, or wild wood, are his familiar friends.[43]

But Hawthorne was no naturalist; plainly he was easily impressed by whatever unspecified "secrets" Thoreau might have shared in their few meetings, having little time to be a genuine observer of beasts or flowers himself. The best to be drawn from this brief entry is that Thoreau spent a goodly amount of time in the woods and fields of Concord and that he carefully watched the behavior of flora and fauna. The degree of his knowledge remains obscure.

That Emerson was impressed with Thoreau's abilities as a field naturalist, there can be no doubt. Two years before meeting Henry, Waldo had dreamed of writing a "Natural history of the woods around my shifting camp for every month in the year. . . . No bird, no bug, no bud, should be forgotten on his day & hour." Emerson never had time to train himself to such a study, but in Thoreau he perhaps saw someone uniquely qualified for the task. Certainly Emerson saw wild nature more clearly in Henry's company. A walk to the Fair Haven Cliff early in their friendship brought Waldo "a new scene, a new experience."[44] Another walk recorded in Emerson's journal during the autumn of 1839 well illustrates the older man's impressions of his protégé's ability.

> 20 November. Ah Nature the very look of the woods is heroical and stimulating. This afternoon in a very thick grove where H.D.T. showed me the bush of the mountain laurel, the first I have seen in Concord, the stems of pine & hemlock & oak almost gleamed like steel upon the excited eye. How old, how aboriginal these trees appear, though not many years older than I. They seem parts of the eternal chain of destiny whereof this sundered Will of man is the victim.[45]

Emerson was never able to concentrate his attention on the minutia of nature for very long. Two sentences of botanical observation seemed to him enough to draw a moral applicable to human experience: young trees quickly became links of the eternal chain of destiny. How could such a man as this, his head full of his quest for the spirit that lay separate from Nature, ever assess the natural history abilities of his young friend? Reading Emerson, it becomes obvious that Thoreau was the more careful and discerning naturalist of the two; but then, that was not so terribly difficult.

The observations of Thoreau's older friends are no more helpful than the memories of his young students in assessing his abilities as a naturalist. There is no real basis upon which to independently judge Thoreau's early proficiency.

Having exhausted the independent possibilities, the log of Henry Thoreau's readings, along with his own writings—both his private journals and his published works—become the only real sources for an honest appraisal. The news is not good. The record of his readings in a few natural history books indicates a very low level of interest; the nature observations surviving from his journals between 1837 and 1846 are few and desultory; the nature material incorporated into his published writings for the same period is sketchy where it occurs at all. If Thoreau was an expert naturalist during this period, he disguised the fact very, very well.

In the years of transcendental apprenticeship, Henry examined roughly a dozen books that might be considered works on natural history. Several of these he read in 1842 for a review at Emerson's behest. Thoreau studied the remainder, including such classic authors as Audubon, Lyell, and Linnaeus, for self-enlightenment.[46] As the notes in surviving remaining journals suggest, his goal was not in any sense technical knowledge, but rather moral edification and entertainment. After reading Linnaeus in 1839, he wrote of "the quiet bravery of the man." He read Audubon in December 1841 in search of "a thrill of delight," noting that "books of natural history make the most cheerful winter reading." He admitted in 1840 that "a very meagre natural history suffices to make me a child—only their names and genealogy make me love fishes." And, in 1856, after he had gone a long way toward becoming an expert botanist, Thoreau recalled using Bigelow's *Plants of Boston and Vicinity* twenty years before, "looking chiefly for the popular names and the short references to the localities of plants, even without any regard to the plant. I also learned the names of many, but without using any system, and forgot them soon."[47]

Very little of Thoreau's early journals exist. Originally, he envisioned the journals as a kind of literary workshop, a commonplace book for recording ideas and roughing out initial drafts of lectures and essays. Often he tore actual leaves from the journal books to better collate and assemble his materials. The few remaining pages fell into tatters. In 1841, living at Emerson's and preparing to write new works for *The Dial,* Thoreau recopied such of his entries that had survived this self-inflicted piracy. Any analysis of the first four years of Thoreau's journals must be based on this copy. Henry continued to take leaves from his journals through 1849, though he grew more circumspect as the years went by.[48]

Occasional entries in the remnants of these early journals do show that Thoreau was a good and patient observer of nature. He recognized the track of an otter in the snow, sighted a fox at Fair Haven Pond, distinguished the call of the veery. But these notes are very few and far between amidst long pages defining proper virtuous behavior, criticizing the literary merits of one author or another, constructing poems. Perhaps the original journal volumes contained more, but it seems unlikely, as essentially none showed up in later writings. If Thoreau did record additional natural phenomena between 1837 and 1841, he did not regard the material as important enough to recopy into the new volume while at Emerson's. Such nature writings as Thoreau saw fit to save—brief, to the point, and generally bearing a tedious moral—seem almost orphaned in the company of his other materials.[49]

Given Emerson's injunctions concerning the uses of natural history, which Thoreau read at least twice in the book *Nature,* the scant attention paid to the subject in Henry's surviving journals should not seem surprising. For Emerson, nature was mere symbol and perhaps nonexistent; scientific nature study was second-rate knowledge, useful only for providing perspective on the important matters of life. When Thoreau did take the time to record nature observations, he was careful to toe the transcendental line:

> Oct 27th 1837
>
> The Fog.—
>
> The prospect is limited to Nobscot and Annursnack-. The trees stand with boughs downcast like pilgrims beaten by a storm, and the whole landscape wears a sombre aspect.
>
> So when thick vapors cloud the soul, it strives in vain to escape from its humble working day valley, and pierce the dense fog which shuts out from the view the blue peaks in its horizon, but must be content to scan its near and homely hills.—[50]

The division of this entry into two paragraphs reflects young Thoreau's effort to trace the transcendental moral in what his senses revealed. The first paragraph, just two sentences, painted a vivid picture of Concord enshrouded in a dreary autumnal fog. But this was mere fact, an observation given importance only by the stricture provided in the second half of the entry. Just as the fog obscured the town, so too was the human soul obscured in its quest of lofty spiritual visions on the distant horizon. The voice of Emerson's *Nature* is loud and clear in this nature observation, and in several others scattered through the journals through 1845. The natural surroundings of Concord were of secondary interest to Thoreau in this period.

Just how good a naturalist was Henry Thoreau during the 1830s and early 1840s? Recalling the ornithological notebook he shared with siblings John and Sophia, with the fewer than sixty identifications they managed, it is very tempting to answer that he was not very good at all. In March 1840, he found himself unable to identify several bird species returning northward with the spring. Happy to find that these new arrivals did not come within the scope of his science, he celebrated birdsongs "sung as freshly as if it had been the first morning of creation, and had for background to their song an untrodden wilderness—stretching through many a Carolina and Mexico of the soul." (One of the very few surviving instances from this era in which Thoreau employed the Latin, Linnaean name for a bird—the *Fringilla Juncorum,* or field sparrow—came in a letter written to his brother in 1838.)[51]

To give some credence to the various witnesses who recalled his expertise so vividly (if inaccurately), it seems likely that he could put names to the more prominent birds and animals of the town and that he could both name the important flowers and provide the months of their blossoming. That is not much, really, but it may well have been enough to make him the most expert naturalist in Concord at the time. (The claim is a little bit like labeling someone the best cricket player in Point Barrow, Alaska; perhaps true, but what is the competition?)

It is more important to recognize that Henry Thoreau was not primarily interested in nature study during the period, and was at times at pains to avoid the subject. He was primarily interested in answering the summons of his new and influential friend. Emerson had issued a call for a uniquely American scholarship, an especially American poetry. Above all else, Henry Thoreau dreamed of becoming that American scholar and poet.

Emerson had Thoreau at least partially in mind when he wrote his essay, "The Poet"; Waldo lifted portions of an 1844 journal entry concerning Thoreau for the essay. By that time he had become somewhat discouraged and exasperated with Henry's poetical abilities, but there was no escaping that he had been Thoreau's great inspiration.[52]

The problem Thoreau faced lay in Emerson's high-flown and obscure demands for a literature reflecting the peculiar American spirit. Yes, the country needed its own voice, but what exactly was that voice to say? And how was the message to be expressed? Attempting to puzzle out the answers for himself between 1837 and 1846, Henry gathered several arrows into his quiver and shot them off more or less at random. That he was determined there was no doubt ("H.T. is full of noble madness lately, and I hope more highly of him than ever," Emerson wrote to Margaret Fuller in 1841).[53] But determination and raw talent were not enough; Henry's efforts to fit the transcendental mold became a struggle with mixed and meager results.

Newly graduated, Henry's attention was at first taken up with the task of building his career in teaching. Squeezed between letters of application and academy preparations, his public literary output was confined to a Concord Lyceum lecture on "Society" and a newspaper notice concerning the death of one of Concord's oldest residents. He confided poem after poem to his journal, and also began experimenting with the essay format, but had no ready outlet for his writings.[54]

Emerson and his fellow transcendentalists meanwhile wrestled with a similar sort of problem: how to get their views aired in public. Waldo continued to lecture with increasing popularity, but the major New England journals routinely rejected most transcendental essays, criticism, and poetry. Critiques of the transcendental message ranged in adjective from merely silly to outright blasphemous. To resolve this difficulty, the group finally agreed to undertake their own journal. *The Dial* was born in July 1840, with Margaret Fuller as editor.[55]

Thoreau's response to the opportunity *The Dial* presented is an excellent indicator of his own assessment of the relative merits of his talents. Between July 1840 and January 1842, he submitted several poems, an original essay defining the proper behavior for a well-rounded individual, and some translations of Greek mythology. There was no nature writing, save perhaps a few airily descriptive lines scattered through his ill-metered poetry.[56] Henry had determined to become America's poetic voice, and to that end, he had to become superior to nature. In a journal entry for March 3, 1839, Thoreau explained the necessity to himself.

> The Poet
>
> He must be something more than natural—even supernatural. Nature will not speak through but along with him. His voice will not proceed from her midst, but breathing on her, will make her the expression of his thought. He then poetizes, when he takes a fact out of nature into spirit—He speaks without reference to time or place. His thought is one world, her's another. He is another nature-Nature's brother.[57]

With Emerson standing behind him, encouraging every word, actively soliciting material for *The Dial*'s pages, Thoreau might well have thought that the perfect springboard for a poetical career had been presented him. He did not reckon with Margaret Fuller.

Fuller, the daughter of a Cambridge, Massachusetts, lawyer and congressman who believed in equal education for women, had attended the best schools. By the 1830s she was recognized as a brilliant conversationalist, one of the leading intellectuals of her generation. Although she had been a charter member of the Hedge Club and had published a highly respected translation of Goethe, the transcendentalists persuaded her to edit *The Dial* primarily because of her reputation as a literary critic.[58]

Margaret Fuller was far more honest with Thoreau than Emerson could ever be. Despite enormous pressure from Waldo, she steadfastly refused Thoreau's poorer attempts at poetry, either rejecting them outright or demanding revision after revision. She also refused the one essay he tendered, a piece called "The Service," which he never published anywhere. Fuller edited the first seven issues of *The Dial.* Thoreau's total appearances in those numbers amounted to four poems and one translation essay. Becoming the American scholar was more difficult than met the eye. When the Concord Academy closed down in April 1841, Thoreau inspected several farms and seriously entertained the notion of becoming a farmer. Encouraging this idea, Margaret Fuller thought he would become "a successful and happy man."[59]

Emerson refused to be discouraged. He invited Thoreau to live with him, offering room, board, and access to his considerable library in exchange for his young friend's services as a handyman. Soon afterward, Emerson wrote to Thomas Carlyle that a poet now lived with him. By September, Thoreau wrote to an acquaintance that he had composed more than three hundred verses. Two months later he began to compile an anthology of great English poetry, a project that would occupy much of his attention for the better part of three years and eventually come to nothing.[60]

Frustrated with the continuous demands on her time and lack of remuneration, Margaret Fuller turned the editorship of *The Dial* over to Emerson after the April 1842 issue. Thoreau's opportunities for publication improved correspondingly. In the next two years, *The Dial*'s pages would include eleven more of his poems, four more translations from the Greek, five sets of selections from Asian spiritual literature, and four original essays. The subject matter of the essays included such solid transcendental subjects as ancient poetry, anti-slavery reform, and the inward spiritual journey. The fourth essay was a review of books concerning what was for Thoreau highly unusual subject matter: natural history.[61]

Early in 1842, Emerson had given Thoreau the set of natural history volumes recently published at the behest of the Massachusetts Legislature. Hoping to steer Henry's creative energies in a positive direction, Waldo suggested that a review essay might be in order. Thoreau responded with "The Natural History of Massachusetts," which appeared in *The Dial* for July 1842.[62]

From the perspective of the twentieth century, this essay appears prototypical of the best Thoreau work to come, but it is very misleading to view the piece in that fashion. For the Henry Thoreau of 1842, this was just a single arrow from his quiver of ideas, and a not very important one at that. Even the general public regarded basic nature writing as a minor form of literary art, an estimation richly shared by the transcendentalists.[63]

Following the model of composition set forth by Emerson, Thoreau fashioned his essay by mining his journal for entries concerning natural history subjects. The piece reads as an episodic flow of ideas joined by a very general overarching theme, which indeed it was. The essay's comments on Audubon come from the journal entry of December 1841; those on Linneaus were written originally in November 1839. Comments made on fish in February 1840 were worked in, along with the tale of fox spotting from January 1841. The essay is in fact a quilt of virtually every surviving natural history observation Thoreau jotted down between 1837 and 1841. As such, it represents a summary of Thoreau's gleanings from nature through that date.[64]

Thoreau is careful in the essay to adhere to Emerson's standard transcendental creed, arguing that "we do not learn by inference and deduction . . . but by direct intercourse and sympathy." Denouncing the Baconian scientific method as false, he concludes that "we cannot know truth by contrivance and method." The best use for the facts of natural history were to point the way to greater spiritual truths. In keeping with that attitude, Thoreau barely remembered to mention the titles of the books he was supposedly reviewing.[65]

"The Natural History of Massachusetts" was the only essay Thoreau published in the first ten years of his writing career in which he directly addressed the subject of nature. While he wrote repeatedly about such virtues as bravery and friendship, spent considerable time collecting the works of the English poets, became active in the anti-slavery movement, read the great works of Asian religion, and researched historical figures such as Walter Raleigh, he seems to have purposely avoided the natural world as subject matter. This one essay he wrote at Emerson's urging, and the experience did not inspire him to write more. Plain nature was not a worthy theme for the American poet.[66]

Apart from the material placed in *The Dial,* Thoreau managed to publish only one other piece through early 1843. This was "A Walk to Wachusett," published in the January issue of the *Boston Miscellany.* Both this essay and "A Winter Walk," which appeared in *The Dial* for October 1843, were travel essays, a common format that Thoreau adapted for transcendental purposes. In each, the described journey is heavily symbolic of the inner search for spiritual understanding. The nature descriptions in these essays were exceedingly general and incidental to the story line.[67]

In "A Walk to Wachusett," Thoreau and a companion set their sights on a lofty and distant goal—Wachusett, a mountain visible on clear days in Concord. The journey is a record not so much of their observations as their thoughts, which became appropriately elevated as they ascended to the heights. Atop Wachusett, they are able to see farther than their fellow beings, even perceiving the hand that made the mountain. "So is the least part of nature in its bearings referred to all space."[68]

"A Winter Walk" extends this theme, describing a journey through the woods and fields of Concord the morning after a winter storm. All the world is shrouded and quiet, and familiar objects present such an unusual face that the walker intuits their existence on a higher plane. The essay suggests that even in homey and familiar surroundings the traveler could journey inward.[69] In both this essay and "A Walk to Wachusett," any nature description is highly generalized and "emblematic," intended only to point the way to greater spiritual achievement.

"A Walk to Wachusett" might have been a triumph of sorts for Thoreau—the first sustained essay for which he received monetary payment—except that the *Boston Miscellany* never paid him. (The journal closed down after one more issue.) He had by that time been writing for five years without a cent to show for his effort.[70]

Emerson had no such problems. In the spring of 1841 he published a new book, a collection entitled *Essays, First Series.* Acclaim in the major urban centers of both the United States and Great Britain was profuse and immediate. In 1842 he lectured in New York City, and in the winter of 1843 undertook a lecture of several eastern cities. For the first time, Ralph Waldo Emerson became truly famous, both nationally and internationally.[71]

Although a sharing of personal tragedies bound them more closely together (Thoreau's brother John died of lockjaw on January 11, 1842; Emerson's son Waldo died of scarlatina eleven days later), Emerson's success made the friendship between the two more unequal. Waldo did insure that Henry's work appeared regularly in *The Dial,* but he also felt compelled to give a more honest appraisal of his friend's verses. This came in the autumn of 1842; very shortly after that Thoreau burned most of his three hundred or more poems. Both Emerson and Thoreau felt the time had come for the young man to make a change. In May of 1843 he sailed to Staten Island, New York, to take a job as tutor to the three sons of William Emerson, Waldo's brother.[72]

A major component in Thoreau's decision to move was the fact that he would have access to the major literary markets of New York City. He had little luck. Henry did manage to sell two minor pieces to John O'Sullivan's *United States Magazine and Democratic Review,* but the process involved too much compromise with the editor to be edifying. When O'Sullivan suggested he write an essay employing the nature themes more familiar to him, Thoreau refused outright.[73]

Perhaps Henry's most important accomplishment in New York was to establish a friendship with fellow New Englander Horace Greeley, the powerful editor of New York's *Tribune.* Greeley subsequently served as Thoreau's literary agent, successfully placing several of his most important essays.

More than anything else, Thoreau was homesick on Staten Island. He heartily disliked New York City, got on poorly with his three charges, and above all, missed Concord. After spending six months writing long and miserable letters to his mother, his sisters, and to Lidian Emerson, he made a brief Thanksgiving visit, and quickly thereafter came home for good. This was the last time he made any serious effort to leave his native soil.[74]

The New York experiment was a sad failure, and the outlook at home soon diminished as well. *The Dial,* barely able to recover publication costs, passed out of existence with the April 1844 issue. Deprived of his chief outlet, Thoreau would not appear in print again for almost a year. Henry worked closely with his father throughout 1844, making pencils, building a new house on Texas Street. In April he took an extended walking tour, climbing Mount Greylock with a new friend, poet Ellery Channing (who was trying not to be at home while his wife gave birth). No Thoreau journal exists for this period. Having reached low ebb, it is likely that Henry had ceased to make day-to-day entries. Emerson meanwhile brought out a second acclaimed series of essays and began working on a collection of his own poems. His star continued to ascend. Thoreau's discussions with his mentor became correspondingly sharp in their disagreements.[75]

A sad yet revealing incident provided a capstone of sorts to this phase of Thoreau's career. On April 30, 1844, Henry embarked on a boating excursion to the source of the Sudbury River with a former student, Edward Hoar. They got no further than Fair Haven Bay when they halted to fish for their evening meal. Hauling in a considerable catch, they quickly kindled a fire in a grassy recess to broil their prize. A mistake. The spring had been dry, the river low. The two took no precautions, and when the fire jumped into the dry grass, the flames rushed out of control toward the nearby woods. More than three hundred acres burned. The owners were understandably angry, along with several villagers who joined to fight the fire through a long night.[76]

Six years would pass before Thoreau could bring himself to write of this incident. If his friends and students thought of him as a friend of nature, many of his fellow townspeople now considered him a "damned rascal." The whispered words "burnt woods" followed him for years. Surely the fire of 1844 was a carelessness no true naturalist would care to contemplate.[77]

By fall, Henry Thoreau, perhaps sobered but essentially undaunted, had begun to think of new directions for himself. He determined to continue his efforts to earn his bread by writing—a brave decision in the face of his success to that point. His poems and essays largely a failure, his reputation as a friend of nature tarnished; there was much to prove.

There was also the matter of his brother. Despite various rivalries, Henry had truly loved John, had taken his death very hard. The sorrow needed expression; his brother needed a fitting elegy. Thoreau called to mind a journey the two had taken back in 1839, a two-week excursion to the White Mountains undertaken by sailing the Concord and Merrimac Rivers. Henry had written little of the trip at the time, but now the adventure assumed new and symbolic meaning. He began writing all that he could recall.[78]

To this end, Thoreau acquired a new notebook, taller than the predecessors he had employed in his journalizing. Recopying old journal entries into this "long book," drafting new thoughts and observations, he began to organize past and present materials to shape a long account of the actual and the symbolic journey along the two rivers. Provided he could find the time and the peace and quiet, Henry Thoreau had decided he would write a book.[79]

I wish to go away and live by the pond, and when my friends inquire I have no better reason to give—than that I shall hear the wind whispering among the reeds.

— The Long Book, 1844(?)

3 THE POND AND THE MOUNTAIN

THE WRITING LIFE IMPELLED Henry Thoreau. Despite the repeated failures, reversals of fortune, and inability to make money, writing remained the only career to hold any attraction for him. Reduced to almost critical circumstances by 1844, Thoreau made a series of decisions that collectively rescued his chances for success in the field. Most important among these determinations, he resolved to write a book, and to move to a cabin by a pond to accomplish that task without undue distraction. Neither decision was directly related to any casual interest Henry may have had in nature. His conscious knowledge of nature's ways remained weak and superficial; the thought of writing natural history offered no appeal. Yet, in going to live at Walden, Thoreau incidentally created for himself the opportunity to genuinely see and understand something of nature's ways for the first time. By the time he left Walden in 1847, his view of nature had changed forever, and with it his entire approach to life and to the craft of writing.

native, no other hope for you. Eat yourself up; you will eat nobody else, nor anything else."[6]

Soon after, Henry concluded a bargain with Emerson, then borrowed an axe and began felling timbers for framing. By May he raised a roof on his cabin, with the help of a distinguished transcendental company including Channing, Emerson, and Bronson Alcott. On the Fourth of July, 1845 he moved in, although the tiny house was not yet complete.[7]

Few houses in American history have been more intimately described than the little cabin in Walden Woods. Still, actual drawings of the structure and its setting can surprise. In the most contemporary rendering, drawn from memory by Sophia Thoreau in 1854, the high-pitched roof initially draws the eye. Judging by the angle of the peak, Henry expected a great deal of snow. The careful shingling of walls and roof convey the owner's sense of dignity—this was no temporary shack, but the private home of a responsible citizen. Twelve-on-twelve windows centered in the side walls firmly establish that the resident was a New Englander.

Ironically, the woodcut made from Sophia Thoreau's drawing, used on the title page of the first edition of *Walden,* shows the wrong kind of trees in the background. Rather than firs and hardwoods, a stand of pitch pines dominated the backdrop of Thoreau's home. No trees at all grew on the one-hundred-foot slope separating the cabin from the pond. Clear cut by woodsmen for fuel, the sterile ground had given over to low-lying shrubs and herbs, including strawberries, blackberries, life-everlasting, and shrub oak. Henry's view down to his favorite swimming cove was unobscured.

The cabin sat at the edge of one of the largest remaining woods in Concord, a survivor of the general Puritan destruction of the New England wilderness. Far from being an outpost on the great American frontier, Henry's house nestled in an island of forest surrounded by fields and pastures. The wood was an anamoly in the town, standing on an isolated pocket of unusually porous sandy soils left by the glaciers. Scrubby populations of pitch pine, shrub oak, scarlet oak, black oak, and hickory occupied the ground. Generations of townspeople had mined these woods for fuel, but the land was not fit for agriculture. This piney sand barren was instead the home of such feathered neighbors as brown thrashers, "chewinks" (rufous-sided towhees), whippoorwills, and great horned owls. Gray squirrels scrambled from tree to tree, while eastern chipmunks occupied burrows among the tree roots. Cottontail rabbits sometimes approached Henry's door, and the occasional red fox threaded a path among the pines, oaks, and hickories. Wild nature surrounded Thoreau in Walden Woods. Within a year's time, these neighbors would become impossible to ignore.[8]

Apart from the desire to live life deliberately and write in peace, Henry wished also "to know beans." Even before taking up residence he planted two and a half acres in beans in an old field some two hundred yards northeast of his house. He also planted small amounts of potatoes, corn, peas, and turnips. The crop netted him eight dollars and seventy-one and a half cents at harvest. This, along with a little money earned by surveying and day labor, proved his only sources of income for the year. In moving to Walden, Thoreau was forced to make a virtue of simplicity; he had almost no money at all. The long homily on economy that forms the first chapter of *Walden* was inspired as a matter of necessity. Having failed to make a significant income from writing, Henry seized on the fact that there is a second way to be rich: to want little.[9]

Many in Concord must have felt it especially appropriate that the woodsburner had gone up the hill to live near Walden Pond. Traditionally, Walden had attracted Concord's outcasts. A freed slave by the name of Cato Ingraham had lived there, and another named Brister Freeman; also Zilpha, a poor "colored woman," and several poor white farmers answering to the names Stratton, Breed, Nutting, LeGross, and Wyman. All that remained in 1845 were the abandoned cellars of their houses, evidence of a poverty-ridden existence now rapidly disappearing into the forests. The latest of these outcasts, an alcoholic Irishman named Hugh Quoil, died not long after Henry moved in. Walden Woods was not the home of the commonly accepted members of the Concord community.[10]

Although Henry appreciated the beauties surrounding his isolated woodland home, he did not go to Walden Woods to study nature. The few nature observations he entered into his initial Walden journals read as sporadic afterthoughts, reflective and very short interruptions to the matters Thoreau took far more seriously.[11]

In the published version of *Walden,* Thoreau created emotional and spiritual distance between himself and his village family and neighbors by failing to mention or describe his actual distance from them. A brisk walk of only one and a half miles along the railroad tracks connected him with the village. He regularly entertained visitors at the pond, both his family and his friends as well as chance wanderers, and he went to town every two or three days. There he attended dinner parties, transacted business, called on acquaintances, spent time with his parents and sisters. Although he had little patience for the rigid formalities of Victorian society, Thoreau was much devoted to his family and enjoyed the community of his friends, especially Bronson Alcott, Ellery Channing, and the Emersons.[12]

The Walden stay was in no sense a pure experiment in domestic economy. Henry lived the simple life because that was the hand fate dealt him, and he learned enough to educate others of the possibilities at great length. But he often accepted lavish gifts of food, and he remained determined to make as much money as possible by writing. His first real monetary success as an author derived from works completed while he lived in the woods.

Judging from the surviving content of the three Walden journals (a little more than half of which survives),[13] various writing projects provided the essential focus of Thoreau's life in the woods. In the face of his disastrous experiences of 1843 and 1844, he had determined to continue his career as a writer and to concentrate on a book dedicated to the memory of his brother. This decision, made in 1844, dictated a profound reorientation in Henry's work habits. Unlike his failed poetry, which he could dash off in an afternoon's inspiration and work into shape in a day or two, or even unlike his early essays, which he composed by quilting together thoughts mined from his journals, a book required the creation of a powerful organizing concept and the ordering of a vast array of materials to cohere to that theme. In short, the book required concentration, close attention to detail, and above all, large blocks of uninterrupted peace and quiet.

Blocks of time were exactly what Thoreau had not possessed at his parents' home on Texas Street. Scrupulously honest about paying a fair room and board, Henry had worked long hours in his father's pencil factory to earn the money. When he was free from that responsibility, his parents' house was often too clamorous for serious scholarly work—the family took in boarders to make ends meet. Between the pencils and the noise, the Thoreau house was just not the proper environment for an aspiring writer. The desire to compose new essays and books ordained the need to move away from home.[14]

Settled in at the pond, Thoreau set to work on an array of writing projects. Although the elegy for his brother was the most pervasive of these, Henry recognized the need to continue his efforts to win name recognition with the reading public. Besides the work on his book, written out in the Long Book journal, he took along to the woods the beginnings of a long essay on Thomas Carlyle and two new blank notebooks. Wisely refusing to confine himself to a single undertaking, he had two endeavors in hand as he moved in, and was keeping a weather eye for further inspirations.[15]

The Carlyle essay proved the first fruit of the Walden stay. Henry completed a lecture draft for presentation to the Concord Lyceum in February 1846, and sent a polished copy to Horace Greeley for marketing the next autumn. When Greeley wrote back in October that *Graham's Magazine* would pay handsomely for the privilege of printing the work, it was the most uplifting news for Thoreau's writing career in three years.[16]

The fact that two blank journal notebooks accompanied Thoreau to Walden seems to imply that Henry saw enough potential in his living experiment to maintain a record of his stay. He used the two books in tandem, the first intended as a journal of his daily thoughts and activities (especially his developing criticism of contemporary society), the second as a notebook for his literary drafts, including both his book and the Carlyle essay. This artificial division of thought eventually disappeared as Henry began filling every available blank space with whatever ideas occupied his thoughts at the moment.[17]

The work that would become *A Week on the Concord and Merrimack Rivers* presented by far his knottiest problems. Back in 1839, Thoreau had written only the sketchiest of notes of the journey taken with his brother. Beginning in 1844, he tried to reconstruct the adventure from memory as well as he could, making entry after entry in the Long Book as details came back to him. Although he tried to discipline himself to write out the skeleton of the story in proper chronological order, the task was impossible. One of the first challenges at Walden was to sort out the disorder of the Long Book.[18]

From the outset, Henry did not intend *A Week* to be a strict accounting of the exact thoughts and activities he and his brother shared. While the book, tentatively titled "An Excursion on the Concord and Merrimack Rivers," was to tell the story of their travels in nature, the narrative would concentrate on the journey to higher and better thoughts they undertook as the week progressed. The action of boating on the two rivers would provide the framework for the contemplation the book was principally to relate.[19]

Materials for the contemplative side of *A Week* did not present a serious problem. The journals he had kept since 1839 were full of thoughts on virtue and proper behavior, on great men and the significance of the historic past, on literature and philosophy, on Eastern religion. For this aspect of his book, Thoreau need merely to pick and choose from among a wealth of entries and then organize the writings into a coherent framework.[20]

The material activities of the week's travels on the rivers was another matter. The journey had of course been almost entirely an outdoor experience—the days spent boating on the Concord or Merrimac, the nights spent camping along the shores. While this action may have been only secondarily important to Henry, it was necessary (if the book was to have any credibility) for the natural surroundings he described to be right. Here was a serious problem. Henry simply could not remember that much detail, and there was very little in his journals to go on.[21]

The Long Book compiled a variety of nature descriptions, some taken from memory, others from journal entries of 1842 and earlier. There was a certain desperation to the search for natural history materials. The actual journey was of two weeks' duration in late summer (August 31 to September 13, 1839), but Thoreau wrote into the Long Book journal entries ranging from the spring to the late fall over several years, hoping somehow to make them work. Some of the material fit quite smoothly—descriptions of robins, herons, bitterns, and bobolinks bore the proper aspect for a late summer river journey, whether the brothers saw them in August 1839 or not. A passage from the first draft in which he mentions that "we watched the flight of the robins & blackbirds which at this season may be seen flying directly high in the air especially over rivers" actually derived from a journal passage of July 1842, recorded eight months after John Thoreau died.[22]

Other nature observations posed even more of a struggle. The weather had turned from summer warmth to distinctly autumnal wind and chill during the last night of the actual voyage, and Thoreau used this as an excuse to introduce a discussion of natural phenomena associated with fall. A purple finch, which passed through New England only in April and October, wandered into the first draft of *A Week* through this device, as did a discussion of witch hazel, a shrub that bloomed in Concord in mid-

October. Notes on the trill of the song sparrow and an encounter with a fox entered into the Long Book proved too unseasonal to force into the first draft at any point.[23]

Lacking the personal observations necessary to flesh out the backdrop of his journey, Thoreau turned to books, especially to the natural history volumes he had reviewed for *The Dial* back in 1842. In February 1845, Henry for the moment completed the raids on his older journals for material to be entered into the Long Book. He turned to writing a lecture for the town Lyceum on the subject "Concord River," presumably to clarify his thoughts on the matter of streams, material and figurative. To lend reality to his subject, he devoted a major portion of this address to descriptions of the fish to be found in the river. Some of this came from his own experience as a skillful angler (Emerson and others often compared him to Izaak Walton), but the preponderance he drew from David H. Storer's *Report on the Fishes of Massachusetts.* This lecture proved to have more genuine nature observation than all the other material he had gathered for *A Week* combined.[24]

Once established at Walden, Thoreau began reorganizing the content of the Long Book into a single coherent narrative. To give the book's beginning a firm anchor in nature, he adapted his lyceum lecture on the Concord River for use as an introductory chapter, to be followed by seven additional chapters, each devoted to a day of the sojourn. Henry began the work bravely, adapting the array of moral contemplation, literary commentary, classical allusion, and Asian inspiration to comfortably fit the location, scenic background, and tone of each day as he remembered it. By the time he was halfway through, the fact that this first effort was in many ways inadequate had become obvious to him. The polished paragraphs that characterize the first pages of the draft gave way in several instances to hurriedly composed notes, often with incomplete sentences connected by dashes. The chapter entitled "Thursday Sept. 5th" took up just a single manuscript page. A great deal of work remained to be done before Thoreau could call this manuscript a book. He would work through draft after draft before beginning the search for a publisher in March 1847.[25]

While dividing much of his writing time between the Carlyle essay and *A Week,* Henry also devoted several pages of his new journals to thoughts and experiences enkindled by his life in Walden woods. Household economy, bean cultivation, classical reading, an arrest for refusal to pay taxes, writing projects on Carlyle, the *Week* journey, and life at Walden; Thoreau had plenty to occupy his attention. Yet, he could not live so fully in the woods without nature making some imprint on his mind. As he spent day after quiet day absorbing the peace of his surroundings, nature crept slowly into his thoughts, leading him in new and unexpected directions.

The problem of nature had bothered Henry even before he came to live at the pond. Sometime (probably) in 1844, he entered into the Long Book: "I feel that I draw nearest to understanding the great secret of my life in my closest intercourse with nature. There is a reality and health in (present) nature; which is not to be found in any religion—and cannot be contemplated in antiquity—I suppose that what in other men is religion is in me love of nature."[26]

He returned to these musings three more times in the Long Book, deciding that "all parts of nature belong to one head," and that the laws of nature were not science, but morality. He railed against the popular view of nature incorporated into the school curriculum, maintaining that "every child should be encouraged to study not man's system of nature but Nature's."[27]

These Long Book entries indicate that Thoreau, as he prepared to live at Walden, still interpreted nature in the familiar Emersonian framework ("NOT ME"). This intellectual process continued along similar lines during the first months at the pond. In August 1845, Thoreau observed that "All nature is classic and akin to art—The sumack and pine and hickory which surround my house remind me of the most graceful sculpture." In December he discerned "a civilization going on among brutes as well as men," and in the following February he noted that "all the laws of nature will bend and adapt themselves to the least motion of man."[28]

The fertile serenity of his first spring lived at Walden wrought the beginnings of a change in Henry Thoreau's ideas about nature. In March and April of 1846, as the world turned green once more, Henry listened attentively to the distant song of a robin in the forest, the honking cries of a wedge of geese rising through the mist over Walden Pond. These were matters too precious to dismiss, Emerson fashion, as perhaps not existing at all. No morals, no transcendental lessons accompany the journal entries describing these visions. Simply a lump in the throat in watching nature's overawing beauty.[29]

On April 18, 1846, Thoreau posed himself a new question in his journal:

> What are these pines & these birds about? What is this pond a-doing? I must know a little more—& be forever ready. Instead of singing as the birds I silently smile at my incessant good fortune but I don't know that I bear any flowers or fruits—Methinks if they try me by their standards I shall not be found wanting—but men try one another not so. The elements are working their will with me.[30]

The elements were indeed working their will with Henry. Two journal entries from May 1846 suggest that Henry was in a sense less self-assured about the conception of nature he had been assuming since 1837. On May 3, he simply wrote, "I heard the whippoorwill last night for the first time." No philosophizing, no drawing of the moral. A simple observation of natural fact. After he wrote this one sentence, he skipped a space, then began a long entry on Carlyle. For Thoreau, the simple fact of the whippoorwill had assumed an importance in its own right. In the next journal entry, May 5, Henry made a further, simple note on the whippoorwills before going on to write about (of all things) human sexuality. These two entries mark a change in response to the questions he had asked back on the eighteenth of April: What are these birds about? The tone of both foreshadows the style of Thoreau's journals of the 1850s.[31]

By late June 1846, Thoreau had become enamored enough of natural facts to spend several paragraphs in his journal minutely describing a chivin he had caught in the river. He measured the distance between various points on the fish's body, carefully described the coloration, and painstakingly related the character of each individual fin. There is not so much as a romantic adjective anywhere in these paragraphs—the entire entry is a meticulously scientific description of a chivin. It stands out like a cactus in a rainforest when examined in the context of the rest of the Walden journals. Henry was experimenting, trying to look at nature from different perspectives.[32]

Still, he was very busy writing and getting a living. At this point in his life he was apparently not prepared to embark on a careful and prolonged study of nature's ways. The observations of fact that occasionally occurred in the spring of 1846 were not sustained through the sporadic journal entries of the ensuing months. Thoreau did not suddenly throw himself into the process of becoming a scientific naturalist. He had simply recognized that there were ways of looking at nature other than the one prescribed by Waldo Emerson. A door had opened. Commitments to the Carlyle essay and *A Week* kept him from immediately stepping through.

The questioning mood of the spring of 1846 did mentally prepare Thoreau to boldly reinterpret his perception of nature when the opportunity arose. The occasion came late that same summer, when Henry embarked on what was perhaps his greatest single adventure: his first journey into the wilds of Maine.

Thoreau was invited to journey to the upper Penobscot River country by his cousin, Bangor lumber investor George Thatcher. He left Walden on August 31, reaching Bangor two days later. Superficially, the trip was not much different from others he had taken. Although the prospect of leaving Concord for good left him homesick and despondent, Henry enjoyed short vacation excursions. He had visited relatives in Bangor in 1838, and had undertaken mountain climbing expeditions in 1839, 1842, and 1844. These travels offered the chance of a fresh perspective, and perhaps the raw material for new essays as well.[33]

What separated the Maine expedition from previous journeys was the opportunity to visit genuinely wild country. Although Henry had climbed wild mountains before, they had risen from thoroughly settled surroundings—the peaks offered homely vistas of human occupation of the landscape. By contrast, the upper Penobscot was almost totally unoccupied country, well beyond the boundaries of civilization. Timbermen prowled the lowlands in search of white pine, but the uplands had been only sketchily explored by white New Englanders. This would be Thoreau's first look at genuine wilderness.

Henry and his cousin left Bangor on September 1, riding the stage inland through heavy rain for two days before reaching the tiny village of Mattawamkeag. There they met two Thatcher associates before journeying four miles on foot to the farm of George McCauslin, a fifty-two-year-old pioneer in the region. Enjoying the farmer's frontier hospitality, the travelers waited there two days for Indian guides who never showed.[34]

Thoreau and Thatcher had hired an Algonkian, Louis Neptune, to guide them to the mountain. When Neptune failed to arrive at the appointed rendezvous, the disappointment for Thoreau cut two ways. Henry knew that Louis had guided previous expeditions to the peak, that the man's experience was second to none. More importantly, Henry had made this excursion in part to study the ways of the Indians closely at first hand. The disappointment would become a pessimistic counterpoint to an otherwise positive and enthusiastic narrative. Thoreau for the moment concluded that the onslaught of white civilization had debased the Indians to a condition comparable to the urban rabble of America's growing cities. "He glides up the Millinocket and is lost to my sight, as a more distant and misty cloud is seen flitting by behind a nearer, and is lost in space. So he goes about his destiny, the red face of man."[35]

Disappointed but determined, Thoreau and Thatcher persuaded "Uncle George" McCauslin to accompany them northwards. They first walked four miles upstream to the home of McCauslin's son-in-law, skilled boatsman Tom Fowler Jr., who also joined the excursion. Taking to bateaux, the six-man party threaded their way through a series of lakes joined by the swiftly flowing waters of the Penobscot River. Two days brought them to their goal, the foot of Mount Ktaadn, highest peak in Maine.[36]

What happened during this time in the wilds? Perhaps no single incident of Henry Thoreau's life has engendered as much misunderstanding as whatever happened to Henry while journeying to Ktaadn. Authorities of diverse background and sentiment have viewed this visit to the mountain as a pivotal event in Thoreau's intellectual development. One oft-cited argument contends that as a result of climbing Ktaadn, Henry came to see the wild forests as the source of evil, reenforcing his preference "to think of himself as a man of mind, not of nature." A corollary to this argument holds that prior to Tuesday, September 8, 1846, Thoreau had idealized the wild as infinitely preferable to the civilized. After actually viewing the true wilds of Maine, however, Thoreau supposedly began to steer toward a more cozy romantic middle ground, emphasizing a balance between wilderness and civilization.[37]

These theories make sense only if one accepts the traditional picture of Thoreau as a man passionately devoted to wild nature from the outset of his writing career. But that is simply not true. Henry had not in any way idealized the wild before journeying to Maine; in fact, he had demonstrated minimal interest in the natural world in any form prior to 1846. Thoreau climbed Ktaadn only a few months after his first genuine appreciation of nature stirred at Walden Pond. Journal entries had just begun to exhibit this new interest. That September in Maine, Henry viewed wild nature with freshly opened eyes. The result was not a rejection of what he saw from the mountaintop, but a further awakening. All of Thoreau's most celebrated writings praising wilderness came after this moment. Ktaadn became his great inspiration; the history of his writings about the journey reflect this critical fact.

To genuinely comprehend what happened to Thoreau on Ktaadn (and something did unquestionably happen), it is necessary to understand that Thoreau's treatment of the event occurred on two separate but integrated levels. There was the event itself, shaking yet powerfully moving, and then the act of describing the experience on paper. At each level, the previous nine years of life as a frustrated poet and author created the frame of mind that made the impact of the mountain so stirring.

Thoreau climbed the mountain after living roughly fourteen months at Walden Pond. He labored very intensively during this period, producing the first draft of *A Week,* completing the Carlyle essay, writing much of the journal material that would evolve into his civil disobedience essay and the early chapters of *Walden.* Practice had strengthened Thoreau's abilities as a writer immensely. At the same time, by living in the woods, he had begun to see nature in a different, more insistent light than Emersonian transcendentalism would allow. Thoreau ascended Ktaadn with his senses wide open and his confidence as a writer brimming over.

In terms of personal preparation, perhaps the most marked difference between this and previous expeditions at the outset was that Thoreau applied the lessons derived from wrestling with the manuscript of *A Week on the Concord and Merrimack Rivers.* The lack of proper notes from the 1839 journey had made reconstruction of the events a nightmare. This time Henry took brief daily notes of his adventures during the actual trip and began writing detailed descriptions of what had happened as soon as he returned home, while memories were still fresh.[38]

His eye more sharply attuned to the natural world by his introspections at Walden, Henry wrote of the wilds exactly as he saw them, creating a vastly different record from the artificially recreated journey of *A Week.* Although the goal of this expedition was to climb another mountain, Thoreau determined to provide a full description not merely of the climb, but the week's travels to get there. Wide-ranging and often contrasting spectacles arrested his attention, from the condition of the forest to the condition of the original inhabitants; from the construction of a bateau to the skill of the men who guided the boats upstream, often literally uphill, through the whitewater. This was an adventure rich in natural physical detail, and he worked exactingly to get things right.[39]

On Monday, September 7, Thoreau and his companions camped below the timberline at Rum Mountain, in the shadow of Ktaadn. If Henry's reaction to the wild view of the mountains was to suddenly intuit nature as an evil entity, he gave no hint of the fact in his recorded notes. The field notes for September 7 are limited to a single phrase encapsulating a preliminary ascent partway to the top: "mount by moon light."[40] The field entry for the following day, when the entire party attempted the climb (Thoreau outpaced and climbed higher than the rest), reads this way:

> Tuesday 8th
>
> Hard bread—& pork getting short—go up—Mount Cranberries and blueberries clouds—wind—rain rocks lakes return down stream 8½ marks of freshet—trout all come from top the inlet trout
> —slipping sliding—jumping—brook runs S & SW wet feet—climb tree see meadow hard bread & pork—allowance—Moose tracks muddy water—Burnt lands—batteau 2½ fish in sun
>
> ---
>
> return 4½ swiftly dropped batteau over Abolcarmegus falls carry around Pockwockomus Falls—Camp at Oak hall carry leaving boat to bring over in morning—old camp high wind & smoke—goes down before morn—[41]

If Thoreau discovered by peering from the mountain that the wilds were evil, the fact seems not to have had any immediate impact on his notes. If anything, the sketch conveys the impression that he was primarily concerned with getting enough to eat. Nor do the remainder of the notes sketching the three day return down the Penobscot to Bangor contain the least hint of adverse reaction to the wilds.[42]

Back home in Walden woods, Thoreau set about the process of fleshing his field notes into a possible essay almost immediately. Significantly, he undertook the task not in chronological order, but wrote first of his experiences on the mountain. This was the important part of the journey, the portion he wished to write down while the memories were still vivid. At this stage, his thoughts on the lesson of the mountain took this form:

> Coming down the Mt perhaps I first most fully realized that this was unhanselled and ancient Demonic Nature, natura, or whatever man has named it.

> The nature primitive—powerful gigantic aweful and beautiful, Untamed forever. . . . The earth seemed recent—and I expected the proprietor to dispute my passage—When then did my ancestors acquire the preemptive right? But only the moose browsed here, and the bear skulked—and the black partridge fed on the berries and the buds.
>
> The main astonishment at last is that man has brought so little change—And yet man so overtops nature in his estimation.[43]

Clearly this was an extension of the newfound awareness of nature Thoreau had first exhibited in the spring of 1846. Henry was no longer blindly accepting the assumptions that had guided his writing since his first acquaintance with Emerson—that nature was merely symbolic, of secondary importance, perhaps nonexistent. In the spring he had wondered what the pond, the trees, the birds were "a-doing." On the mountain, he was struck full by the impact of his question. There was nature, raw nature, "powerful gigantic aweful and beautiful." His simple question had suddenly grown to overwhelming proportions, dwarfing the petty concerns of human institutions. He employed the adjective "Demonic" not to indicate his acceptance of the notion that the wilderness was the dwelling place of evil, but rather to mock the very idea that wild nature had anything to do with human concepts at all. "Demonic" was simply one of a list of inadequate and silly terms people had employed to describe a natural world they did not comprehend in the least. That humankind could even think of themselves as important in the face of nature's power had become astonishingly foolish. And as to the idea that people believed they could own or even manipulate true nature. . . . Following Ktaadn, nature, powerful and beautiful, would occupy center stage in the growth of Henry Thoreau's ideas.

The memories of his adventure fully and safely committed to paper, Thoreau forced himself to turn to the more pressing business of his life at the pond, re-drafting *A Week* and writing the two lectures that would become the anchors for the first draft of *Walden.*

In February 1846, Henry had delivered a prototypical version of his Carlyle essay at the Concord Lyceum. His audience gave him an encouraging and sympathetic hearing, but many expressed disappointment that he had not chosen to talk about his life in the woods. There were plenty of questions just about his everyday experiences. Why had he gone to live there? Did he really wish to cut himself off from society? How could he stand to live in such rude discomfort? Wasn't he frightened, out there by himself?[44]

Here was the opportunity Thoreau needed. This time he had kept his records carefully, knew just how he had spent his time, how much the experiment had cost, and how much he had profited. By the winter of 1847 he had prepared an answer to all the questions, molded into a Lyceum lecture he entitled "A History of Myself." This and a second lecture given in Concord two weeks later became the foundation for "Economy," the first chapter of *Walden*.[45]

Response to these lectures was overwhelmingly favorable. Opposition to Thoreau's way of life came from many quarters, ranging from those who simply viewed Henry as a woodsburning disappointment to his parents to those who understood something of transcendental ideas and were appalled. Yet, as Waldo Emerson reported in a letter to Margaret Fuller, all "were charmed with the witty wisdom which ran through it all." Sustained by the success of his lectures, Thoreau now knew he had the makings of a second book. Although the exact order of his writing projects cannot be fully determined, it seems very likely from the content that Henry wrote the first ninety leaves of the *Walden* draft straight through, a task that occupied him into the spring of 1847.[46]

This original version of *Walden* is a remarkable document. Carefully scanning the two-thirds of the draft Thoreau wrote early in 1847, the reader is forced to ask a most astonishing question: Where are the woods in this book? For a story about a man who went to live in the midst of nature, the natural world is remarkably absent. The first seventy pages of the first draft of *Walden* is one more demonstration that even at the time Henry went to live by the pond he did not consider nature a primary theme for his writing efforts.[47]

Virtually all of the first draft (with amendations and editing) survived into the seventh draft, the one Henry published. The first two-thirds of this draft comprise the framework for the first six chapters of the final work, namely "Economy" and "Where I Lived and What I Lived For," "Reading," "Sounds," "Solitude," and "Visitors." Internal evidence suggests Thoreau conceived and wrote out these first ninety-odd leaves from the outset as a single coherent sketch of his purposes and experiences. The content clearly demonstrates the focus of Henry's own understanding of the Walden experiment as he began and lived it.[48]

The subject matter was human life. The crux of Thoreau's argument in this original rendition of Walden was that his fellow New Englanders led unnecessarily complicated lives. By addressing themselves so totally to the acquisition and management of properties they did not really need, they had frittered away altogether too much of their physical, emotional, and intellectual potential. Henry's Walden life revealed the essence of human need—a little food, a small shelter, a limited but earnest labor were enough to make a living. Thoreau lived simply, yet boasted robust good health, enjoyed the company of good society when it suited, absorbed the heavenly pleasures of solitude when he wished. He was by no means poor in spirit. And the time! Time for reflection, time for the real work of improving one's self. He read the good books, contemplated their deeper meanings, worked hard to come to an understanding of this human life. Thoreau's intent as he began drafting his *Walden* essay was to write for and about people.[49]

The fact that he lived in the woods seems almost incidental in these pages. On the twenty-first leaf of the manuscript he mentioned hearing "the woodpecker & vireo & other birds" as he began work on his house. Seventeen leaves later he again remembered the subject, relating that sleeping in his unfinished cabin he "imbibed the influences of nature with as little alloy as a bird in its nest amid foliage." On leaf sixty-four he found time to mention the autumn wildflowers and shrubs growing around the house, and beginning on leaf seventy-four he wrote a long series of paragraphs describing the calls of whippoorwills, blue jays, bullfrogs, and owls—all sounds heard at the door of his cabin. If Henry intended this original version of *Walden* to describe living in a house surrounded by nature, his emphasis was certainly on the house.[50]

Yet, as nature reawakened all around him once again in the spring of 1847, Henry appears to have hesitated momentarily, taking stock of what he had thus far described of his experiences. And the fact was inescapable; a critical element of the Walden life was missing. Flipping to the inside back cover of one of his journals, he sketched a new outline, listing all the themes that had thus far eluded him in telling his story. The topics: songbirds, waterfowl, eagles, groundnuts, foxes, moles, and several others; twenty items in all, virtually all of them elements of nature. In the last fifty-nine leaves of the first version of *Walden,* Henry Thoreau finally came outdoors.[51]

Henry constructed a bridge joining the indoor and outdoor elements of his woodland experiment by first discussing his toils in the two and one-half acre beanfield. He followed this with a description of his frequent treks to town, a device that enabled him to introduce the larger panorama of the forest surrounding his home. He was then able to move quickly but fluidly to the observations of nature that had begun to make such inroads in his journal beginning in the spring of 1846. Phoebes, robins, passenger pigeons, field mice, raccoons became the centering figures of the latter two-fifths of his Walden story. The wonder is that Thoreau created the impression that they had all been important to him from the very beginning in 1845.[52]

He freely admitted in these pages that he did not possess any profound knowledge of nature's ways. Following a discussion of his hikes into Concord village, Henry turned to a description of the local ponds and their fishing potential. Acknowledging his prowess as a fisherman, he confessed that his enthusiasm for angling indeed waxed from time to time, to his own disgust. "I feel that it would have been better if I had not fished," he wrote. The temptation lay not only in the taste of the fish: "It tempts me continually because *it is a means of becoming acquainted with nature*—not only with fishes—but with night and water—and the scenery—which I should not otherwise see under the same aspects" (emphasis added).[53] The pages following this admission became a virtual catalog of the nature he had come to know since moving to Walden.

The essential element tying together the miscellaneous pieces of this catalog were the sections devoted to the return of spring. Drawing heavily on his journal entries from April and May of 1846—when nature first genuinely attracted his literary attention—the spring section invested the whole latter half with a sense of wholeness, as if the man, the house, and the nature surrounding had entered into the season of renewal together. There were still critical elements lacking in this initial rendering of spring. Thoreau had not discovered in 1847 that nature existed as an ongoing cycle, nor had he made any decisions regarding the relationship between nature and the spirit. At this juncture, he had gone far enough only to recognize that he and Emerson disagreed about the importance of the natural world.[54]

Thoreau's celebration of spring spanned nine leaves in the initial draft of *Walden*. To draw this section—and the draft as a whole—to a vigorous conclusion, Henry turned to the Ktaadn experience that had so forcefully reoriented his ideas about nature. Although he never once mentioned the mountain in the *Walden* text, the brooding lessons of the summit pervaded the last pages of the first draft: "Our village life would stagnate, I think, if it were not for the unexplored forests and meadows which surround it. We need the tonic of wildness,—to wade sometimes in meadows where only the bittern and the meadow-hen lurk, and hear the booming of the snipe; to smell the whispering sedge where only some wilder & more solitary fowl builds her nest, and the mink crawls with its belly close to the ground."[55]

It was here, in the original conclusion of *Walden,* that the idea of wildness became a synthesizing concept in Thoreau's thinking and literary art. In the ensuing paragraph he continued: "We can never have enough of nature. We must be refreshed by the sight of its inexhaustible vigor, vast features and titanic—the sea coast with its wrecks, the wilderness with its living and its decaying trees,—the thunder cloud—and the rain that lasts 3 weeks and produces freshets. We need to witness our own limits transgressed, and some life pasturing freely where we never wander."[56]

The echoes of Ktaadn ring sound and clear through these sentences. The inspiration drawn from a knowledge of places where humanity does not dominate, the humbling of insignificant humankind by omnipotent nature, the very necessity of wildness were the lessons discovered on the mountaintop. Use of the word "titanic" is especially suggestive; Henry would draw on the imagery of mythological giants three times more in drafting his mountain experiences for publication. That Thoreau would employ these messages as a vehicle to draw all the themes of *Walden* to a conclusion is indicative of the mountain's effect on his thinking. Nature had not merely become important to Thoreau; he had discovered that his growing awareness of nature's ways gave new meaning to his entire existence.[57]

Henry found still another impetus for nature study that spring, in the form of specimen requests from two Boston naturalists. Horatio R. Storer, a student at Harvard, wrote to enlist Thoreau's assistance in locating rare species of birds and obtaining egg specimens. Henry's reply was ambivalent. On the one hand he confessed to "a little squeamishness on the score of robbing their nests," but allowed that he might consider stealing an egg or even resorting "to the extreme of deliberate murder" if science were to be advanced. Pleading that he had become a poor observer of bird life, Henry warned that he would prove little help. More than anything, he tried to pour cold water on the entire project. Still, the flicker of interest in the scientific study of nature stands in stark contrast to the dismissal of scientific facts that concluded his essay "The Natural History of Massachusetts," written back in 1842.[58]

His interest in the scientific study intensified in April and May of 1847, the result of an inquiry by James Elliot Cabot, assistant to Louis Agassiz. Agassiz, an internationally recognized expert in comparative zoology and fossil studies, had journeyed to the United States from Switzerland in October 1846. Finding the opportunities for scientific study in America virtually limitless, he settled in Boston and began to assemble as complete a collection of American flora and fauna as possible. Agassiz directed Cabot to seek as many potential contributors as he could find. Henry Thoreau was among the names enlisted.[59]

Thoreau and Cabot carried on a brief but wide-ranging correspondence in May and June 1847. Because of his research for the introduction to *A Week,* Henry was best acquainted with Concord's aquatic species, fish and turtles especially. He sent off a host of specimens to Cabot, who reported back that Agassiz was "much surprised and pleased at the extent of the collections you sent." The shipments to Agassiz did not continue beyond June of that year, but they did serve to establish a practice Thoreau would continue for the rest of his life. (In 1850, after sending a rare goshawk to the Boston Society of Natural History, he was elected a corresponding member. Eight years later, the society would confirm that Henry had discovered a new species of bream.) The habits of the scientific naturalist had their roots in the Walden experiment.[60]

Henry brought the first draft of *Walden* to a close in the late summer of 1847. He left the house in the woods that same September, for not as good a reason as had brought him there. Waldo Emerson, preparing to depart for a European lecture tour, had asked him to join Lidian and the Emerson children as caretaker during his absence. Thoreau obeyed the summons.[61]

It is difficult to assess Waldo's feelings about the whole Walden business. He had of course given Henry permission to build the cabin on his land in the first place, and had even helped to raise the roof. Soon after, he made out a new will, bequeathing the Walden woods to Henry should he die. There is every indication that Emerson was much enthused about the literary work Henry undertook at the pond, especially portions of the first draft of *A Week,* which Henry read to him in 1847. Still, Emerson had his misgivings. When Henry agreed to serve as caretaker at Bush, Waldo purchased the Walden cabin—perhaps to insure that Henry would never return to the woods.[62]

At Bush, Thoreau fell into the once familiar role of household handyman and gardener, with the added responsibilities of tending to Lidian, who became very ill over the winter with jaundice, and entertaining the three Emerson children. Despite these added obligations and distractions, he maintained the intense beat of literary effort developed at Walden. Henry had now been writing steadily on one project or another for better than three years. His range, his vocabulary, his descriptive ability, his entire ability as a writer had grown into a powerful engine. Much of this he poured into revisions of *A Week on the Concord and Merrimack Rivers.* But his essay of the Maine woods, "Ktaadn," was the first fully realized fruit of this newfound mastery of language. He initially wrote up the essay for delivery before the Concord Lyceum in January 1848, then quickly expanded the work, sending the finished piece to Horace Greeley for marketing at the end of March.[63]

The care Thoreau invested in this essay—from his immediate effort to maintain good field notes through his determination to write down the bones of his experience while still fresh in his mind—is evident in every page. Even prosaic descriptions of boating up the West Branch of the Penobscot took on an assured and measured tone: "To add to the danger, the poles are liable at any time to be caught between the rocks, and wrenched out of their hands, leaving them at the mercy of the rapids—the rocks, as it were, lying in wait, like so many alligators, to catch them in their teeth, and jerk them from your hands, before you have stolen an effectual shove against their palates."[64]

It is difficult to believe that this was the same man who only two years before had settled for the words, "Verily that was a long pull from Balls Hill to Carlisle Bridge—sitting with our faces to the south—and a slight breeze rising from the north," to describe boating on the Concord River.[65]

Thoreau brought the full strength of his maturing prose to bear in describing his experience atop the mountain. Carefully studying the journal notes of his initial reactions to the mountain, he decided to heighten the impact of his vivid realizations by dividing them into two longer portions, placing separate paragraphs in different parts of the narrative.

Two elements had figured in his original description: the sudden comprehension that the mountain seemed new and unfinished, and his own reaction to the sudden exposure to this raw and unforgiving nature. Both elements were critical to the message he wished to convey. The recognition of "recent" and "primitive" nature he now moved into the depiction of his ascent of the mountain, at a point in the narrative when he had departed from his companions, but had not yet gained the peak. His awe-inspiring discovery is made to take place as he picks his way over the rock-strewn mountainside: Ktaadn was "an undone extremity of the globe." Thoreau relates the profound effect of this revelation on the solitary climber straying into this inhospitable quarter:

> He is more lone than you can imagine. There is less of substantial thought and fair understanding in him, than in the plains where men inhabit. His reason is dispersed and shadowy, more thin and subtile like the air. Vast, Titanic, inhuman Nature has got him at a disadvantage, caught him alone, and pilfers him of some of his divine faculty. She does not smile on him as in the plains. She seems to say sternly, why come ye here before your time? This ground is not prepared for you. Is it not enough that I smile in the valleys?[66]

Here, in some of the most powerful prose Henry Thoreau could produce, was the new understanding of nature grasped on Ktaadn. Waldo Emerson was wrong, very wrong. Nature definitely existed, and it did not exist merely as some benign symbol of the spiritual. Nature stretched far beyond the simple understandings of humankind, "Vast, Titanic, inhuman." Henry was thrown out of his reckoning, had been forced to admit both that nature was an elemental force that demanded knowing and that, for all his time in the woods, he knew nature almost not at all.

In the essay, Thoreau laid out this discovery over several contemplative paragraphs. But he could not sustain the pensive mode; the mountain demanded too much of him in a purely physical sense. Staring at last at the true face of nature, he was forced in the narrative to continue his ascent to the peaks not in symbolic imagery, but in a purely literal account embodying toil, sweat, and confusion. Nor was nature offering any rewards for the climb. Clouds obscured all but the briefest glimpse of the wilderness surrounding him. Nature was for the most part hidden. Recapturing the event on paper, Henry could find nothing metaphorical in attaining the mist-enshrouded peaks; the real dangers of the climb were more than enough to describe.[67]

Thoreau placed the second portion of the contemplation of his discoveries at a point only after his party had safely descended Ktaadn and determined their exact location in the open lands below. Still deep in the forest, they had come to relatively familiar ground, where the normal processes of thought could reassert themselves. Here Thoreau confessed to ruminating over the realizations of the ascent all the way back down. "It is difficult to conceive of a region uninhabited by man," he mused. Yet he had now seen one, and had come to understand that the world was far more than a mere stage for human activity. The earth was not made for humanity at all—"Nature made it, and man may use it if he can. Man was not to be associated with it."[68]

This realization shook Thoreau to the foundation of his beliefs. Ktaadn had challenged his comfortable ideas of nature so thoroughly that it seemed to obligate a whole new and fundamental reexamination of his relationship with the world. For the published version of the essay, Henry found just words enough to suggest the turmoil he felt:

> I stand in awe of my body, this matter to which I am bound has become so strange to me. I fear not spirits, ghosts, of which I am one,—*that* my body might,—but I fear bodies, I tremble to meet them. What is this Titan that has possession of me? Talk of mysteries!—Think of our life in nature,—daily to be shown matter, to come in contact with it,—rocks, trees, wind on our cheeks! the *solid* earth! the *actual* world! the *common sense! Contact! Contact! Who* are we? *where* are we?[69]

In no sense was Henry Thoreau turning his back on wilderness in this passage; nor was he seeking any compromise with nature. These are the words of discovery, the anguished cries of a man who after nine years has abruptly recognized that his assumptions about nature had been woefully inadequate. To dismiss nature as mere symbol had been a sad mistake, one that he would not repeat. He had already incorporated the lessons into the concluding paragraphs of the first version of *Walden.* With the crafting, execution, and publication of "Ktaadn and the Maine Woods," he portrayed these lessons to the most exacting of his ability and announced them to the world at large. From September 1846 on, nature—the real nature he had glimpsed from the mountain—occupied center place in his thinking.

Publication of "Ktaadn and the Maine Woods" was a rare success story for Thoreau. Horace Greeley was able to place it with *Sartain's Union Magazine* almost immediately; the piece ran in five installments between July and November 1848. Thoreau received fifty dollars. This was in sharp contrast to the publication of "Thomas Carlyle and His Works," the essay Henry had toiled over in his first year at the pond. Greeley had found a home for the piece at *Graham's Magazine* soon after Thoreau sent it in 1846, but the essay did not actually appear until the following March. Worse still, *Graham's* did not pay until Greeley forced them, in April 1848. In every sense, the adventure in the Maine woods was an unparalleled success.[70]

The labor of writing continued into the summer of 1848. With his mountain story successfully told, Henry turned his attention to a new draft of *A Week,* expanding the manuscript to roughly ninety thousand words. He attended to his *Walden* draft as well, making stylistic changes, writing a revised copy. The dream of publishing two books, one on the heels of the other, was a very attractive one.[71]

Waldo Emerson returned home from Europe on July 27; Thoreau moved back to his parents' home on Texas Street that same day. The year had strained the friendship of the two men. Thoreau, observing Lidian's ill health and her husband's lack of compassion, grew less enamored of Waldo's saintly demeanor.[72] In the meanwhile, the European tour apparently soured Emerson altogether on the American wilds as a source of inspiration, for Thoreau or anyone else. Soon after returning home, he commented in his journal: "Henry Thoreau is like the wood-god who solicits the wandering poet & draws him into the antres vast & desarts idle, & bereaves him of his memory, & leaves him naked, plaiting vines & with twigs in his hand. Very seductive are the first steps from the town to the woods, but the End is want & madness."[73]

Emerson had lost none of his distrust for the sensate knowledge now enticing his closest friend. In October 1848, he wrote: "H.T. sports the doctrines of activity: but I say, What do *we?* We want a sally into the regions of wisdom & do we go out & lay stone wall or dig a well or turnips? No, we leave the children, sit down by a fire, compose our bodies to corpses, shut our hands, shut our eyes, that we may be entranced & see truly."[74]

Shutting his hands, shutting his eyes, Henry would have seen or felt exactly nothing atop Ktaadn. Waldo had gone to Europe, Henry to Walden and to Maine. Journeying on wholly different planes, they had forever lost the ability to influence one another. By 1848, Thoreau had rejected Emerson's devaluation of sensate knowledge, and was well on his way to denying Emerson's construction of the spiritual universe as well.

Emerson still sought to encourage Thoreau's literary career. Enthused by "Ktaadn and the Maine Woods," which he considered one of the first American essays worth binding in ten years, Waldo sought lecture engagements for Henry beyond Concord. He accomplished little. Still, Thoreau's star had risen enough to attract invitations on his own. Nathaniel Hawthorne, now residing in Salem, asked Henry to speak there in the winter of 1849. The lectures, which Sophia Peabody Hawthorne found "enchanting," were sufficiently successful to draw other invitations. The Gloucester Lyceum heard him once and never again, but the city of Worcester engaged him for a series of three presentations at the behest of Harrison Gray Otis Blake, and invited him back virtually every year thereafter. Portland, Maine, also hired him to lecture in March 1849. Thoreau had made something of a name for himself in New England.[75]

All things considered, Thoreau could take heart in his writing by the close of the 1840s. Certainly his career was in far better shape than it had been on going to live at the pond in 1845. He had succeeded in publishing major essays in leading journals and actually getting paid for them. Towns other than Concord were engaging him to speak. His first booklength manuscript seemed ready for publication, a second waited in the wings. He could take a quiet pride in the development of his art in the past four years. The "Ktaadn" essay especially reflected the growth of his prose composition and the resultant profits—spiritual and pecuniary. Moreover, he had succeeded largely on his own, without the assistance of Emerson or the other transcendentalists. When the group attempted to establish a successor to *The Dial* in 1847, Thoreau refused to contribute.[76]

Riding the crest of a modest success, Thoreau could look forward in 1849 to the culminating event of his struggle to become a writer, one that would, with any luck, propel him to the front ranks of American literature. In February, he contracted to publish the latest of several drafts of *A Week on the Concord and Merrimack Rivers.*[77]

Despite the almost endless series of difficulties Thoreau had encountered in composing *A Week,* he had maintained a marvelously single-minded confidence about the work's eventual publication. Often ignoring the well-intended advice of his friends, particularly Bronson Alcott and Emerson, Henry worked steadily to create a work answering to the entire array of his interests; literary, poetic, political, economic, philosophical, and much else besides. He did enlist Emerson's help with marketing, making a concerted effort to find a publisher for a draft he completed early in 1847, but all their inquiries came to naught. Waldo left for Europe still urging Henry to find a publisher as quickly as possible, and to pay the costs himself if necessary. Emerson, after all, had paid for the publication of both *Nature* and his first series of essays.

Thoreau decided instead to revise and expand the work once more, a task that occupied much of his time through February 1849. To lend greater accuracy to the travel sections of the book, he even retraced portions of his route with Ellery Channing in the summer of 1848. The resulting draft was a truly eclectic work, comprising in part a travel and nature essay, in part a series of commentaries on literature, philosophy, and history, and in part a compendium of old material written in the early 1840s. Henry now included in his book much of "The Service," his first major essay, which Margaret Fuller had rejected for *The Dial* nine years before. Most of the essays he did publish in *The Dial* also found their way into the manuscript at one point or another, along with previously undeveloped passages from his early journals and a goodly number of his poems. Weakly strung together by the skeletal framework of a week's travel along the rivers, the thoughts and digressions composed from this early material represent the full array of subject matter Henry explored at the beginning of his career. Clearly Thoreau intended *A Week* to be a summation of all his endeavors prior to the Walden years. One gets the impression that Henry was cleaning out his literary attic.[78]

Although the tone and substance of *A Week on the Concord and Merrimack Rivers* for the most part represented Henry Thoreau as he understood himself and his work in the years before Ktaadn, the published version did include a few passages in which he distanced himself from his fellow transcendentalists. He wove a severe critique of Goethe into "Thursday" to demonstrate a distinct separation of his ideas from those of Emerson and Margaret Fuller, both of whom revered the German poet as an inspiration for transcendental concepts. And in "Friday," the concluding chapter of the book, Henry confronted Emersonian notions of nature head on, a foretaste of what was to come in newer works:

> Are we to be put off and amused in this life, as it were with a mere allegory? Is not Nature, rightly read, that of which she is taken to be the symbol merely? When the common man looks into the sky, which he has not so much profaned, he thinks it is less gross than the earth, and with reverence speaks of "the Heavens," but the seer will in the same sense speak of "the Earths," and his Father who is in them. "Did not he that made which is *within* make that which is *without* also?" What is it then, to educate but to develop these divine germs called the senses?[79]

A Week was the capstone of the first decade of Thoreau's literary efforts, and again he concluded the work with the lesson of the mountain. Nature was not symbol, not allegory, but the essence of existence itself. And something more besides. Emerson denied Nature in his effort to better communicate with the realm of the spiritual. In concluding his first book, Henry now suggested that in studying nature, true and genuine nature, he studied the spiritual and the material at once. There was no division; both existed together, inseparably.

Having explored that possibility into existence, the next step would be to inquire carefully and more fully into the spiritual and material reality of nature. In 1849, Henry Thoreau understood that he had not yet done more than cross the threshold in the study of nature. But with the elegy at long last out of the way, the time had come.

The printing of *A Week on the Concord and Merrimack Rivers* in May 1849, brought to a close five years of intense literary effort on the part of Henry Thoreau. Quietly confident of the abilities he had developed over the previous five years, Henry finally published the work with James Munroe and Company, paying the expenses himself. The road to literary success had been anything but smooth, but the general outlook in the spring of 1849 seemed promising indeed. But, even as he arranged for the release of his book, reversals and misfortunes began to fall, one by one, like the blows of a hammer. The twenty-one months between October 1848 and July 1850 proved the most disastrous and personally shaking Henry Thoreau would ever experience.

I saw the moon sudden reflected full from a pool—A puddle from which you may see the moon reflected—& the earth dissolved under your feet.

— *Journal,* June 13, 1851

I seem to be more constantly merged in nature—my intellectual life is more obedient to nature than formerly—but perchance less obedient to Spirit—I have less memorable seasons. I exact less of myself. I am getting used to my meanness—getting to accept my low estate—O if I could be discontented with myself! If I could feel anguish at each descent!

— *Journal,* October 12, 1851

4 ABSORBING NATURE

IN THE EARLY MONTHS OF 1849, Henry Thoreau could define himself as a successful author. While his appreciation of nature had grown at Walden, he made no serious attempt to improve upon his superficial knowledge of the natural world. Writing demanded too much of his time. With a book and two major essays to his credit, he fronted the world of letters with a seemingly well- founded self-assurance. Determined to establish himself, Henry envisioned rapid publication of a second book to further secure a literary reputation.

This confidence was clouded by nettlesome irritations in his social relationships, disturbing events that gnawed at his sense of well-being. Unfortunately, such distractions were to prove portents of more and far worse to come. By autumn, Thoreau was rudderless and floundering, at a loss for a literary project, unsure about his life's work. Only after more than a year of false starts and tentative experiments would he finally embark on the inquiry that would nourish and sustain his intellect for the remainder of his life: the study of the complex patterns in nature.

In the summer of 1848, the largest irritation in an otherwise reasonably successful intellectual life was Thoreau's association with Waldo Emerson. Once his chief source of revelation, Henry had outgrown his devotion to Waldo's ideas, had subtly challenged them in his mountain essay, "Ktaadn," and was preparing to contest them more fully in print in his conclusion to *A Week.* On a more personal level, any illusions Henry may have possessed regarding Emerson's saintliness were largely destroyed by his firsthand observation of the great man's treatment of Lidian.

A shot fired from a completely unexpected quarter transformed this vexatious friendship into a completely intolerable one. On October 31, 1848, that oh-so-clever New England poet, James Russell Lowell, published a long doggerel entitled "A Fable for Critics," which included the following lines:

> There comes ______, for instance; to see him's rare sport,
> Tread in Emerson's tracks with legs painfully short;
> How he jumps, how he strains, and gets red in the face,
> To keep step with the mystagogue's natural pace![1]

The verses go painfully on in this vein. Readers (and there were many) readily assumed that the lines referred to Thoreau and Ellery Channing. How galling. The four years Thoreau had spent creating physical and intellectual distance between himself and Emerson, abruptly erased in the public mind by a few lines of idiotic verse.

In response, Thoreau poured still more of himself into *A Week,* the work representing the culmination of a decade's literary effort, the conclusion a frank declaration of independence from Emerson's dismissal of nature as mere symbol. The work went on in the shadow of family tragedy. Henry's sister Helen, whose health had been gradually weakening from tuberculosis for at least six years, became gravely ill in the winter of 1848. She died on June 14, 1849, fifteen days after the publication of *A Week on the Concord and Merrimack Rivers.* Thoreau's triumph was inextricably alloyed with profound sorrow.[2]

Little is known of the relationship between Helen and Henry, but such indications as exist indicate that they were very close, as indeed were all the members of the Thoreau family. Years later, people remembered the entire family gathering together to sing in the parlor. Sophia played the piano—Scottish melodies were a family favorite—while Henry added the "silvery tones" of his flute. The Thoreaus were also remembered as a family of great talkers, Henry included.[3]

It was Helen who soothed Henry's tears at the prospect of leaving home for Harvard back in 1833. Later, Henry was drawn to the abolitionist cause because of the work of Helen and their mother. Facing the fact that his sister was dying, he arranged for a photograph to be taken of her, a solicitous gesture she much appreciated. And when she died, he expressed his grief in one of the last poems he would ever write.[4]

Helen's death was the first in a series of tragic and disastrous events that would severely test Henry's hard-won self-confidence, throwing his entire life off-stride for more than a year. The next blow cannot be specifically attributed to a single date, but can be generally assigned to a season: the autumn of 1849. As the last flowers of summer bloomed in September, Thoreau faced up to a humiliating fact. *A Week on the Concord and Merrimack Rivers* was a failure. The publisher, James Munroe and Company, managed to place fewer than three hundred copies in the hands of readers, and several of those were given free to reviewers.[5]

The book received scant notice in the press. Munroe did little advertising, and the leading journals devoted little or no space to reviews. Such reviews as were printed were not unkind, although most portrayed the work as a simple travel book. A few deplored its "pantheism," a familiar criticism of the works of perceived transcendentalists.[6]

Thoreau's own chagrin was blended with bitter anger directed toward Emerson. In personal discussions with Henry between 1847 and 1849, Waldo had been lavish in his encouragement of the forthcoming book, although he privately admitted to misgivings concerning the complex layers of its content. Moreover, he had, since 1847, pushed Henry to publish the work as rapidly as possible, finally urging him to pay the price of publication himself. When the book failed to sell, Thoreau found himself in debt for close to three hundred dollars, a staggering sum for a man who made a virtue of simplicity.[7]

When Munroe sent the 706 unsold copies of *A Week* to his home in October 1853, Henry was able to treat the incident with a certain wry humor, but four years had by then passed in which to get used to the idea.[8] In September of 1849, the failure burned deep, and he rounded on Emerson in his anger. Vitriol served as ink in paragraph after paragraph entered into the journal of September 1849:

> I had a friend, I wrote a book, I asked my friend's criticism, I never got but praise for what was good in it—my friend became estranged from me and then I got the blame for all that was bad,—& so I got at last the criticism which I wanted.
>
> While my friend was my friend he flattered me, and I never heard the truth from him, but when he became my enemy he shot it to me on a poisoned arrow.[9]

If nothing else, the crushing realization of the failure of *A Week* confirmed Thoreau's determination to distance himself intellectually from Ralph Waldo Emerson. This was perhaps a negative in a life that had become suddenly directionless, but it was at least an indication of the bearing to avoid.

Henry had placed an advertisement at the close of *A Week on the Concord and Merrimack Rivers,* advising readers that a second book, *Walden,* would soon follow. The almost universal neglect of the first book left him with little heart to continue the second, and for the moment he dropped all work on the "Walden" manuscript.[10] Casting about for a reliable theme for new writing, he seized once again on the travel format that had brought him his greatest success. This time he decided to extend his "excursions to the seashore." He and Ellery Channing left for Cape Cod on the ninth of October 1849.[11]

Disaster overtook him once again. The brig *St. John,* crammed with immigrants fresh from Ireland, had wrecked off Cohasset in a violent storm two mornings before. Bodies were still coming ashore when Thoreau reached the scene; the beach was strewn with human wreckage; stories of anguish, suffering, and outright horror flowed all along the coast. Hastily supplied coffins often contained mother and child together; muted survivors watched the wreck pounded by the waves a mile out to sea.

This time the tragedy was not in any way personal—Thoreau was a disinterested onlooker. But the somber occasion was affecting, as much as Henry tried to deny it. "If this was the law of Nature," he wrote, "why waste any time in awe or pity?" He went on to suggest that the beauty of the coast "was enhanced by wrecks like this, and it acquired thus a rarer and sublimer beauty still." Yet the dark and threatening power of the sea took charge of Thoreau's imagination, pervading all he would ever write about Cape Cod. He drew the material for a successful series of lectures and essays from this and three further journeys to the Cape, but in the end the experiences gave him no new direction.[12]

Back home, the painful aftertaste of publishing *A Week* left Thoreau almost aimlessly adrift for close to a year. He did not begin to work seriously on the "Walden" manuscript again until the winter of 1852. Although he continued his journal in the meantime, the entries for the rest of 1849 and the first nine months of 1850 were desultory and sporadic, as if he had little motivation for any kind of literary undertaking.[13] In January of 1850 he confided to his journal

> seeds beginning to expand in me, which propitious circumstance may bring to the light & to perfection. If I look within all is as indistinct as the night—unless there is a faint glimmer & phosporesscence, a sort of boreal light—there—and perchance there is heard the breathing of crickets under the sod—and as the darkness deepens I may see some twinkling stars. I know not whether it is the dumps or a budding extacy—Were there too many slap jacks or is it the incoming God?[14]

In the next July, he confessed to uncertainty about where even to go for his daily walk, and complained that "Nature is as far away from me as God." He even admitted to a momentary desire for fewer frogs, owls, and mosquitoes in his swamps—actual and figurative. And another entire year after that, he was dismayed to discover that "Here I am 34 years old, and yet my life is almost wholly unexpanded."[15]

Henry continued to walk, and spent additional time out of doors in consequence of a growing new vocation: surveying. He had become acquainted with the art while teaching school early in the 1840s, and undertook his first professional surveys while living at Walden Pond. As his reputation for precision and impartial honesty spread, demands for his services grew among the townspeople. In the autumn of 1849, faced with heavy debts because of the failure of *A Week,* he began to maintain a notebook devoted to survey work and to accept fairly extensive employment. Often the work left him an ill taste. A perambulation of the town's boundaries in the fall of 1851 threw him in with politicians whose company he loathed, and too often he was asked to survey woodlots that were consequently sold at auction and cut. In January of 1858 he was even forced to survey a portion of Walden Woods for subsequent cutting. At least the work allowed him many profitable hours (monetary and otherwise) outside, and the delineation of odd boundaries took him into the wilder portions of Concord's woods and swamps.[16]

Slowly, the threads of nature study—taken up so briefly at Walden, only to be discarded as literary efforts consumed so much of his time—began to reclaim Henry's attention. In May of 1849 he identified the partridge-berry in Tarbell's Swamp, one of the very few identifications he made in that entire year. In the fall, while still coming to grips with the lack of sales of *A Week,* he apparently began to plan a more exhaustive study of nature. Sometime between the eleventh of September and the fifteenth of October (the journal is not clearly dated), Thoreau began to compile a detailed list of the wilder places in Concord. In this same period, he read William Jones's "Topographical Description of Concord" in the *Collections of the Massachusetts Historical Society.* Uncharacteristically, he put down no reason for assembling such a list, but it is clear that he was considering visits to those places where the more unusual flora and fauna of Concord might be found.[17]

In the months that followed, Henry began to enter nature observations into his journal more often. There was still no regular pace or rhythm to these sightings—there is nothing to suggest that he had embarked on a regular program of natural field studies—but his interest in nature had intensified. In February 1850, he noted the activities of redwing blackbirds, robins, and "cherry birds" at Flint's Pond; two months later he was recording the spring blossoming and observing the "turtle doves." Desultory nature observations at Walden and the Concord River continued into May, when he realized that the "year has many seasons more than are recognized in the Almanace."[18]

But July of 1850 saw one last in the great series of disasters befall, a disaster that nearly shook the entire sense of purpose Thoreau had begun to nurture so carefully within himself. On the nineteenth, Waldo Emerson received word that a ship carrying Margaret Fuller, her husband the Marquis Ossoli, and their infant son had wrecked off Fire Island. Fuller had gone to Europe as a foreign correspondent for Greeley's *Tribune* in 1846; she fell in love with Ossoli during the 1848 Italian Revolution, a revolution that forced them to flee to America. Now all were dead. Waldo persuaded Henry to go and head the search for the bodies and for Margaret

Fuller Ossoli's manuscript detailing the revolution.[19] Thoreau spent five days in the almost fruitless task, and returned home in a black mood ill-suited to nature observation. The material world for the moment had lost its appeal:

> We are ever dying to one world & being born into another—and probably no man knows whether he is dead in the sence in which he affirms that phenomenon of another—or not. Our thoughts are the epochs of our life—all else is but as a journal of the winds that blew while we were here.
>
> I do not think much of the actual.
>
> It is something which we have long since done with. It is a sort of vomit in which the unclean love to wallow.[20]

Slowly the blackness ebbed away, the habit of observation returned. He began again to note the phenomena of nature, continuing through the summer, and at the end of August wrote a long, detailed, and very precise catalog of the flowers and berries he encountered as autumn weather neared. By this time, neighbors were bringing to him for study the rarer birds they had managed to shoot. He was seeking still more secluded places where "some rare things grow." When he reached the end of a journal volume in mid-September, he devoted the last page to a list of plants, noting in some cases their Linnean classifications or outstanding botanical features. Nature study, and botany especially, seized Henry's imagination.[21] As winter came on, he began to prepare himself for still more thorough studies in the next year. In November, he noted that "I have no doubt that a dilligent search in proper places would discover many more of our summer plants . . . lingering till the snow came, than we suspect."[22] Anxious to begin investigations even as the snow began to fly, he reminded himself that "In winter I can explore the swamps and ponds."[23]

During this confused and at times aimless period of Thoreau's life, what interested him was perhaps not so much nature as it actually existed and behaved, but rather an idealized vision of nature that he called "The Wild." The concept probably owed more to romantic ideals of beauty and truth than to observations of nature in the raw. What mattered was not what the observer saw, but the observer's response to seeing. Pure views of strange and wild nature evoked a sense of awed fulfillment, a touch of the mind of God. "The Wild" was an elusive concept suggestive of mystery and poetry, more easily described than defined or explained.[24]

The relationship between actual nature and The Wild was a very strong one, and in time the idealized notion would be subsumed in the more complete understanding of genuine natural behavior Thoreau would acquire. In most celebrations of The Wild, he complained, "there is plenty of genial love of Nature, but not so much of Nature herself."[25] But in 1849 and 1850, the evidence indicates that Henry intended his nature studies to feed and support his idealized vision of The Wild, rather than the other way around.

In September 1849, he argued in his journal that "a town is saved not by any righteous men in it but by the woods and swamps that surround it." Soon after, he wrote, "How near to good is what is wild. There is the marrow of nature—there her divine liquors—that is the wine I love."

He did not limit his vision of The Wild to nature. Considering such great works of literature as *Hamlet* and *The Iliad,* he concluded that "it is only the wild that attracts us," the "free-thinking." A year later he decided that no poetry "adequately expresses this yearning for the wild. the *wilde.*" Thereafter he began to seek The Wild of his imagination more exclusively out of doors. "To see wild life you must go forth at a wild season," he advised. "When it rains and blows, keeping men indoors, then the lovers of Nature must forth. Then returns Nature to her wild estate." In June of 1852, he was prepared to argue that the spirit was fed in places where the most beautiful wildflowers blossomed.[26]

By far the most important product to emerge from this embrace of what was wild in nature and human affairs was a lecture he initially composed for the 1850–51 lecture season. Entitled simply "The Wild," Thoreau delivered the lecture before the Concord Lyceum on April 23, 1851. In the months and years that followed, Henry expanded and reworked the basic arguments, eventually developing enough material to divide the work into two separate lectures. After contracting his last illness, he reunited the two into a single long essay, which he published in the *Atlantic Monthly* under the title "Walking."[27]

"The Wild" and "Walking" were together the most powerful and uncompromising statements regarding nature Thoreau publicly espoused in his lifetime. The opening paragraph set the defiant tone of the piece, a tone comprised in equal parts of a desire to claim his own intellectual frontier, to awaken his neighbors from their dull complacency, and to celebrate the awe-inspiring nature that made America unique. Standing before the

Concord Lyceum, he first observed, "I wish to speak a word for Nature, for absolute freedom and wildness, as contrasted with a freedom and culture merely civil,—to regard man as an inhabitant, or a part and parcel of Nature, rather than a member of society. I wish to make an extreme statement, if so I may make an emphatic one, for there are enough champions of civilization; the minister and the school-committee, and every one of you will take care of that."[28]

This was Henry Thoreau without apologies. His book may have failed, as the whispers and cackles of the townspeople reminded him,[29] but he would back away from exactly none of the sentiments that had informed that work. The love of nature, the scalding criticism of human institutions, the "pantheism" for which he had been so roundly criticized, all were promised in this opening paragraph.

In the pages that followed, Henry argued the necessity of balancing the outdoor and the indoor life. A life spent too much in the outdoors produced a roughness of character, but too much time spent inside led to "a softness and smoothness, not to say a thinness of skin." In public at least, Henry was willing to strike a balance between civilization and the wild. Yet it was essential for Americans to understand that the continued existence of wildness was critical to the survival of the rough-hewn, ambitious, and expanding national character. Reminding his listeners of the continued presence of the untamed lands to the west, he contended that "The West of which I speak is but another name for the Wild; and what I have been preparing to say is, that in Wildness is the preservation of the World." After citing the story of Romulus and Remus and like examples from history and myth, he went on to say that "Life consists with wildness. The most alive is the wildest. Not yet subdued to man, its presence refreshes him."[30]

Thoreau fully understood that his fellow townspeople had little understanding or appreciation for the wild he venerated. In the essay he portrayed himself as living "a sort of border life," standing on the edge of wild nature, beckoning his fellow citizens to neglect their petty allegiances and look honestly at the greater world of which they were a part. "We hug the earth," he accused, "how rarely we mount. . . . We might climb a tree, at least." Drawing from his journals, he told of finding "my account" by climbing a white pine, and there discovering, in the topmost branches, uncomparably delicate and beautiful cone blossoms. Carrying a spray of the flowers to town, he showed them to all the good and industrious citizens—farmers, lumber-dealers, jurymen—none of whom had ever seen one before. "We see only the flowers that are under our feet in the meadows," he lectured, but there are other and greater visions for those who care to look. If Concord would avoid the listless and deadening fate of the overcivilized, its citizens, Thoreau insisted, must look beyond their ledgers and at least into the treetops. More preferably, they should look to the west, where nature remained free and wild. "In wildness is the preservation of the World."[31]

Thoreau folded several elements of his research and experience into his essay on "The Wild," and in that effort at least momentarily dispelled the sense of aimless drifting that so pervaded his journals. Although he had no clear purpose in doing so, Henry determined to carry on research in several different areas immediately following the failure of *A Week.* On the seventeenth of September 1849, he wrote to Jared Sparks, president of Harvard, seeking permission as an alumnus to borrow books from the university library. Sparks granted permission for a one year period; Thoreau used the privilege until he died.[32]

One of the most important and intensive of Thoreau's efforts was his renewed research in Eastern religion, especially Hindu literature. Henry had first become acquainted with Eastern scriptures during the youthful days of *The Dial,* when he had abstracted quotations, primarily on morality and proper living, from such diverse authors as Confucius and Manu. Access to Emerson's library gave him the opportunity for close study of several Eastern works, and his interest persisted through the 1840s. He carefully studied the *Bhagvat Geeta* during his stay at Walden Pond, and included some discussion of Oriental literature in the final manuscript of *A Week.* In 1848 he noted in his journal that "The contemplations of the Indian sages have aided the intellectual development of mankind."[33]

In the maelstrom of disappointment over his book, Thoreau seems to have decided to begin a new and more systematic study of Eastern doctrines, maintaining that "The Hindoos by constitution possess in a wonderful degree the faculty of contemplation," so different from Westerners who thought "only with ruinous interruptions & friction." In September 1849, he borrowed a two-volume French translation of one of the key works of Hindu religion, the *Mahabharata,* from the Harvard Library, along with a history of Hindu literature. Thoreau examined the *Mahabharata*—which collected a wide assortment of vedas, prayers, cautionary tales, laws, and other material—most carefully, even taking the time to write out an English translation of one story, "The Transmigration of the Seven Brahmans." By October he had concluded, "Why should we be related as mortals merely—as limited to one state of existence—Our lives are immortal our transmigrations are infinite—the virtue that we are livs ever."[34]

In the next year and a half, Thoreau borrowed the *Vishnu Purana* and the *Sankya Karika,* both works devoted largely to the proper living of one's life; the *Sama Veda* and other Vedas; the *Sakoontala;* and a collection published by the Asiatic Society of Bengal that included the *Upanishads.* The reading confirmed in his mind that the "Hindoos are more serenely and thoughtfully religious than the Hebrews." In 1851 he extended his studies to include Chinese works, specifically translations of Confucius and Mencius.[35]

On the surface, Thoreau's purpose in studying these various texts was to obtain insight into living a more perfect intellectual life, to discern the proper moral paths conducive to the achievement of higher, more spiritually pure, thought. Quoting the *Sankhya Karika,* he noted that, "By attainment of perfect knowledge, virtue & the rest become causeless; yet soul remains awhile invested with body, as the potter's wheel continues whirling from the effect of the impulse previously given to it."[36]

The moral element of Hindu thought was important to Thoreau, but given the conclusions he had reached atop Mount Ktaadn and in the final "Friday" chapter of *A Week*—that the world of the spirit and the sensate world of nature were not separable—his interest in this aspect was muted. In "The Transmigration of the Seven Brahmans," the one portion of the *Mahabharata* Thoreau found instructive enough to translate, the story involves the spiritual quest of seven individuals who had committed indiscretions in their quest for greater spiritual attainment. In consequence, the Brahmans had to undergo several further incarnations. Those who remained most true to the quest for spiritual fulfillment lived the lives of stags, of geese, of swans before achieving transmigration. In short, they lived in nature.[37]

More important to Henry was a second, related aspect of Hindu thought, one that had attracted his interest quite early, and which he pursued carefully during the early 1850s. This was the Hindu vision of the creation of the world.

Several of the great Hindu works, including the *Harivansa,* the *Bhagvat Geeta,* and Manu's *Institutes of Hindu Law,* relate the Hindu story of creation. Thoreau first took note of such stories in 1841, when he abstracted several portions of "The Laws of Menu" for publication in *The Dial.* Although he did not include the creation story in the published selections, Henry was impressed enough to copy the entire creation chapter into his literary notebook. In this version, Manu, speaking the words of the creator, related how God first created the water, in which he planted a protective seed which grew into an egg. Brahma, the primary incarnation of God, was born in the egg. For an entire year the egg sat inactive, then split into two equal portions, heaven above and earth beneath. Having thereby pervaded, "with emanations from the Supreme Spirit," all of the universe, "He framed all creatures." The chapter concludes with a verse noting that "All transmigrations, recorded in sacred books, from the state of BRAHMA, to that of plants, happen continually in the tremendous world of beings, a world *always* tending to decay."[38]

Two important themes emerge from this story: the universe, in both its spiritual and sensual aspects, emanates directly from God; and the physical world is in a state of constant flux.

Thoreau encountered the Hindu vision of creation again in January of 1850, when he read the *Vishnu Purana.* In this work, a student, Maitreya, questions his teacher, Parasara, regarding the origin and nature of the universe. Parasara then prays to Vishnu ("the preserver"), another version of Brahma, for enlightenment. In the fifth chapter of the work, Parasara explains that Vishnu made the universe in a series of six creations, beginning with the "developments of indiscrete nature," including intellect, elemental creation, and organic creation (the world of the senses). Then followed the secondary creations, the various classes of wild and domestic animals, the lesser divinities, and human beings. All were creations from Brahma's own body. For example, the fifth order of the animal classes, the birds, were formed from Brahma's "vital vigor."[39]

The *Harivansa,* which Thoreau took up in May of 1851, further considered the problem of creation. Henry studied the work at length, and in a journal entry dated "Monday May 6th 1845," abstracted several passages bearing on the presence of spirit in nature:

> The Harivansa describes a "substance["] called *Poroucha,* a spiritual substance known also under the name of Mahat, spirit united to the five elements, soul of beings, now enclosing itself in a body like ours, now re-

turning to the eternal body; it is mysterious wisdom, the perpetual sacrifice made by the virtue of the *Yoga,* the fire which animates animals, shines in the sun, and is mingled with all bodies. Its nature is to be born and to die, to pass from repose to movement. The spirit led astray by the senses, in the midst of the creation of Brahma, engages itself in works and knows birth, as well as death.—The organs of the senses are its paths, and its work manifests itself in the creation of Brahma.[40]

Henry had previously encountered commentaries on the spirit in nature in his studies of the *Bhagvat Geeta,* which he had read closely at Walden in 1846 and took up once again in 1854. The *Geeta* was written as a folk story intended for the instruction of all Hindu peoples, and its messages are plainly written and direct. The book comprises eighteen lectures, each written as a dialogue between the warrior Arjoon and the god Kreeshna, another form of Brahma. Kreeshna, answering Arjoon's doubts about a great battle soon to take place, advises the warrior to seek asylum "in wisdom alone," and then explains the true nature of the universe. Mincing no words, the god states in the tenth lecture that "I am the soul which standeth in the bodies of all things." Three lectures later he elaborates, telling Arjoon: "Know, O chief of the race of *Bharat,* that every thing which is produced in nature, whether animate or inanimate, is produced from the union of *Kshetra* and *Kshetragna,* matter and spirit. He who beholdeth the Supreme Being alike in all things, whilst corrupting, itself uncorrupting; and conceiving that God in all things is the same, doth not of himself injure his own soul, goeth on the journey of immortality."[41]

The *Bhagvat Geeta* clearly argues that even a contemplative life must be an active life; the world changes, and even to stand still a person must work. The important thing is to understand the true purpose of this work, which is neither to achieve a specific goal nor to gain material reward, but merely to understand.

The literature of the Hindus is broad, rich, and subtle in content. Thoreau read extensively in these works between 1849 and 1854, drawing any number of impressions and applying them to the various projects at hand. A passage from the *Vishnu Purana* on the liberating duty of discovering true knowledge found its way into his lecture on "The Wild" in the winter of 1851. He worked many, if not all, of the quotations from Oriental literature into his "Walden" manuscript at the same time, practically the only work he did on the book between the autumn of 1849 and the winter of 1852. He also continued to reflect on Eastern ideals of the life properly lived, recording thoughts in his journals from time to time.[42]

More importantly, the reading assisted Thoreau to develop a view of nature unique in the Western society of his time. The prevailing American and European view of nature was to hold that only God and humanity possessed a spirit, that nature was spiritually dead. This view, promoted by the Judeo-Christian tradition and reenforced by the science of Descartes, Newton, and others, promoted the objectification of the natural world. Emerson's heresy was to suggest that the world of God and the spirit did extend to plants and animals, but he had done so in a framework that denied the value of the objective, sensate world, the bodies of animals and people alike. Thoreau rejected Emerson's heresy, only to embrace a far more heretical view of his own: the spiritual and the natural world were inseparable and present all around him. Spirit not only existed in nature, its existence was there to be understood, if one was mentally prepared to do the work.[43]

Thoreau understood that he was not really saying anything new. His ideas were echoes of the Hindu sages, who had concluded that all the universe was simply the body and mind of God long before the birth of Christ. By reinterpreting these beliefs in a Western context, Thoreau challenged the notion that nature existed merely for the use of humankind. Out of this conclusion would come the impetus for a new way of looking at nature in Western society, one that eschewed utilitarian values and sought the presence of the universal spirit in animals and trees.

Henry's readings in Oriental literature did more than reenforce his belief in the presence of spirit in nature. By suggesting that all of nature was just one thing—each creature was really a part of Brahma's own self—these works encouraged Thoreau to look at the natural world in a profoundly unscientific way; as a complete and interworking whole rather than as a series of carefully delineated and discrete parts. If one God pervaded all of nature, then each animal, each plant, was a functioning part of a greater unity. As Thoreau came to apply himself more completely to the study of nature, he would retain the image of nature as an interrelated wholeness. His studies would combine minute examination of each part of nature he encountered with reference to the principles that held all the parts together.[44]

A second research project further supported Thoreau's highly unusual view of nature. As part of his work on *A Week on the Concord and Merrimack Rivers,* Thoreau undertook a study of the history of the American Indians. In a notebook begun in 1847, Henry recorded materials discovered in various local and regional histories of New England, much of which would inform his discussions of the geography he encountered during the one-week excursion. In 1850, for reasons both unknown and highly debated among scholars, he decided to expand the scope of this research, beginning seven new notebooks on the subject in a space of little more than two years. (Four more notebooks were begun after 1854.) Most were completely filled in the course of a few months. Whenever possible, he supplemented this research with visits to Native American peoples. In November of 1850, he devoted several pages of his journal to a description of his visit to a temporary Indian encampment near Concord. Trips to Maine in 1853 and 1857 were made primarily to obtain fuller information from Algonkian Indians who served him as guides into the wilderness.[45]

Much of the material in the notebooks was topically arranged. In an era when virtually every citizen of the United States viewed the Native Americans as savage enemies, it is to Thoreau's great credit that he was interested in them as people. Most of the histories of the period limited the discussion of Indians to war encounters, but Henry sought to discover as much as he could on a wide range of topics, including religion, lifestyle, government, and art. Although virtually all the information he discovered was derivative—Indian practices as recorded by often misapprehending or biased Europeans and white Americans—he attempted to glean as fair a view of Indian life as possible. His own commentaries editorially balanced the observations copied from other sources at several points in the notebooks.[46]

Thoreau never produced any specific writing based exclusively on the notebooks, although he incorporated materials from his research into *Walden,* "Cape Cod," his nature essays, and various journal entries. As close as he ever came to writing an "Indian book" were two essays recounting his trips to Maine: "Chesuncook," partially published in the *Atlantic Monthly* in 1858, and "The Allegash and East Branch," published posthumously as part of a book entitled *The Maine Woods* in 1864.[47]

Perhaps more important than any specific writings derived from this vast quantity of research was the perspective he obtained from readings in the Native American religions. In October 1852, Thoreau concluded in his journal that "The constitution of the Indian mind appears to be the very opposite to that of the white man. He is acquainted with a different side of nature."[48] He apparently based this observation in large part on his study of Native American creation stories, many of which he recorded in the third and fourth of his "Indian notebooks." Drawing from Henry Roe Schoolcraft, Adrian Van der Donck, John Heckewelder, and several others, Thoreau carefully noted the Indian belief in gods for each aspect of nature, and over these "one great God & one great evil one." Reacting to a paragraph taken from Schoolcraft's *History of the Indian Tribes of the United States,* Henry wrote that they "see the great spirit in everything." Drawing later from Heckewelder, he copied down a passage stating that "The Indians consider the earth as their universal mother."[49]

Just as he took inspiration from the Hindu belief that all the universe was God, Thoreau took also to heart the Native American belief in the universal great spirit. His readings, combined with the two Maine experiences in which he employed Indians as guides, gave Thoreau tremendous respect for the close relationship to nature he perceived in them. As his own studies of nature deepened, he looked often to Native American lore for instruction on the ways of plants and animals.[50]

He also adapted their perspective to his own growing understanding of the universal spirit in nature. Writing the story of his 1853 expedition to Chesuncook Lake, Henry observed that a pine tree "is as immortal as I am, and perchance will go to as high a heaven, there to tower above me still." (When the *Atlantic Monthly* published the essay in 1858, the editor, that paragon of moral virtue, James Russell Lowell, recognized the lack of proper Christian sentiment in this sentence and struck it out. Thoreau was furious.)[51]

Henry's combined reading in Hindu and Native American religion provided him a firm foundation to look at the natural world as a functioning whole imbued with the spirit of God. For Thoreau, there was no separation between the spiritual and earthly planes of existence, nor was the spirit of God limited to the souls of human beings. Spirit, whole and inseparable, was present in all of nature.

Thoreau's excursions into the world of the intellect during the early 1850s did not end with his studies of Oriental and Native American literature. Although he had no clear idea of where his mind was taking him, Henry was systematically expanding his knowledge in several additional directions.

Thoreau immersed himself in the writings of natural scientists, especially botanists. He seems to have begun in the fall of 1849 with Alexander von Humboldt's *Views of Nature; or Contemplations on the Sublime Phenomena of Creation.* Humboldt had ushered in the age of systematic scientific exploration with a five-year expedition to South America at the beginning of the century. In *Views of Nature,* he envisioned a science encompassing and comprehending the whole of the natural world. To attain such a goal, Humboldt contended, it would be necessary above all to master an understanding of the interconnections among nature's parts, rather than cataloging each part discretely. Thoreau readily concurred.[52]

After reading Humboldt, Henry undertook a methodical study of botanical works, beginning with Harvard scientist Asa Gray's *Manual of the Botany of the Northern United States.* Between October of 1850 and March of 1852, he read several more, ranging from such comparatively modern experts as Nuttall, Micheaux, Bigelow, Lindley, and Gray, to the father of modern classification, Linnaeus, to such classical naturalists as Theophrastus. Much of this material he abstracted for insertion in a separate natural history notebook. For broader perspective, he took up Charles Darwin's journal of the voyage of the *H.M.S. Beagle* and Gilbert White's *Natural History of Selborne.*[53] One especially instructive work was William Bartram's *Travels through North and South Carolina, Georgia, East and West Florida,* a book that combined descriptions of close botanical observation with rousing tales of adventure—science and romance.[54] The book, published in 1791, was tremendously popular in a period when it was still possible to unconsciously combine science and art.

Any blend of artistic endeavor and scientific inquiry met increasing skepticism as the nineteenth century advanced. Well-recognized romantic writers, including Coleridge and Goethe, had pursued scientific investigations and incorporated their findings into essays and poetry, striving to combine accuracy of observation and facility of expression. By the 1840s, however, a small but growing coterie of scientists began to frown on such works, arguing that the blend of inductive observation and personal intuitive reaction to the results biased the entire process. Professionals such as Asa Gray and Louis Agassiz asserted that all good scientific writing should be value-neutral; the reporter uninvolved in the observations. As the scientific professions gathered strength, books devoted to discussion of proper scientific methodology multiplied. Thoreau personally found works in which the observer removed himself from the discussion painfully sterile. Others saw even greater danger. Both Emerson and Carlyle warned against a mechanical and materialistic science that denied a role to the creator.[55]

Desiring to write an exacting portrait of nature while retaining his own presence, Thoreau studied the works of the great landscape painter William Gilpin, seeking perspective on the best manner in which to translate sensate observation into art. As the months went by, Thoreau became increasingly adept in his understanding of science and art, drawing from his readings such information as he needed while maintaining an independence of judgment. Writing on Nuttall's *North American Sylva,* he noted that "It is sapless, if not leafless." Becoming exasperated with Gilpin, he observed, "I wish he would look at scenery sometimes not with the eye of an artist. It is all side screens and fore screens and near distances and broken grounds with him."[56]

At the same time, Thoreau sought to increase his exact scientific knowledge through personal contact with naturalists, especially Thaddeus William Harris, Harvard librarian and one of America's leading entomologists. Henry traveled to Cambridge to borrow books three or four times a year, and always availed himself of the opportunity to discuss matters scientific with Harris. They discussed botany, entomology—Thoreau occasionally brought specimens for Harris to identify—and the woodlore of the American Indians. Henry also made a habit of stopping at the Boston Society of Natural History, making careful study of their extensive bird exhibits to assist him in his own field identifications.[57]

After more than a year of intensive research, Henry in the fall of 1850 apparently decided on a specific course of action. On the eighth of November he entered a long and vividly executed description of nature in the autumn, ranging among sights and sounds; the colors of decaying vegetation, the cry of birds, the stillness of the woods.[58] Eight days later, he observed: "My journal should be the record of my love. I would write in it only of the things I love. . . . I feel ripe for something yet do nothing—can't discover what that thing is. I feel fertile merely. It is seed time with me—I have lain fallow long enough."[59]

Five days after that he sat on the shore of Fair Haven Pond, basking in the view of the still water between the island and the shore while two fish hawks sailed overhead. "I did not see how it could be improved," he wrote. "Yet I do not see what these things can be. I begin to see an object when I cease to *understand* it—and see that I did not realize or appreciate it before—but I get no further than this. How adopted these forms and colors to my eye—a meadow and an island; what are these things? Yet the hawks & the ducks keep so aloof! and nature is so reserved! I am made to love the pond & the meadow as the wind is made to ripple the water."[60] Henry had decided that his journal should be a record of the things he loved, and he had decided that he loved nature. A journal of nature stood on the horizon.

Thoreau did not plunge into keeping a detailed nature journal without reservation. For the next three years he kept up a profound argument with himself over purpose, revealing a deep ambivalence regarding both the content of his journal entries and the means of composing them. Throughout the year 1851, the threads of this running debate with himself crop up among his nature observations with fair frequency. In January he reminded himself that the journal should contain "those thoughts & impressions which I am most likely to forget," thoughts that would signify, "in one sense the greatest remoteness—in another the greatest nearness, to me." In February he argued that "My desire for knowledge is intermittent; but my desire to commune with the spirit of the universe . . . is perennial and constant." By late spring he was proud to be one of the few who "observed the minute differences in the seasons." He then envisioned "A Book of the seasons," each page written outdoors in nature and describing the actual season at hand. But in August he concluded that "It is narrow to be confined to woods & fields and grand aspects of nature only." He was feeling the need to look at the behavior of people. At the same time, he resolved to live his life more deliberately, to "read no book—to take no walk—to undertake no enterprise but such as you can endure to give an account of to yourself." September saw him striving to record "Whatever things I perceive with my entire man," believing "it will be poetry." Standing in the moonlight at Fair Haven three nights later, he studied "The stars of poetry & history—& unexplored nature looking down on the scene. This is my world now."[61]

Autumn brought a new and stiffer sense of determination. On the tenth of November 1851, he wrote: "I come from the funeral of mankind to attend to a natural phenomenon. The so much grander significance of any fact—of sun & moon & stars—when not referred to man & his needs but viewed absolutely—Sounds that are wafted from over the confines of time."[62]

On Christmas day, he pointedly told himself to "not be in haste to detect the *universal law,* let me see more clearly a particular instance. Much finer themes I aspire to—which will yield no satisfaction to the vulgar mind." By that date he seems to have largely settled himself to the idea of a nature journal, a journal that would record nature in its most minute aspects while constantly bearing in mind the universal structures and themes that made all of nature a working whole. To create a viable record of such an enormous subject, the journal itself would have to become the vehicle; no poem, essay, or book could ever be large or flexible enough to properly convey the subject matter.[63] In January of 1852 he noted: "I do not know but thoughts written down thus in a journal might be printed in the same form with greater advantage—than if the related ones were brought together into separate essays."[64]

From this point forward, although Henry drew regularly from the journals to create lectures for the Concord Lyceum and other places, he never again set about deliberately to write a descriptive nature essay for publication. Even though, as he wrote on February 8, 1852, "Thoughts of different dates will not cohere," the journal itself now became his primary literary vehicle, an ongoing experiment in the comprehension and expression of the natural world. The journal was to be a project itself, and not simply raw material for other projects.[65]

Faced with the enormity of understanding and recording all of nature in Concord, Thoreau slowly evolved a methodology to assist him in the task. His daily walks became longer in time, but perhaps shorter in distance—five miles or less—as he came to recognize the incredible range of phenomena coming to his attention with every step. The abundance threatened to overwhelm him, and he sought not to look so much as to saunter with his eye. Still, he came to rely on his senses more than ever, watching closely for the specific date of each flower's blossoming in the spring, noting by eye and ear the arrival of new birds with each change in the season. The sense of smell too became important, revealing "what is concealed from the other senses." He found it necessary to be outdoors, "to get experience of wholesome reality, as a ballast to thought and sentiment." Any discovery of a new natural fact brought him a sweet satisfaction, "suggesting what worlds remain to be unveiled."[66]

The new spirit of inquiry that came to pervade Henry's journal was best characterized by the seemingly constant barrage of questions asked of himself. Gone is the placid self-assurance accompanying the few and random nature observations of the early journals. By the early 1850s, Henry wanted to know everything, thoroughly and reliably. This made for several entries containing queries to himself regarding plant and animal identification, coupled with subsequent investigation and occasional self-correction. For example, while boating in November 1851, he encountered "minute yellow coccoons" in a field flanking the river. "What is the insect?" he asked. Two months later, he observed a curious white cleavage in the cracks of the ice at Fair Haven, leaving him to wonder "what is their law?"[67]

Thoreau worked carefully to answer his own questions, often relying on the written works of experts to assist him. In May 1851, he drew from his botany reading to distinguish between the black and white ashes at Miles Swamp, detecting a subtle but unmistakable difference between two closely related species he had not previously noticed. At times the lessons unfolded over a period of several years. In May 1853, he tentatively identified a bird song heard in the woods as that of a chickadee, but later crossed this out and wrote in "myrtle bird" in its stead. In 1858, he crossed out "myrtle bird," definitely identifying the songster as a white-throat sparrow.[68]

Henry also began employing tools to assist his field identification work. First and foremost were scratch paper and pencil, carried into the field daily. Generally he crafted rough notes of his observations and adventures while actually outdoors, and then constructed the actual journal entries at the writing table in his room, taking care to retain the sense of outdoor immediacy in each entry. In the early 1850s he also carried a botany (either Bigelow or Gray) and wore a large hat that he used as a "botany box" for carrying specimens. In June 1853, he borrowed a spyglass to aid his identification of the various hawks he encountered, and in the spring of 1854 acquired one of his own. (The purchase was instantly rewarded; his first sighting with the new glass was a "white-headed eagle," the first he recognized in Concord.) Thoreau's use of these accouterments—aids to memory, to identification, to the sense of sight—indicated the depth of his commitment to a close study of nature's ways.[69]

The results of this study were copious and complicated. What Thoreau had in mind was from the beginning something more than a mere catalog of natural observations. Always in the back of his mind was the fact of the spirit in nature, a knowledge that encouraged him to look beyond the minutia of everyday observation, to seek the interrelationships among organisms and to discover the patterns of birth, growth, and decay in all the species he identified. "I make it my business to extract from Nature whatever nutriment she can furnish me," he wrote in 1853, "though at the risk of endless iteration."[70]

By the summer of 1851, Thoreau's journal featured pages upon pages of laborious plant notes, identifying species, enumerating distinguishing details, noting both the places where they grew and the kind of habitat. In the following spring Henry began listing the flowers he encountered in chronological order of appearance, a practice he maintained with each change of season over the next several years. By 1853 he could predict the order of blossoming and foretell the number of species left to bloom.[71]

In March 1853, Henry listed the hawks he found in Concord, and beginning in summer 1854 kept a careful list of the appearance of new birds in the town. In addition to the bird lists, he undertook a study of ornithological habits, including feeding, preferred haunts, and nesting, which completely overshadowed the sketchy notebook he had maintained with his siblings back in the 1840s.[72]

Thoreau was by 1854 a fully committed naturalist, able not merely to identify hundreds of species of plants and animals, but to organize his observations into predictive patterns that described the turn of the seasons. In April, he delineated four stages in the season of spring, beginning with the emergence of a few radical leaves in March, ending with the first great crop of leaves and grass in June.[73]

As Henry delved more and more deeply into the secrets of nature, he found the going increasingly lonely. While many of his neighbors may have shared a general if superficial interest in nature, Thoreau now devoted himself so fully to the subject that he found himself cut off from much of society. More than one Concord resident branded him a "loafer." He hoped that by conquering "some realms from the night" his townspeople might think better of him, but he was none too sanguine about the possibility. As early as November 1850, he spoke of some "bitter-sweet dissatisfaction" with some of his friends, and subsequently complained that "you cannot have a deep sympathy with both man & nature."[74] In July 1852, he elaborated.

> By my intimacy with nature I find myself withdrawn from man. My interest in the sun and the moon, in the morning and the evening, compels me to solitude.

> The grandest picture in the world is the sunset sky. In your higher moods what man is there to meet? You are of necessity isolated. The mind that perceives clearly any natural beauty is in that instant withdrawn from human society. My desire for society is infinitely increased; my fitness for any actual society is diminished.[75]

Later journal entries spoke of the pain and loneliness Thoreau felt at times, although by 1854 he had hardened himself. Seeking solitude "with infinite yearning and aspiration, . . . more and more resolved and strong," he came to see any desire for society as a "genial weakness."[76]

Uppermost in Henry's mind when thinking of friendship and society was, of course, Waldo Emerson. Emerson apparently criticized Henry's solitary walks openly, while Thoreau continued to resent the fact that the general public saw any fame in him as reflected from the great man. The arguments and misunderstandings continued. In the autumn of 1851, Henry lamented that they were "almost a sore to one another."[77] By the spring of 1853, the situation had become almost a caricature of itself: "P.M.—Talked, or tried to talk, with R.W.E. Lost my time—nay, almost my identity. He, assuming a false opposition where there was no difference of opinion, talked to the wind—told me what I know—and I lost my time trying to imagine myself somebody else to oppose him."[78]

Fortunately, other of Thoreau's friendships were on firmer ground. Ellery Channing continued to share outdoor excursions with Henry, and Bronson Alcott was a regular visitor. Alcott, caught between Emerson and Thoreau, once observed that he visited Waldo as the equivalent of fine wine, and Henry as the equivalent of wild venison. Henry was pleased by the comparison.[79]

If Henry was criticized for making a withdrawal from society in the early 1850s, the accusation was in some ways justified. In July 1852, he told Emerson outright that nature was more interesting than people.[80] To his fellow citizens, Henry had long been associated with a variety of reform ideals, ranging from the general state of the economy to the specifics of abolition. As previously noted, Henry in the 1840s had fitted several arrows to his bow, attempting both to find a voice and a subject matter. He now settled almost exclusively on the subject of nature, treating matters of morality and politics as virtually extraneous subjects. During the 1850s—the most crucial and bitterly divisive in the history of the American nation—Henry could be distracted from his nature studies only by events of surpassing moment. The Compromise of 1850, the Nebraska-Kansas Bill, Bleeding Kansas, all occurred with very little notice from Thoreau. He continued to materially assist fugitive slaves, but took little part in abolitionist activities. The Anthony Burns case roused him to fierce denunciation of slavery and the state, as did John Brown's Raid, but the passion never lasted long. "To what purpose have I senses," he asked, "if I am thus absorbed in affairs My pulse must beat with nature."[81]

In addition to the criticisms brought forth against Henry Thoreau by his friends and fellow townspeople was that leveled by Henry himself. If he was not much impressed with the goals set for him by his neighbors, he was very much determined to refine and accomplish the ideals he envisioned for himself. To that end, he carried on an intensive journal review of his methods, practices, and processes of thought.[82]

Henry's greatest concern was that in studying the minutia of nature he was growing cold and scientific. "I fear that the character of my knowledge is from year to year becoming more distinct & scientific," he mused in August 1851. "I see details not wholes nor the shadow of the whole. I count some parts, & say 'I know.'" For ten days in September, he actually quit looking for flowers or carrying his botany book. But the study of nature beckoned more strongly than ever and he began again, only to rehearse the same arguments with himself the following spring. "Once I was part and parcel of nature," he bemoaned, "—now I am observant of her."[83]

Thoreau sought what he envisioned as the poetry of nature. This was perhaps a little difficult to define, but Henry was reasonably certain that it was not to be found while using a botany or a hygrometer. "The poet must bring to Nature the smooth mirror in which she is reflected," he wrote in 1853. "He must be superior to her, something more than natural." One could not purposely go out as an observer and expect to find nature—nature was to be experienced "in the fullness of life." Yet Henry did go to nature as an observer, carrying a botany and perhaps a hygrometer as well. By June of 1852 he suspected that "I am less thoughtful than I was last year at this time." He believed his senses strained from the habit of constant attention while in the woods and fields, and felt "dissipated" by the wealth of observations he had collected, wishing to be "the magnet in the midst of all this dust and filings."[84]

This self-criticism was largely an outgrowth of Henry's continued allegiance to the amorphous ideals of transcendentalism. Although his bickering with Emerson had reached embarrassing proportions, Thoreau continued to think of himself, and all good thinking people, as transcendentalists. "The fact is," he wrote, "I am a mystic, a transcendentalist, and a natural philosopher to boot."[85]

In his transcendentalist moods, Thoreau tended to swing to the view of nature as symbol, rather than as sensate reality. Perhaps he best conveyed the essence of this mood in observing that "My thought is a part of the meaning of the world, and hence I use a part of the world as a symbol to express my thought."[86]

Most often, particularly in the early 1850s, these occasional returns to Emersonian visions of transcendentalism came in the dead of winter, when contact with living nature was necessarily limited. In winter, Henry observed, "A man is constrained to sit down, and to think."[87] The fields of literature and thought remained open when harsh winter weather closed the fields of nature. Thoreau understood this perfectly well: "The alert and energetic man leads a more intellectual life in winter than in summer. In summer the animal and the vegetable in him are perfected as in a torrid zone—he lives in his senses mainly—In winter cold reason & not warm passion has her sway—he lives in thought & reflection—He lives a more spiritual & less sensuous life."[88]

Of course, winter was also the lecture season at the Concord Lyceum and in other New England towns. Thoreau's yearly commitment to lecture at least locally may have helped to inspire the intellectual endeavor he associated with the cold weather months.

As the winter season wore on, Henry's appreciation of the opportunities for quiet thought wore thin. In February of 1852, he complained that his muse was failing him, that original thoughts were as rare as birdsong in winter.[89] A month later, he was happy to be outdoors at last. "It affects one's philosophy, after so long living in winter quarters, to see the day dawn from some hill. . . . Sucking the claws of our philosophy when there is game to be had!"[90]

By the mid-1850s, Henry learned to appreciate the possibilities offered by nature in winter; the opportunities to see new birds, to observe the behavior of the ice, to induce animal behavior from footprints. Bundling up, he forewent his philosophy to spend more time out in the cold.

At the heart of Thoreau's self-criticisms was his ambivalent relationship with science. Since his years at Walden Pond, Henry had understood and in some ways celebrated the great possibilities of the scientific method. At his most generous, he argued that "The man of science is the man most alive, whose life is the greatest event." But Henry also perceived the growing division between science and art. As the scientific disciplines developed, they eschewed art in practice and presentation, creating a view of the world that seemed to Thoreau and others artificially cold and distant. This was a science Henry could not value. "I suspect," he wrote, "that the child plucks its first flower with an insight into its beauty & significance which the subsequent botanist never retains." Although Thoreau understood and valued the methods of science and learned much from scientific writings, he could neither call himself a scientist nor condone their attitudes. Scientists saw only the parts, never the whole, and those from a supposedly neutral position, never "humanly" as Thoreau put it. The scientific was to him something less than the poetic.[91]

John Shepard Keyes, a fellow resident of Concord, later recalled that Thoreau "was more Indian like in his observations, not scientific."[92] Probably Henry would have agreed. He regarded the Native American way of viewing nature as an expansion of the scientific method, a more instructive way of viewing the whole. After attending a lecture delivered by an Anishinabe Indian in March 1858, Henry considered the crucial differences between traditional science and Indian modes of observation:

> Our scientific names convey a very partial information only; they suggest certain thoughts only. It does not occur to me that there are other names for most of these objects, given by a people who stood between me and them, who had better senses than our race. How little I know of that *arbor-vitae* when I have learned only what science can tell me! It is but a word. It is not a *tree* of *life*. But there are twenty words for the tree and its different parts which the Indian gave, which are not in our botanies, which imply a practical and more vital science. He used it every day. He was well acquainted with its wood, and its bark, and its leaves. No science does more than arrange what knowledge we have of any class of objects.[93]

Edward Neally, a young Irish contemporary, understood the difference between Thoreau and Harvard scientist Agassiz perfectly. Agassiz always wanted to kill his specimens, dissecting the remains to determine how they differed from other specimens. But Henry "liked to study 'em living. He didn't like to have 'em killed, . . . but he would rather know what they'd do."[94]

Henry's criticisms of science were quite specific and extended well beyond the growing scientific rejection of artistic expression. He found what he considered fatal flaws in the foundation of science itself. Most importantly, he believed the oft-cited practice of neutral observation to be impossible. In July of 1851, while making field observations, he recognized that he, the supposedly neutral observer, was always and unavoidably in the center of the observation. The point of view was always the same. In the spring of 1854, he stated flat-footedly that "There is no such thing as pure *objective* observation."[95]

Thoreau was further put off by what he called the "inhumanity" of science, characterized by the scientist's willingness to kill other creatures in the name of inquiry. In the early 1840s, Henry's brother John (and perhaps Henry as well) had followed the time-honored practice of using a gun to assist the identification of ornithological specimens—a bird dead in the hand is much easier to identify. By the 1850s Henry had confirmed the presence of the spirit in nature, and the idea of shooting even difficult-to-identify species disgusted him. This was not the way to acquire true knowledge. "To be serene and successful we must be at one with the universe," he concluded in May of 1854. "The least conscious and needless injury inflicted on any creature is to its extent a suicide."[96]

But, less than three months later, Henry found himself so carried away in a scientific investigation of turtles that he actually killed a "cistudo" for the sake of science. Never again. By no trick of mental gymnastics could he excuse himself of what amounted in his mind to murder. "It affects my day injuriously," he confessed. "I have lost some-self respect." Such an action was at bottom inconsistent with "poetic perception," and would negatively affect all his observations. What of life could be learned from a dead turtle?[97]

Nor could science answer what Thoreau regarded as the genuinely crucial questions. Scientists could describe the physical forces that created the lightning that struck and killed a favorite tree, but they could not explain the "moral *why*" of the occurrence any better than the lay person. Science did not even begin to get at the really essential truths of life as Thoreau saw them, and was therefore presumptuous in any claim to being a final authority. At best, science was a tool, a means to achieving a broader understanding. At bottom, he believed people to be closer to the essential of life "in their superstitions than in their science."[98]

Each year, Henry leafed through several scientific reports, including such publications as the *Annual of Scientific Discovery.* He was a corresponding member of the Boston Society of Natural History, and was invited to join the Association for the Advancement of Science. He knew science, but he perceived also an essential poverty in scientific investigation, as there was no science that considered the higher law. Science may have spoken a highly technical language, but this merely disguised a great ignorance of all that was meaningful.[99]

In his darker moods, Henry became so disillusioned with his habits of scientific observation that he threatened to give up nature study altogether. Nature became shallow. Such a mood struck in June of 1852, and again in May 1854:

> We soon get through with Nature. She excites an expectation which she cannot satisfy. . . .
>
> I go about to look at flowers and listen to the birds. There was a time when the beauty and the music were all within, and I sat and listened to my thoughts, and there was a song in them.[100]

The ill-humor never lasted for very long. The day following this entry he composed a long and exacting chronological list of the budding and leafing of all the plants he had encountered that spring. He then went off to observe nature anew, heeding the advice he had given himself two years before: "If you would be wise learn science & then forget it."[101]

Thoreau could rise above the narrow and confining demands of science because of his most basic belief in spirit in nature, a spirit that unified the myriad parts of nature described by science into an indivisible whole. "The earth I tread on is not a dead inert mass," he emphasized, denying science and Western culture generally. "It is a body—has a spirit—is organic—and fluid to the influence of its spirit—and to whatever particle of that spirit is in me." He truly loved nature, loved its sincerity, found in it the sustenance of moral, intellectual, and physical health. Admittedly, this love assumed some of the characteristics of religious fervor, as Henry found himself striving to live a more pure and moral life in order to preserve his relationship with nature.[102]

Listening carefully to the sounds of the natural world, especially to the crickets in summer and autumn, Thoreau strained to hear a more universal song, the song of the earth itself. Away from the prickly mess of human institutions, Henry found "a different kind of light," and strove to comprehend the truth suggested by the Hindu mystics, that God, nature, and Henry Thoreau were really all the same thing. His life partook of infinity. Echoing the lessons derived from the *Vishnu Purana* and the writings of Manu, he saw the heavens and the earth as one vast flower. "The earth is the calyx, the heavens the corolla." Finding his own thoughts to be identical with those of the thirteenth-century poet Sadi, he saw no difference at all between the poet and himself. Both were a part of the same God.[103]

Thoreau entertained these thoughts in the context of his nature work, studies that would make him a comprehensive botanist, an excellent bird-watcher, a sympathetic observer of all nature. This work too would yield important perspective. In August 1851, upon finding the Hieracium Paniculatum, he observed: "I have now found all the hawkweeds. Singular these genera of plants—plants manifestly related yet distinct—They suggest a history to Nature—a Natural *history* in a new sense."[104]

In the spring of 1852, the search for nature's minutia, combined with the search for God, brought him to an entirely new and potent manner of seeing the universe in nature:

> For the first time I perceive this spring that the year is a circle— I see distinctly the spring arc thus far. It is drawn with a firm line. Every incident is a parable of the great teacher. The cranberries washed up in the meadows & into the road on the causeways now yields a pleasant acid.
>
> Why should just these sights & sounds accompany our life? Why should I hear the chattering of blackbirds— why smell the skunk each year? I would fain explore the mysterious relation between myself & these things. I would at least know what these things unavoidably are—make a chart of our life— know how its shores trend— that butterflies reappear & when— know why just this circle of creatures completes the world.[105]

Armed with a formidable scientific knowledge of the natural world and an exceedingly rare awareness of God in nature and in himself, Henry Thoreau had asked a question that only he was in a position to answer: How did all of the different components of nature work together to make a complete whole? The question was not a scientific one, for it argued that the whole was something other than the sum of the parts—a kind of being in itself. The question was not a religious one, at least not in any Judeo-Christian sense New England, America, or Europe would understand, for it argued that the natural world was God. This was a glimpse of a new and enticing vision, an image of nature's complexity and wholeness without parallel in Western thought. Entirely on his own, Henry Thoreau had asked the question that would lead to the development of what we would now label an ecological view of the world.

But how to answer such a question? Thoreau was so far in advance of his contemporaries there was nowhere to turn for advice or models of inquiry. His only recourse was to watch nature carefully, to record the actions of each species, the interactions among species, the effects of climate and geography on all species—and armed all the while only with a vague and incomplete idea of what exactly to look for. How does one demonstrate for others the certain knowledge that all of nature works together in myriad complex ways because it is all God? Small wonder that Henry grew discouraged from time to time.

Henry had begun his close studies of nature in 1851. After asking his great question in the spring of 1852, the journal of his observations grew even more detailed and precise. He devoted long hours to close observation in remote and difficult parts of Concord, made special studies of the behavior of turtles, birds, and other creatures. Meanwhile, his new vision served to inform and inspire still another project. The "Walden" manuscript, abandoned after the disaster of *A Week,* took on new potential.

Troubled by the question of why he had ever left his home in the woods at all, Thoreau renewed work on his Walden story in the winter of 1852. As in the 1840s, materials from his journals became important elements in a manuscript intended for publication, although the emphasis was different. By 1852, the journal had become a continuous work in its own right; Thoreau borrowed journal entries, but he no longer sacrificed the journal's completeness for the sake of other writings. The journals remained bound and largely intact.[106]

In the next two years he worked to rewrite and expand the Walden manuscript almost continually, eventually producing four revisions before writing out a clean copy for the printer in February and March 1854. To create the final, published version of *Walden,* Henry wedded his original story to the realization he had recorded in his journal long after leaving the pond: nature is a circle; all the world is one thing.[107]

Ironically, as Henry reworked his manuscript, the face of the woods he loved was changing drastically. Consumption of cordwood and lumber for ties by the railway companies created an enormous pressure on New England's woods, and the forests surrounding Walden Pond felt the axe along with several other of Concord's woodlots, all privately owned. Shocked by the devastation to the trees he loved, he resolved in 1852 to go to Walden less frequently. Yet even as the demands of industry razed portions of the landscape, Thoreau continued to draw direct inspiration and material from his outdoor experiences. Incidents, observations, and ideas initially entered in his journals often found their way into the Walden manuscript. A game of tag played with a loon at Walden Pond in October 1852 became one of the most stirring parts of the chapter entitled "Brute Neighbors."[108]

The diverse elements Thoreau folded into the final version of *Walden* blended successfully because of his perception of the cycle of nature. The book is, in effect, two distinct poles of thought firmly anchored in an assurity. The lightning passing between these poles gave the work its rare power and majesty.

The first pole, both in order of introduction in the book and in original inception, was his critique of the human economic order. The essence of his criticisms—the fact that a sumptuous house made its owner poor, that inheritance of farmland was tantamount to imprisonment, that factories were not the best way to make clothing, as the real goal was to make money instead—was present from the very first draft of the story. Thoreau sharpened and added to this commentary with each succeeding draft, creating a devastating indictment of economic illusion and outright folly.[109]

That the book does not read as a bitter attack on human foibles is due to the presence of the second pole: a subtle and profound celebration of Thoreau's vision of the natural world. Arguing that there may be "a civilization going on among brutes as well as men," he retained from the first draft the clear statement that "We can never have enough of Nature."[110]

In the later drafts, Henry goes much further than this, discovering in any number of encounters the presence of the same spirit in nature as in himself. In the first paragraph of "Solitude" he describes himself as a part of nature, and a few pages later acknowledges that he was never truly alone at the pond, thanks to visits from the maker of Walden and the creator of the fertile herb gardens of the wilderness. Then, in "Winter Animals," he listened to the wild discordance created by the echoing calls of a flock of geese and an owl, only to find in the argument "the elements of a concord such as these plains never saw or heard." The image of nature Thoreau painted in *Walden* was the image of a single thing. In "Brute Neighbors," he even reiterated the great question from his journal: "Why do precisely these objects which we behold make a world?" What was in the mind of the creator? It is possible to discover the answer, Henry reminded his readers. "Heaven is under our feet as well as over our heads."[111]

Thoreau anchored the contrast between economic folly and natural serenity in his newfound discovery of the cycle of the universe. In the much-revised and expanded chapter entitled "Spring," Henry drew for his readers the circle that encompassed the universe. He spent more than two years at the pond, but in the book he compressed the essential experience into the cycle of a single year, beginning and ending with spring. The second year was in effect the same as the first, just as every year is the same in nature. Progress was an illusion, a trick, an invention of the human mind.[112]

Henry found the perfect image to express this idea in a natural phenomenon discovered at the "Deep Cut," a passage dug through a sandy hillside near Walden for the railway. Thoreau often walked along the railway on excursions between pond and village, and in the spring of 1848 first noted the existence of what he came to call the "sand foliage." As the frost thawed in the raw, unvegetated earth along the steep sides of the Deep Cut, uneven expansion and heaving of the soil layers forced wet sand to ooze from walls. The sand assumed wild and amazing patterns, a kind of flowering of the earth itself. Henry returned to the sand foliage year after year, reveling in this expression of the earth's own artistry. Several experiments in describing the event occupy successive volumes of the journal; in March of 1852 he even described the cause of the event scientifically.[113] But in *Walden,* he used the event in a completely different way, seeing the sand foliage as a demonstration of nature's cycle at work:

> Thus it seemed that this one hillside illustrated the principle of all the operations of Nature. The maker of this earth but patented a leaf. . . . This is the frost coming out of the ground; this is Spring. It precedes the green and flowery spring, as mythology precedes regular poetry. I know of nothing more purgative of winter fumes and indigestions. It convinces me that

> Earth is still in her swaddling clothes, and stretches forth baby fingers on every side. Fresh curls spring from the baldest brow. There is nothing inorganic. These foliaceous heaps lie along the bank like the slag of a furnace, showing that Nature is "in full blast" within. The earth is not a mere fragment of dead history, stratum upon stratum like the leaves of a book, to be studied by geologists and antiquaries chiefly, but living poetry like the leaves of a tree, which precede flowers and fruit,—not a fossil earth, but a living earth; compared with whose great central life all animal and vegetable life is merely parasitic.[114]

Although Thoreau added a concluding chapter to *Walden,* this passage was truly the climax of his story. The same laws that govern the behavior of each and every creature (including humanity) on the earth, govern also the earth itself. All the universe is a single expression of the mind of God. In the ultimate spiritual sense, when Thoreau played his complex game of tag with the loon on Walden Pond in October of 1852, the loon, the man, and the pond were really all the same thing. This is the ultimate mystery spelled out in the *Bhagvat Geeta,* one of Thoreau's favorite companions at the pond. Loon and man perceived themselves as separate and different because they were under the magic spell of Maya, victims of their material senses. As Kreeshna explained to Arjoona in the *Geeta,* to pierce that spell, to understand that the world and everything in it is the god himself, is the proper spiritual goal of humankind. Echoing this lesson in *Walden,* Thoreau contended that if a person understood all the laws of nature, the faithful description of any one event would enable that person to infer all that would follow. That person would know the poetry, the song of the earth.[115]

Walden appeared in print in August 1854. Notices and reviews in the public press were generally more favorable than those for *A Week,* and sales, though sluggish, were enough to assure the book's sustainabilty. Since Thoreau's death, *Walden* has never been out of print. In his own time, critics focused primarily on the critique of societal economics—even that was difficult to swallow for an America bound to the idea of material progress. The writings on nature were most often treated as rustic and quaint; the few who understood the belief in the spirit of God in nature again strongly rejected the book's "pantheism." America was not prepared to find spirit in rocks and trees.[116]

Henry himself treated the publication with a quiet confidence. True, the book provided him the greatest measure of fame he would ever personally enjoy, but Henry by 1854 was too deeply immersed in discovering the answers to the questions posed in *Walden* to become overly elated by the work's mild success. He even regretted the Eastern lecture tour that would tear him away from the wilds of Concord in that November. In the fall of 1854, and for virtually all the months that followed over the next six years, Henry was busily at work—observing, recording, comparing, compiling—attempting to perceive the patterns in nature. Envisioning that project in his mind, *Walden* stood as little more than a progress report.

We are favored in having two rivers, flowing into one, whose banks afford different kinds of scenery, the streams being of different characters; one a dark, muddy, dead stream, full of animal and vegetable life, with broad meadows and black dwarf willows and weeds, the other *comparatively* pebbly and swift, with more abrupt banks and narrower meadows.

—*Journal,* July 5, 1852

The year is but a succession of days, and I see that I could assign some office to each day which, summed up, would be the history of the year. Everything is done in season, and there is no time to spare.

—*Journal,* August 24, 1852

5 THE RIVER

FOR ANYONE INTERESTED in the work of Henry Thoreau, perhaps the most daunting challenge lies in the massive content of the journals he kept between 1851 and 1861. While several biographers and analysts have delved into these journals, they have most often chosen to mine only a few of the more striking or unique natural history passages to illustrate Henry's interest in nature.[1] Yet, most of what Thoreau recorded was not spectacular, but rather a diary reflecting the elemental beat of ordinary natural occurence. For Henry, significance lay not in the sublime or sensational, but in the simple passing of everyday life. What was typical was perhaps most important of all. "Undigested" is the adjective authors most often use to characterize the intimidating preponderance of nature observation Thoreau recorded in the 1850s. To truly understand Henry, one must envision the vast scope, the excruciating detail, the very grind of his labors. The effort to record nature's actions on a daily basis was no small committment of time or energy. It was an all-consuming way of life.

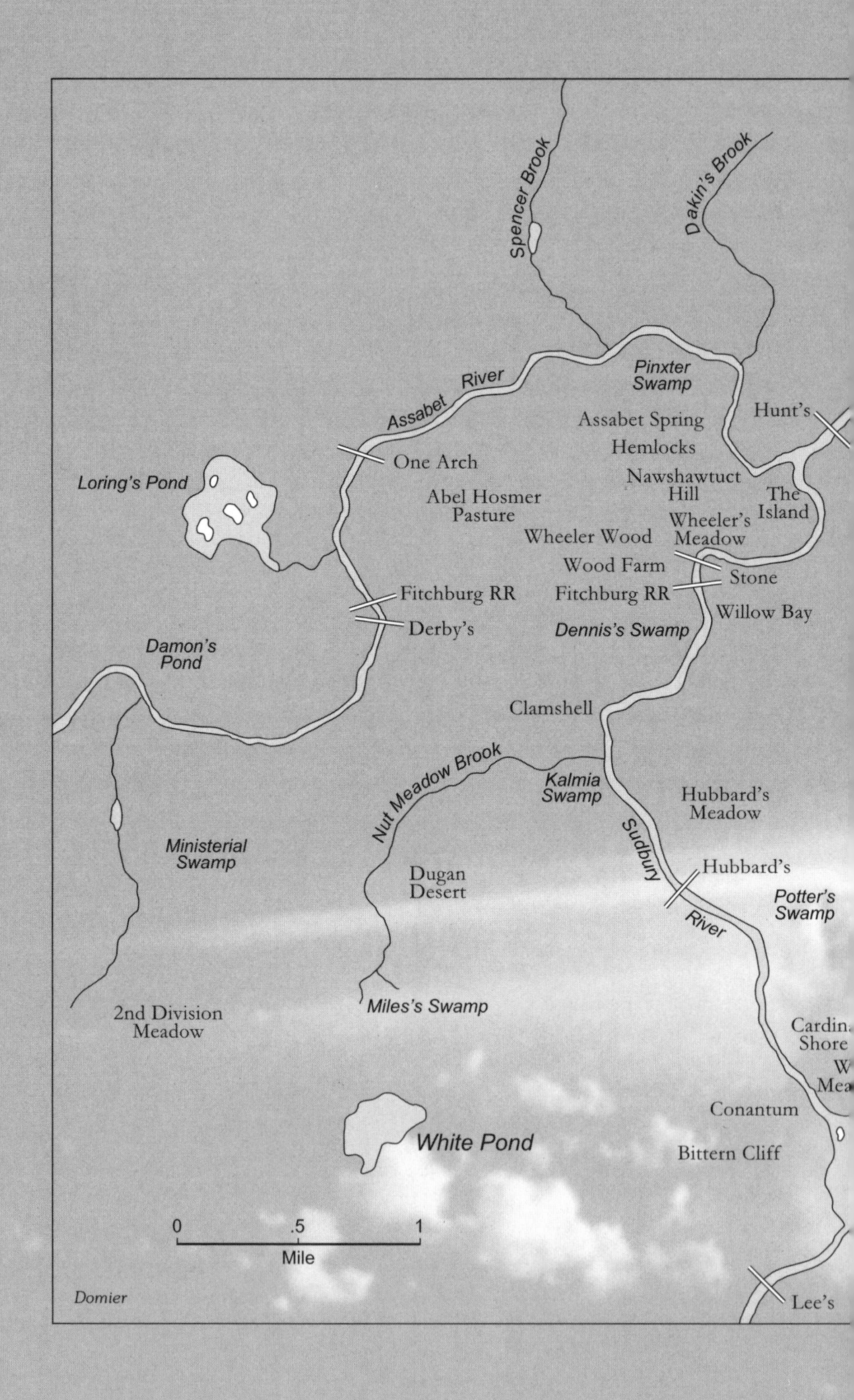
Spencer Brook
Dakin's Brook
Assabet River
Pinxter Swamp
Assabet Spring
Hemlocks
Hunt's
One Arch
Loring's Pond
Abel Hosmer Pasture
Nawshawtuct Hill
The Island
Wheeler Wood
Wheeler's Meadow
Wood Farm
Stone
Fitchburg RR
Fitchburg RR
Willow Bay
Derby's
Dennis's Swamp
Damon's Pond
Clamshell
Nut Meadow Brook
Kalmia Swamp
Hubbard's Meadow
Sudbury River
Hubbard's
Potter's Swamp
Ministerial Swamp
Dugan Desert
Miles's Swamp
2nd Division Meadow
Conantum
Bittern Cliff
White Pond
0
.5
1
Mile
Domier
Lee's

Tarbell's Meadow
Buttrick's Hill
Ball's Hill
GREAT MEADOWS
River
Moore's Swamp
Mill Dam
Mill Brook
Saw Mill Brook
Goose Pond
Walden Pond
Flint's Pond
Andromeda Ponds

Beginning in 1850, Henry carefully honed his skills as a naturalist and nature writer. He then employed these faculties on an almost daily basis over a ten-year period. Generally spending hours each day in the wilder parts of Concord—the rivers, the ponds, the woods—he recorded as much as he could of what nature was up to. Special inquiries into specific subjects, such as the reproductive habits of turtles or the growth patterns of various tree species, at times occupied him for weeks together. The record of this activity comes down to modern readers as an intimidating and often confusing welter of natural history information.[2]

Thoreau himself was neither intimidated nor confused. He not only wrote the entries, but he examined and reexamined each passage time and again, searching for the patterns that would help him to understand nature's ways. Within the journals, there is little to explain the structure or purpose in his research, but the structure was there. Henry carried the general methods of his research in his head, organizing his daily inquiries so as to increase his general knowledge of the systems in nature. He also retained an intimate and exact knowledge of the geography of Concord, to which he could refer while studying and adding to his journals.

As we have neither Henry's mind nor his geographical knowledge to guide us in reading his journals, we must fall back on more mundane means to discern the patterns in the research Henry undertook in Concord. By carefully scrutinizing each journal entry with an eye to specific time and place, it is possible to bring order out of the seeming chaos. Thoreau was interested in the natural behaviors associated with several different "ecosystems." He of course spent considerable time studying the ways of nature at Walden Pond and in the surrounding woods. The woodlots along the Old Marlboro Road were another favorite spot, as were Concord's higher grounds, Nawshawtuct and Ball's Hill. Finally there were the rivers and their associated meadows, a grand avenue of wild nature meandering through the middle of the town. By organizing Thoreau's journal entries according to which of these areas he visited and at what time of year, it becomes possible to derive some notion of the principles Thoreau applied to his investigations. Just what exactly was he trying to find out?[3]

The subject matter of this chapter is Thoreau's ongoing studies of the environment of the Concord River and its tributaries. By examining only those journal passages pertaining to this ecosystem and organizing them according to season and specific place, the purpose and content of Thoreau's visits to these places become more clear. Henry visited the rivers regularly every year at every season, recording the changes in botanical growth, the behavior of fauna including fish, turtles, mammals, and birds, and the actions of the streams as well. He perhaps studied the rivers more thoroughly than any other of Concord's wild places.

While he was often specifically interested in the life history of one specific species or another at a given moment, he was more generally interested to see how that history fit into the overall pattern of the system. How did the rivers affect the lives of the creatures living near and in them? And how did the behaviors of each creature influence the lives of other flora and fauna sharing the same ground? Thoreau wished to know it all.

Compiling the ten years of his specific record keeping, one can see how much he found out. What follows is a geographic orientation to the Concord River, followed by a compound descriptive analysis of a year in the life of the river during the 1850s, as derived from Henry Thoreau's journals. Literally speaking, this is not something Thoreau wrote, but something he experienced.

In the nineteenth century, the Concord River dominated the landscape, giving shape and boundary to the lives of creatures occupying the Town of Concord. By geographic convention, the Concord rose within the town limits, formed by the joining of the Assabet (North) and the Sudbury (South) Rivers at "The Island," a large rock (also known as Egg Rock) located a half-mile northwest of the village center. Both streams rose in the town of Westborough, some eighteen miles away. The entire watershed drained roughly four hundred square miles.

The Sudbury flowed primarily eastward on its journey to Concord, beginning 274 feet above sea level and falling 150 feet enroute. Much of the drop was in the first few miles. The South River scarcely flowed over the last ten miles before reaching The Island, the incline was so slight. The sluggish stream made for marshy flood plains over much of the distance.

Four miles before reaching Concord village, the Sudbury cut through the glacial kettle pond known as Fair Haven Bay. Fronted by the Conantum Cliffs to the west and Fair Haven Hill to the north, the bay occupied an area of seventy acres; a comparatively wild haunt favored in spring by swallows, bats, and gatherers of flowers. Now well within the Concord town boundaries, the Sudbury headed northwest from Fair Haven as far as Kalmia Swamp, bended to the northeast, north, and east, then described a long, graceful curve to the north around Nawshawtuct Hill to join the Assabet.

The Assabet, or North River, entered Concord at the corner of the southwest boundary. The Assabet flowed more swiftly, falling twenty-six feet in the last six miles before joining the South River. In the 1850s, the river entered the town through Damon's Pond, a small pool constructed for the use of the cloth mill. From Damon's, a crow would fly three miles to reach The Island, but the Assabet flowed four and one-half miles to get there. The river turned east, north, and east again before coming to Nawshawtuct, then looped south and southeast to meet the Sudbury.

The Concord River—Musketaquid to the Algonkians—continued the twisting habits of its sources, describing a series of short bends while tending northeast. The river plain was quite flat, dropping little for over its first ten miles. At Ball's Hill, Musketaquid turned northward to leave the town, journeying to join the Merrimac River at Lowell.

The lands adjoining Concord's three rivers were generally as smooth and featureless as the river beds. The valley topography was that of a large, shallow lake lacking water and filled instead with grass and flowers. Mile after mile, the rivers wound through very slightly undulating open meadows, broken occasionally by closed pools of water. Damp alluvials, marshy bottoms, and acidic peats comprised of the decayed remains of antecedent flora were the dominant soil habitats. Plant species sought to sustain and extend their numbers in a community that underwent changes in pattern yearly. The ebb and flow of the river provided the dynamic, granting one species or another a temporary advantage, soon taken away.[4]

The curving, bending character of the rivers was a product of fluvial actions, simple physical processes that greatly affected the river course and the landscape. Not all the water in the river traveled at the same speed. "On the longest side the river is active, not passive, wearing into the bank, and the river runs there more swiftly," Thoreau noted. This flow differential played a major role in the continual shaping of the Concord and its tributaries.[5]

Over the long centuries, the fluvial actions, modified by the geology of eastern Massachusetts, the activity of beavers, and other factors, shaped the Assabet, Sudbury, and Concord Valleys to their nineteenth-century appearance. And still the process went on, year by year, surely but subtly changing the pattern of the river.

The dynamics of stream hydrology were not fully understood by anyone in Thoreau's time. In his studies of the rivers, Henry did exhibit a basic comprehension of the forces at work in creating the streambeds: "There is a peculiarly long, sluggish, wide, deep, and lake-like reach, muddy in the broadest parts (for Concord), from Fair Haven Pond to Nut Meadow Brook. Though in meadows, it is pretty straight. Not enough current to make a meander."[6]

Human actions affected the behavior of the rivers. Downstream at Billerica, near the mouth of the Concord, millers had dammed the Concord as early as 1708. The Middlesex Canal Company assumed the rights to the dam in 1794, selling them to the Talbot Brothers, grist millers, fifty-seven years later. The dam constricted the flow of water through the entire drainage, slowing the flow of the river and raising the water level. Concord was one of five towns that petitioned to the state legislature for redress in 1859, claiming that the Talbots had raised the dam and permanently flooded portions of the meadows. The town hired Thoreau to compile data demonstrating the effects of the dam, and he spent much of that summer closely surveying depths, meanders, currents, and so forth. The town lost the suit.[7]

Local dams also contributed to the changing patterns of the river. Above Damon's millpond, Knight's Manufacturing Company constructed a new dam in 1851, raising the river level for three miles upstream. Dead trees stood in the water along both sides of the river, delineating the former shores. Five years later, the Warner Pail factory dammed the river south of the one-arch bridge, flooding neighboring fields.[8]

The fluvial process was also much affected by the construction of several bridges across the rivers. Within the Town of Concord, the Assabet was spanned four times (once by the Fitchburg Railroad), the Sudbury three (once by the railway), and the Concord three times. Most bridges were combined wood and stone construction. Each bridge support standing in the stream was an impediment altering the river flow; each bridge effectively narrowed the streambed beneath its span. The stone turnpike bridge across the Assabet narrowed the stream to one-fourth its normal width. Henry noted in 1859 that the resulting increase in the speed of the current had washed away a quarter acre of land during the 1850s. Often, the effects of human construction were most obvious in the vegetation pattern changes near a bridge.[9]

Henry visited Concord's rivers at every season of the year, in every kind of weather. Generally he went on foot, although he was a skilled oarsman and often journeyed on all three streams in his boat. In winter he skated, and occasionally in summer he swam. And in spring, when he wished to draw close to skittish and wary flocks of migratory ducks, he crawled on his belly. Although he most loved the unoccupied, wilder stretches of the rivers, he thoroughly explored every mile of Concord's streams, and knew them intimately.[10]

WINTER ICE

Strange to say, a narrative of life on Concord's rivers based on Thoreau's journal entries must begin in the winter season. Henry discovered that the key to understanding the vegetation patterns of the meadows lay in understanding the work of the river during the season of ice.

In most winters, the rivers froze at some point during the first weeks of December. In 1850, the river skimmed over in the early morning hours of December 13, in 1853 the surface froze on the fifth. Each year was a little different. In the winter of 1852–53, and again in 1857–58, ice closed the river only for brief periods. But this was unusual. In 1852, the river remained solidly frozen as late as March 4, enabling Henry to "take that walk along the river highway and the meadow-which leads me under-the boughs of the maples & the swamp white oaks &c which in summer over hang the water-there I can now stand at my ease and study their phenomena-amid the sweet gale & button bushes projecting above the snow and ice." The winter of 1854–55 was so cold that the river froze completely, allowing Thoreau and others miles and miles of uninterrupted ice-skating.[11]

The ice grew thick in the long, quiet stretches of the rivers, extending across the meadows, into the swamps, even up hillsides. On tempestuous days, high winds blew waters from open spots over the banks and several feet inland, where it froze a foot thick over bushes and tree trunks. At times, the ice ensnared trees. Weighed down by snow and ice, the lower branches of young bankside alders and maples dipped into the rising waters of a thaw freshet. When the river froze once more, the branches were caught. Slowly but surely, the weight of the ice bent the trunk to the ground, often killing the tree.[12]

Even in the coldest winters, a few shallow places along the river were usually open. In 1859, Henry counted eleven open places on the Concord and Sudbury Rivers within the town limits. The largest, on the Sudbury just above The Island, was just over thirteen hundred square yards; most were much smaller. Many of these open expanses were associated with the fluvial activity of the river. Located at the river bends, often where sand bars formed, they remained open because the circulating current continually brought new water to the shallows, inhibiting freezing. Other openings in the ice cover remained where waters from warm springs entered the river.[13]

Muskrats took advantage of these openings, locating their winter lodges at points where the river did not freeze. Some were as large as haycocks, six feet high and fifteen or more feet in diameter. These lodges became small winter islands, homes for burrowing insects and spiders, havens for hibernating turtles and rooting plants, roosts for migrating ducks, shelter for the muskrats, targets for preying foxes, raccoons, and minks. Usually each lodge housed a single muskrat, although several might share a large one—until breeding time. By then, piles of pale clam shells lined the riverbanks.[14]

The muskrats kept their homes in good repair through March, painstakingly raising or even rebuilding the lodges when flood or other disaster struck. Winter was not a stable time for the river inhabitants. A bitter winter was often punctuated by a "January thaw" (which did not always come in January). Overnight, meltwaters poured through the channels and up over the meadows, only to freeze again as the cold descended anew. A sudden flood drove the muskrats out in January 1855.[15]

Inconsistent weather played havoc with insect life. Springlike conditions coaxed honey bees, grasshoppers, crickets, caterpillars, beetles, and ants out of their shelters, only to die when wintry conditions prevailed. A thousand small ants died on the ice of Tarbell's Meadow in early March 1859. Spiders too fell prey to the unseasonable warmth of a thaw. If the cold did not immediately descend, rising melt waters would drown or carry them away.[16]

The freezing, unfreezing, and renewed freezing of the river waters created swirling combinations and contrasting blocks of white, blue, gray, and black ice.[17] The freezing also re-created the meadows each year, a process Thoreau discovered in February of 1851. Walking along the edge of the river on February 12, he saw that every half mile or so the pressure of the ice sheets had broken out thin ice cakes that stood on their edges. Thirteen days later he investigated these ice cakes again, and realized that "a remarkable quantity of the meadow's crust" adhered to the cakes. Large portions of the meadow—enough to resemble small islands in the river—had actually floated free, to be swept downstream. Further studies the following day revealed that the ice was lifting away meadow crust as much as a foot thick.[18]

Thoreau was intrigued. Recognizing this process to be a key element in the continually shifting character of the meadow vegetation, he carefully observed the combined behaviors of river, meadow crust, and ice over several years. Henry also sought illumination from books, consulting Robert Hunt's *The Poetry of Science* to discover the manner in which water conducts heat.[19] Finally, on March 1, 1855, he was able to record in his journal that

> I think the meadow is lifted in this wise: First, you have a considerable freshet in midwinter, succeeded by severe cold before the water has run off much. Then, as the water goes down, the ice for a certain width on each side the river meadows rests on the ground, which freezes to it. Then comes another freshet, which rises a little higher than the former. This gently lifts up the river ice, and that meadow ice on each side of it still has water under it, without breaking them, but overflows the ice which is frozen to the bottom. Then, after some days of thaw and wind, the latter ice is broken up and rises in cakes, larger or smaller with or without the meadow crust beneath it, and is floated off before the wind and current till it grounds somewhere, or melts and so sinks, frequently three cakes one upon another, on some swell in the meadow or the edge of the upland. The ice is thus with us a wonderful agent in changing the aspect of the surface of the river-valley.[20]

The action of the ice thus created in a single process two essential components of the meadow community. The hole left where the earth was torn away became a pool, a small pond in the meadow, a home perhaps for turtles and pouts. The meadow crust deposited downstream shaped a small hillock, a hummock providing new spaces for several species of vegetation. A few meadow plants knew no home other than these hummocks.

The process was annual, and widespread. In the last week of February 1855, Thoreau recorded that the whole of Concord meadows was filled with great chunks of ice, many of twenty-five square feet or more. At Derby's Bridge, the blocks piled four feet deep, most blocks a foot thick and carrying six inches to a foot of sod beneath. In the Great Meadows northeast of the village, one block measured seventy-four by twenty-seven feet. Several pieces of the meadow came to rest in Abel Hosmer's pasture, most covering areas of over one hundred square feet. The ice deposited button bushes, rushes, and even cranberry vines among the hummocks.[21]

The boundaries between the meadows and the rivers—the edges where the button bushes grew—were especially vulnerable. One such hummock in 1854 was eighteen feet long and ten feet wide at its broadest point. Bushes five feet high accompanied the hummocks to points further down the river, together with silkweeds and grasses. Every five yards or so, a portion of the meadow was torn away. Sometimes they came to rest in peculiar places. At the Wheeler Meadow in 1859, one hummock finished in five feet of water offshore. The bushes died.[22]

A farmer named Wood told Thoreau that the ice took two acres of soil from the crust of his meadow in 1851 alone. Eight years later, high flooding rearranged the meadows even more than usual. Six hummocks totaling half an acre of soil halted at Sherman's Bridge. The ice lifted more than two hundred yards of meadow edge from the east side of the Sudbury downstream from the Bittern Cliff. Huge hummocks came to rest near Potter Swamp Meadow, the Cardinal Shore, and the Fitchburg Railway bridge. All contained button bushes, willow shrubs, rose bushes, and water lily roots.[23]

At times, the process was lethal. One year in the 1840s, the ice unroofed the burrows of forty snapping turtles hibernating in the mud. Torpid and exposed to the bitter winter air, they froze to death.[24]

Thoreau calculated that rearrangement of the meadows took place at a much greater pace prior to white settlement of the valleys. The dams and bridges along the length of the rivers slowed the current, limiting the ability of the water to carry the great blocks of ice. Even in the nineteenth century, the recession of the winter flooding revealed a landscape considerably changed. Thick hillocks of soil checkered the meadows, while large patches of bare earth betrayed depressions that became pools after the spring freshets arrived.[25]

SUGGESTIONS OF SPRING

In mid-March, signs of spring began to appear, sporadic, but unmistakable. Henry found skunk cabbage flowering under protected banks on south-facing portions of the meadows. The catkins of pussy willows, bog willows, and aspens, borne since autumn, began to expand. Pale yellow blossoms of golden saxifrage and marsh marigold appeared in sheltered meadow pockets by month's end. Tufts of greenery shot up where springs trickled onto the earth's surface. Snows gradually disappeared, aided by rainstorms—occasionally fierce and accompanied by high winds. A March storm in 1860 blew down pines on the hillsides, shook houses in the village, and toppled chimneys. As snows melted, the world took on a wonderful variety of brown hues, punctuated with the promise of renewed life. Elm buds swelled, willow catkins put out. Earthworms drew close to the surface of the meadows, actually appeared in the water at the bottom of shallow brooks and ditches, where spring came "earliest." Newts, also visible at the bottoms of brooks even in the most bitter weather, became more active. Salamanders ("lizards") began to appear. By the end of March, new varieties of birds appeared, returning from the south, while winter visitors departed. Painted turtles began to sun themselves on rocks and half-submerged logs astride the rivers and pools.[26]

In his efforts to comprehend the cycle of nature, the turn of the season to spring obviously occupied a place of central importance in Thoreau's studies. In March 1853, he asked himself: "What is the earliest sign of spring? The motion of the worms and insects? The flow of sap in trees and the swelling of buds? Do not the insects awake with the flow of sap? Bluebirds, etc., probably do not come until the insects come out. Or are the earlier signs in the water?—tortoises, frogs, etc."[27]

On the meadows at least, one of the earliest signs of spring turned out to be the visitation of the crows. Often these were different birds from the crows of winter. New flocks returning from the south displaced the winter contingent. The summer residents arrived early in March, migrating in groups of twenty or thirty, and remained in flocks until nesting began in mid-May. As soon as the ice departed any portion of a meadow, the crows came in search of food, rain or shine. They were not particular. The fare included carrion, worms, insects, berries, and anything edible the river happened to wash up.[28]

Often it was tempestuous weather that brought migratory ducks temporarily to the Concord meadows. Mergansers ("Sheldrakes") came through sometime between late February and late April, depending on the weather conditions. They sought shelter in a variety of haunts—the Great

Meadows, Fair Haven, the Assabet, or the larger kettle ponds—facing always upstream. Secure from unwanted visitors, they were playful and noisy. A flock resting near the Bittern Cliffs at the end of March 1858 included three distinct groups of activities: the first feeding, the second preening and playing, the third resting quietly; perhaps twenty in all. There were seldom many in a flock, never more than twenty, perhaps because the townspeople shot them, thinking them a threat to gamefish. Mergansers were efficient fishers, equipped with serrated bills especially useful for catching fish.[29]

All the ducks (and Canada Geese as well) returning to ride the Concord freshets were skittish and nervous, secretive. The least intimation of human presence set them flying; odd noises spooked them. From the Gulf of Mexico northward, ducks flew a gauntlet of shotguns twice a year, spring and autumn. No place was a sanctuary, no time a respite. They could only hide. Tall meadow grasses offered shelter, as did secluded ponds and lonely stretches of the rivers. Nowhere in Concord was completely safe; the ducks had always to be on guard. Thoreau at times managed to get close enough to observe their habits—an exceedingly rare sight for nineteenth-century New Englanders—but he did so by making a cautious and painstaking way through uninhabited woods and then crossing the wet meadows on hands and knees, the meadow grasses disguising his approach.[30]

Two varieties of ducks returned to Concord in March to take up summer residence. They would remain until November. Wood ducks occupied several places throughout the town, including marshy areas along all three rivers. They built downy nests as much as fifty feet above ground in the cavities of trees, the nesting beginning late in June. Within a month, the young were fully grown—at least those that survived. Snapping turtles preyed heavily on the little ones, who left the nest soon after hatching.

Black ducks too resided all about the town, nesting on the ground in the vicinity of Fair Haven, Clamshell, several meadows, Flint's Pond, and the Andromeda Ponds. Their spring arrival coincided with the appearance of the aquatic grasses beneath the water surface of the meadows. Usually the black ducks came in flocks of nine to eleven birds, remaining together for a brief span before dispersing to breed.[31]

Fast-flying migratory green-winged teal passed through in March, as did goldeneye ducks driven inland from the Atlantic Coast by heavy storms. Blue-winged teal flew past Concord a month later, resting briefly in marshes and shallow pools. Herring gulls visited briefly in March and April, feeding on newly hatched shellfish, fresh fish, and berries. Other aquatic avians were even more rare. Buffle-head ducks rested briefly on the river one April morning, pushed inland by the weather; and a single "cinnereous [American] coot" flew over Willow Bay on the Sudbury River in April 1856. A farmer shot the bird and turned the carcass over to Thoreau.[32]

As the river ice began to break in March, hunters appeared along the banks and even in boats, searching for muskrats. Furriers valued the skins at fifty cents apiece, and Concord River skins were highly regarded for their size. Musketaquid muskrats were fat. Hunting began in mid-February and continued over two months, usually in the early morning and the evening. Generally the hunters were poorer, landless residents of Concord, men without fixed occupation who sought money from a number of such peripheral pursuits. Ne'er-do-wells in the eyes of Concord's middle class, Thoreau came to know some of them—Goodwin, Melvin, Heavy Haynes—quite well.

The muffled sound of guns echoed up and down the river every two or three minutes, as many as a dozen hunters working at one time. Forty muskrats died on the Sudbury between Hunt's and Flint's Bridges by March 5, 1860. Thoreau heard a rumor that an entire cartload were shot along the Assabet in 1859. A characteristic hunter watched the button bush thickets along the river shore, waiting for a muskrat to peer out. He shot about six in a typical morning, stripping and bagging the pelts, leaving the carcasses to rot along the shore. By April, the skinned bodies lay all through the meadow bottoms. Crows found them good eating.[33]

Spring came in fits and starts. The river channel might open as early as the end of February, or it might remain closed in places until late March. In 1853, snow and ice six inches thick remained on the edge of the meadows on March 29. Spring flooding was equally unpredictable. In 1851, the freshets had inundated the meadows by mid-February; two years later the flood took place in the first week of April. Even in a single season, the waters could wax, wane, and wax again. In 1855, floodwaters took out a bridge on both the Sudbury and the Assabet; the muskrats had to evacuate their lodges as well. The waters subsided only to rise again in April, higher than any point since winter.[34]

The greatest flood of the period took place in 1852. The spring freshet took place in mid-February that year, covering the meadows with yellow water. The last of the snow melted early in March; three weeks later yellow lily leaves began to appear along quiet stretches of the river. Then came April, and two violent snowstorms. The first, on the sixth, dropped six to eight inches of drifting snow on Concord. The second, a week later, brought another six inches. The weather turned warm, and Thoreau began tracking the lethal combination of heavy storms and sudden warmth in his journals. By the sixteenth, the water was high and continuing to rise. A wind and rain storm on the nineteenth turned the meadows into a tumultuous sea, whitecaps dashing against the meadow banks. By the twenty-first, the water had washed over six of the eight roads leading out of Concord, and people had water in the basements of their houses, even on high ground. On the twenty-second, villagers who rarely took note of conditions on the meadows talked excitedly of the "great rise of waters." The waters did not conspicuously recede until May. The meadow grass grew very well that year.[35]

WARMER WEATHER

April usually brought at least the promise of warmer weather. The rivers generally fell back into their normal channels, bounded by masses of button bush hummock a foot and a half thick. As the sun rose higher in the spring sky, plants responded to the increasing light. In the river shallows, common naiads appeared. Greenish sweetflag blossoms opened in marshy grounds along the shores, and meadow saxifrage bloomed on the higher banks. Not many varieties of flowers emerged that early, however. The greatest activity was among the river shrubs. In the shallow water, sweetgales bloomed. In marshy thickets, winterberries, black currants, leatherleafs, slender willows, and common elders came to life. On the banks, the buds of a variety of willows, alders, and maples began to expand.[36]

Thoreau often visited the black willows and white maples that grew along the river and nowhere else in Concord. The black willows—large shrubs or small disheveled trees—hugged the river, demarcating the extent of fluvial processes that ceaselessly changed the river's track. Wherever river eddies deposited sediment to create a sand bar, black willows were among the first plants to take root. Before the mid-1840s, black willows had not grown along the river about the Sudbury River meadows. Henry traced their history in his journals. In 1844, engineers had constructed a causeway and bridge to carry the Fitchburg Railway over the river. The causeway narrowed the river channel, generating a new system of swirls and eddies, leading to the development of new sand bars. Within a few years, wind-blown seeds had grown into a thick hedge of willows lining the causeway and the bars. Willows still grew nowhere else in the area. As the warmer, longer lasting rays of the April sun warmed them, the young trees budded and flowered. Their leaves appeared in early May.[37]

As spring freshets ebbed, spider webs began to appear, woven among new plants and the previous year's stubble. Thoreau made little study of spiders, but did note the placement, size, geometry, and locations of webs at various times of the year. From these notes it is plain that in the meadows he distinguished the webs of two different varieties of spiders. Those of the early spring were of the genus *Agalena,* common in the short grasses found on the meadows in late March and early April.[38]

With the fall of the waters, nocturnal fires appeared here and there on the riverbanks. Built and kindled by fishermen, the fires attracted fish swimming in the shallows. Pickerel, white suckers, and pouts became clearly visible in the firelight, easy targets for wooden spears thrust into the water. Spearing fish was an activity of the early spring and the late autumn, possible only when the plankton life lay close to the shore. Spearers appeared in season no matter the weather—even with snow still on the ground.[39]

By the end of April the shallows warmed and plankton moved toward midstream, bringing the potential for spearing to a close. The unpredictable, often stormy days of early spring gave way to the calmer times of late April and May, the river resumed its normal channels, and people gave up spearing for line fishing. Early May saw the height of the pickerel fishing as the adults spawned in the shallows. Rainy days were best; gentle, straight-down rains that brought the fish to the surface. The fish refused the shiners and chivin deployed as bait on the clear, sunny days. Men and boys were the fishers in that era—village dwellers and farmers alike. For poorer families, fish from the rivers were essential food, the difference between proper nourishment and want. Although the arable lands of Concord were all privately owned in the 1850s, the river was, as Henry Thoreau observed, "an extensive 'common' still left."[40]

Settled weather brought other fishers back to the river. The streams slowed, and the water cleared of sediment. By mid-April, belted kingfishers flew low across the water, seeking fish or crustaceans while establishing territories. Kingfishers preferred areas of shallow, flowing water, where fish were visible from the air. Pairs maintained a regular domain, warning off competitors with a toneless rattling cry. The kingfishers incubated their eggs in early June, tunneling deep into sand or gravel banks to construct a nesting chamber. Across the Concord from the Great Meadows, Buttrick's sandbank sheltered a kingfisher nest. With the birth of five young or more in July, the parents had to catch over seventy fish each day for weeks.[41]

A few early songbirds returned to the meadows with the kingfishers. Rusty Blackbirds passed through in March, bound for Canada. Horned larks came and went a bit later. A very rare incident occurred in April 1860, when a few red crossbills visited a hemlock grove on the Assabet, eating the conifer seeds strewn on the ground. Thoreau suspected that "the abundance of white pine cones last fall had to do with their coming here." A month later, another rare visitor, a single swamp sparrow, sang its trill along the riverbank. Solitary by nature, swamp sparrows occasionally visited the marshy patches of the meadows, never for very long.[42]

Other birds came to the meadows to stay. Large flocks of common grackles (Thoreau called them "crow blackbirds") arrived in early March, feeding omnivorously on virtually all the meadow could offer. The birds unflocked and nested by May, building low in the bushes along the riverbank, or high in trees over the water. The young left the nests and took flight in the latter half of June. Redwinged blackbirds also came in March, flocks of thousands that remained together until May. Mainly seedeaters, the redwings kept close to the riverside, eventually establishing nests in the button bushes along the banks. Hundreds of nests lined the river in June, small cups of grass containing three to five pale blue eggs.[43]

The raucous clucks and screeches of the grackles, coupled with the more musical scree of the redwings, dominated the meadows in March's daylight hours. At month's end, a new and different note punctuated the singing. The lofty whistle of meadow larks ("see-you; see-yeeer") began as the first stragglers appeared with warming weather. The polygamous birds nested in small grass domes concealed in the meadow grass. The young flew at the end of July, and the song of the meadow lark abruptly ceased.

Each spring, the floods left a perceptible water line across the meadows, threaded across hillocks and depressions, comprised of the debris dropped as the river lost energy and retreated toward summer boundaries.

As the season turned, these lines marked the separation of plant and insect communities growing in the meadows. Pontederia stems, black and green, comprised much of the debris, interspersed with cranberries, yellow lily roots and other vegetation, and occasionally, larger casualties of the freshet. In April 1854, Thoreau spied a large rooster floating downstream, headless, apparently the victim of an owl. In 1855 the flooding claimed a gray rabbit.[44] By early May, tiny splashes of color began to spot the debris line left by the retreating waters. The reddish-violet blossoms of coast blue violets sprang up where the highest tides of the freshet had watered the sand or peaty soil. In the forests beyond, the larger deciduous trees began to turn green, growing leaves "about as big as a mouse's ear." As May wore on, many different kinds of blooms emerged, as the meadows began to display the varying characters of their complicated topography. Although the shores and meadows of the Concord rivers were all a part of the drainage community, all affected by the rivers' behavior, there were a number of different habitats; characterized by varying soils, height, moisture content, and proximity to the river. Over seventy such minor habitats coexisted along the rivers, their locations often changing because of the ice and fluvial behavior Thoreau had recognized and described. More than three hundred plants grew on these meadows, banks, shallows, and shores; all adapted to life in one or a few such habitats and able to live only under those peculiar conditions. By the mid-1850s, Henry was able to identify each and every one of them on sight.

In the latter part of May, eight such plants began or renewed life in proximity to the river—each in its own particular habitat. By noting the particular habitat preferences of each, Thoreau was able to use their presence to identify and distinguish among the various plant communities along the river. The white flowers of the rock cress appeared on stony ground near the Assabet, while white grove sandworts flowered in peaty swales such as existed near Lee's Hill. On sandy, burned-over soils near Hubbard's, wild pinks bloomed. Marsh ferns opened in swampy places. Spinulose wood ferns grew spores in shady places along the riverbanks. Four basswood trees—the only ones Thoreau could find in Concord—also blossomed along the banks, growing only out of rich soils. In the river margin beneath the banks, creeping spikerush emerged, a sedge that would line much of the river's edge through the warmer months. And in muddy, shallow waters, white water crowfoots flourished. Eight plants, each suited to peculiar conditions, each unlikely or unable to grow in the domains of the others. Recognizing their particular habits, Thoreau could see that the Concord drainage was a quilted plant community, consisting of numberless patches of ground small and large, each with its own grasses and flowers. This particular knowledge of aquatic plantlife was a special kind of expertise few could match.[45]

Beginning in the month of May and continuing into early June, the meadows took on the greenish hues of summer. The button bushes marking the shores of the river began to leaf out at the end of May. Thoreau allowed that the button bush "is not a handsome bush at this season, it is slow to put out its leaves and hide its naked and unsightly stems."[46]

The "true grasses," rushes, and sedges that dominated the vegetation also emerged at this time—spikerush, wooly sedge, button sedge, hop sedge, inflated sedge, woolgrass, red top, sheep's fescue grass, canary grass, fowl meadow grass, and especially pipes. By the end of June, the meadows were a vast sea of green. Many species of flowers bloomed in the damper portions of the meadows, mostly white initially—winter cress, meadow rue, wild strawberries. Soon the houstonia came, creeping mats of deep green vegetation dotted with tiny blue or white flowers—bluets. Marsh violets also emerged, along with the yellow blossoms of creeping buttercups. As spring wore on and gave way to summer, plants appeared on the drier, firmer portions of the meadows; ferns, cottongrasses, clover, and the parasitic lesser broomrape. As Thoreau learned, this was a plant world shaped by many forces—wind, water, birds, fur-bearing mammals, Native Americans, white people—all under the dominant influence of the river.[47]

As the freshet receded in the spring, shallow, muddy pools began to dot the meadows. Flood waters had filled the depressions left where ice had torn the meadow crust away. At times tenuous rivulets connected these pond-holes to the river, but often they stood apart; tiny, self-contained aquatic worlds.[48] The duration of their existence depended on the size and depth of the depression and the heat of the summer sun. The smaller pools disappeared, sometimes as soon as early summer. The larger endured, perhaps until the following spring, when the ice and meltwater rearranged the meadow surface once more. As long as they lasted, they teemed with life. Tiny crustacea occupied the pools in tremendous numbers; fish preyed on these creatures. Breams and pouts often entered these pools when floods were high, only to find themselves confined as the waters withdrew. Pickerel followed also to prey on the crustacea and the other fish. By mid-April, each little pool swarmed with aquatic life that attracted amphibians, mammals, and birds.

In the river, freshwater mussels—clams, to Henry Thoreau—began to move in toward the shores as the weather warmed. The timing of this migration varied considerably from year to year; in 1860 Henry found the clams lying up "abundantly" at the beginning of May, but in 1854 significant movement did not take place before mid-June. The mussels moved by alternately expanding and contracting a foot, leaving a furrow in the river bottom as they slowly hauled themselves upward. Thoreau found them "chiefly at shallow and slightly muddy places where there is a gradually shelving shore." He found a great many of them. In July 1852, he calculated that a mere twenty rods of such shoreline contained more than sixteen thousand clams. He did not feel they would go extinct any time soon.[49]

As warmer weather came on, marsh birds began to appear, recently migrated from southern climes. Three birds came early in April; snipes, woodcocks, and spotted sandpipers (peetweets, as Thoreau called them). These three species shared much in common: habitat, diet, preferred nesting sites. Yet, the habits of each prevented direct competition with the others. Each possessed a discrete niche in the Concord environment.

Snipes, migrating by night, were the first of the shore birds to arrive, usually as soon as the meadows were bare of ice. Disliking the direct sunlight, snipes were most active in the evening and on cloudy days. Their harsh and varied cries echoed across the meadows all along the river, as did the booming sound of their wings as they dove into the meadows from high above. The activity was clearly audible in the village, as Thoreau noted in his journal.

> April 2 [1859]
>
> As I go down the street just after sunset, I hear many snipe tonight. This sound is heard annually by the villagers, but always at this hour, i.e., in the twilight,—a hovering sound high in the air,—and they do not know what to refer it to.[50]

By May, the noise and the display ceased. Nesting had begun. The nest was little more than a grass-lined depression in the ground, holding a clutch of four brown eggs, black spotted. In so vulnerable a location, silence and concealment were the means of survival. Most often, the snipes nested in the grassy tussocks deposited throughout the meadows by the ice.[51]

Woodcocks were also setting by the beginning of May, but preferred the bushes and thickets at the water's edge for nesting sites. The nest was a small hollow among the dead leaves, holding four brown-spotted buff eggs. The woodcock, mottled brown in color, blended well with its surroundings, relying on this camouflage for protection. Thoreau often heard their call, a loud "beep," but seldom spied one.[52]

Like the snipe, the spotted sandpiper hid its nest, also a slight ground depression lined with grass, among the meadow hummocks. But not at the same time. Arriving in April, the sandpiper sought out (like the others) insects, worms, spiders, and crustaceans in the meadow mud, but waited until July to brood.[53]

As floodwaters abated and pools took shape, other creatures of the river renewed the cycle of their lives. The first frogs began to stir in mid-March, awakening from winter hibernation in the mud of ditches and depressions along the meadows. Each spring, Henry undertook an exacting study of the habits of the several varieties of frogs occupying the river valley, seeking to distinguish each species by its song, habitat, and reproductive habits. The problem was challenging. The rivers and nearby swamps were home to at least six different species of true frogs, plus assorted tree frogs and toads. Although each had its distinctive song, the life cycles of several species overlapped in Concord, making exact call identification very difficult. "My dream frog turns out to be a toad," he sighed to his journal one year in May. Thoreau listened carefully each spring over several years, eventually tracing each song to its source.[54]

The wood frogs, the most truly amphibious variety, appeared first, as early as mid-February, mating and spawning in the small woodland ponds and swamps. Even before the ice completely melted, egg masses had attached to underwater vegetation—as many as 20,000 in a single spawn. Pickerel frogs began to croak in the meadows soon after, depositing their spawn in partially frozen meadow pools. Tadpoles developed by mid-March; at month's end the pollywogs were full grown, still with long tails.

By April, the meadows were alive with the song of frogs, the high-pitched whistle of the spring peepers blending with the rich twang of the green frog, while the snore of the leopard frogs joined in at a lower scale. "One dreamy sound," as Thoreau put it. The song depended on the weather. Rain had little effect, but if the temperature turned cold, the singers remained submerged in the pools, burrowed in the bottom mud and grass. On warmer nights, hundreds collected along the shores. The chorus of the tiny green frogs was brief, two weeks in early April, in which they bred among the debris of fallen trees close to shallow water in the meadows. The leopard frogs prevailed a bit longer, their low snoring pervading the length of the rivers. The great breeding took place early in April, the spawn hatching a month later. At the end of May in 1857, Thoreau found in Moore's Swamp that "the myriads of pollywogs, now three quarters of an inch long, crowding close to the edge, make a continuous black edging to the pool a foot wide."[55]

Unlike the other four, the spring peepers (or hylas) were not true frogs, but tree frogs. They hibernated beneath logs and loose bark, venturing out late in March. The males climbed into the shrubs and trees overlooking the water, emitting their high-pitched ascending whistles to attract a mate. For a month the sound and activity filled the meadows, ending with the spawn lying amid the grasses in ten inches of water, collected in four-inch parcels containing one hundred deposits or more.[56]

As the frogs began to appear in the meadows, so too did the hawks. Marsh hawks preyed on frogs especially. Migrating northward with the change of season, frog hawks appeared in Concord as soon as the ground was bare. Each hawk maintained its own territory, warning off intruders with sharp whistles and cries. As spring gave way to summer, the marsh hawks would nest in mounds of dead reeds and grass among the springy meadow vegetation. By mid-August, the young were flying. Red-tailed hawks reappeared at much the same time as the marsh hawks, hunting small rodents in the meadows before turning to the deciduous woods and swamps of Concord for food and shelter.[57]

Two additional birds of prey passed through the town in April, seeking summer roosts further north. Bald eagles flew over the Cliffs and hunted in Wheeler Meadow in the springs of 1854 and 1858, taking fish, rodents, and small birds. They also passed through on the return trip in late September. Ospreys followed a similar pattern, appearing sporadically in April and May, capturing suckers and pouts all along the river. Crows often called attention to the great fish hawks as they perched on the limbs of riverbank trees. On the first day of May 1858, Henry watched as two crows harassed an osprey near the Assabet, each cawing loudly, although neither came closer than a hundred yards.[58]

The fish hawks arrived to hunt in Concord as the fish breeding season began. Several species of fish moved into secluded shallows to spawn, making them easy prey. Pouts, white suckers, and pickerel began breeding toward the end of April; bream and chivin followed in May. The pickerel, which fed primarily on pickerel frogs and other fish, spawned in the gravel bottom of clear portions of the river or in the kettle ponds. Following the spawn, the hatching young were completely ignored by the adults. By the end of June, the young, grown to four or five inches, began preying on the young of other fish.[59]

Horned pouts assumed greater responsibility for their offspring—a fact that afforded Thoreau great contentment. Seeking to protect the spawn from pickerel, turtles, and other predators, the pouts built nests—shallow depressions sheltered by vegetation or submerged debris. The adults entered through a narrow, straight entrance about twenty inches long. Breeding took place at the end of April, and the young, light colored and mostly head, hatched early in June. The parents remained on guard until the young grew to an inch long and swam freely. Bathing in secluded sections of the river, Henry at times encountered pouts' nests. Standing perfectly still, he watched for long periods as the adult pouts constantly maneuvered to maintain a protective position between the young and any potential danger. So attentive were the adults that Henry was occasionally able to reach into the water with his hand and lift one to the surface for closer examination.[60]

Bream too built nests, digging a large, saucer-shaped depression after carefully cleaning the soft bottom of quiet, weedy waters. In mid-June, each female laid several thousand eggs, which incubated up to ten days while one or more females stood sentinel over the nest. The adult females remained with the young after hatching, attempting to ward off predators. But bream were small, rarely longer than eight inches, and comparatively powerless. The greatest insurance of species survival was sheer numbers. Despite inevitable losses, the population remained stable.[61]

White suckers and chivin bred in the small brooks tributary to the Concord watershed, entering the brooks as they became free of ice. The suckers ran upstream by night early in April, laying their adhesive eggs in the stream shallows. "They are dispersing themselves through the fields and woods," Henry noted, "imparting new life into them." Adults returned to the river with the young in June. The chivin, turned rosy-colored in the spawning season, ascended the creeks in May.[62]

In the eighteenth century and before, a still greater variety of fish lived in Concord waters. Sea-run Atlantic salmon and saltwater alewives hatched in freshwater streams, then migrated to the sea, returning years later to spawn. Dams raised downstream at Billerica and the subsequent construction of the Middlesex Canal obstructed access to the Concord River. The salmon and alewives no longer returned.

The loss of the oceangoing fish had disgusted Thoreau enough in the 1840s that he voiced strenuous objections in *A Week on the Concord and Merrimack Rivers.*[63] As late as 1857 the fact still irritated. On April 11 he confided to his journal: "The very fishes in countless schools are driven out of a river by the *improvements* of the civilized man, as the pigeons and other fowls out of the air. I can hardly imagine a greater change than this produced by the influences of man in nature. Our Concord River is a dead stream in more senses than we had supposed. In what sense now does the spring ever come to the river, when the sun is not reflected from the scales of a single salmon, shad, or alewife?"[64]

Other oceangoing species were more tenacious. Lampreys returning from the sea ascended falls and dams by gripping stones with their large circular jaws. The dam in the end prevented the return of many, but even in the 1850s a few lampreys lived in the Concord River. The adults, after spending a year or two as blood-sucking ocean parasites, migrated back to fresh water in spring to build nests in the shallows. After clearing an area perhaps four feet in diameter, the lampreys surrounded it with stones carried in their jaws. The walls grew one to two feet high. Within, the mother buried the spawn in the silt or sand, then died. The young, blind at birth, hatched two weeks later. They remained buried in the mud from four to six years, burrowing downward in cold weather, consuming microorganisms in the streambed. They grew to six inches long, then emerged to migrate to the sea as a parasitic adult.[65]

Nor did the dams stop the American eel from living in Concord's rivers. The eels migrated to fresh water from the sea when they grew to six inches. Only the females came upstream, migrating by night to take up residence in the Concord and its tributaries, where they lived for the next six to eight years. When the eels reached a length of five feet, they returned to salt water.[66]

During the long stay in Concord, eels had more problems stemming from human activity than anything else. The Algonkians had built weirs to catch eels; Concord's white residents did the same. Even more problematic were mills and mill dams. In 1855, Warren Miles built a sawmill near the headwaters of Nut Meadow Brook. Like most water-powered mills, it ran chiefly in the spring, when melting snow filled the millpond. Visiting the mill in April 1856, Thoreau found that the turning mill wheel crushed eels attempting to climb the dam. In the first week of May, Miles was removing eels from the wheel each night at the rate of three per hour. Nor were eels the only victims. The mill also killed several brook trout, and caught many more in the hollow beneath the wheel. Similar problems existed at the three other water mills located in Concord. For fish, the danger persisted until water in the milldam ran low enough to halt work, usually in mid-spring.[67]

On the floor of the river, other forms of life shrugged off the inactivity imposed by winter cold. The eggs of caddis flies, dragonflies, stoneflies, and mayflies floated or lay submerged beneath the winter ice, awaiting the spring warming of the stream. In mid-March the larvae began to emerge.

Caddis worms appeared first—welcome food for pouts and other fish hungry after the winter dearth. Upon hatching from eggs laid in gelatinous masses on aquatic vegetation, the nymphs spun silken tubes to serve as shelters. Many species elaborated on these simple weavings, imbedding leaves, sticks, stones, or grains of sand to create an elaborate caddis case, shaped as cylinders, cones, pyramids, or even simulated snail shells. By early summer caddis worms pupated in the cases (still moving). Emerging as adults, they remained in the water a short time before leaving the river for a short life in the air.[68]

The dragonflies, stoneflies, and mayflies also lived an aquatic life in the egg and nymph stages, living on the muddy bottom of the rivers and streams. As pickerel, chivin, bream, pouts, and suckers prepared to breed, the presence of these insects assured survival.

NEW VOICES

In late spring, twilight sounds of the river took on a fresh character. The snipe fell silent, and the mixed chorus of peeping hylas and snoring leopard frogs fell off as their breeding season passed. Standing on Lee's Bridge, on the first of June 1852, Thoreau could hear "the midsummer frog, . . . the nighthawk, crickets, the peetweet, . . . the hum of dor-bugs, and the whip-poor-will." A new amphibian chorus now awoke, comprised of thousands of ringing American toads, soon joined by trumping bullfrogs and trilling gray treefrogs. Each night as the weather warmed, the din increased, became more insistent. The toads gathered wherever insects and moisture were available, favoring the ponds and pools dotting the river meadows. The dreamy ringing of hundreds of grayish males filled the night air as they called to mates, larger, reddish-brown females. Warren's Meadow on the Sudbury was the sight of a vast frolic of toads in early May 1857. The solitary males sang, while couples prepared to mate, swimming and leaping through the pool. The ringing went on until mid-August, though most eggs were laid in strings on the aquatic vegetation long before. There were tadpoles free of spawn by mid-May; by the end of July survivors were a half inch long.[69]

In trees and shrubs overlooking the rivers, gray tree frogs took up their song soon after the toads, almost as the hylas ceased. They continued through the summer, coming down from the trees only to breed and spawn.[70] In the rivers and kettle ponds, bullfrogs began at much the same time. Thoreau noted the changing chorus early in his investigation of river life. On June 13, 1851, he wrote

> The bullfrog belongs to summer. The different frogs mark the seasons pretty well,—the peeping hyla, the dreaming frog [toad], and the bullfrog. . . .
>
> The tree-toad's too, is a summer sound.[71]

Sensitive to temperature, the bullfrogs emerged from hibernation in late April, but seldom began their deep, croaking trump before the middle of May. As the weather grew hot, their trumping grew loud, until by summer it dominated the nocturnal atmosphere of the river. Unlike the toads and other frogs, the bullfrogs did not crowd together in mating. Preferring larger territories, a relatively small population stretched along the length of the rivers and pond shores, the males emitting a distinctive "jug o' rum" call in a deep bass. Bullfrog tadpoles grew very large, and took two years to complete the transformation to adult frog. They ate fish, crustaceans, young snakes, small birds, other frogs—essentially, anything they could get into their mouths. In July of 1856, Thoreau watched a young bullfrog swallow whole a pickerel frog, head first.[72]

Snakes also consumed large numbers of young frogs. Two species occupied the Concord meadows in significant numbers, the northern water snake ("water adder" to Henry), and the common garter ("striped snake"). People were their great enemies. "I have the same objection to killing a snake that I have to the killing of any other animal," Thoreau wrote, "yet the most humane man I know never omits to kill one."[73]

Striped snakes emerged from hibernation late in March, preferring wet meadows or marshy territories, where they mated in April. The mother gave birth to live young three months later. Striped snakes swam well. In April 1857, Henry encountered a large one in the Assabet, swimming easily with its head a foot out of the water. Like bullfrogs, striped snakes swallowed anything they could catch—birds, mice, fish, worms, toads, frogs. Occasionally, this led to trouble. In the late summer of 1858, Henry saw a young garter forced to disgorge a toad taken into its mouth. Too big.[74]

Water snakes too consumed a widely varied diet, including frogs, salamanders, fish, small mammals, and baby turtles—all swallowed whole. They mated in April, gave birth in August to thirty or forty live young, each six inches to a foot long. Water adders could range widely in the search for food. In May 1857, a water snake climbed into an apple tree to seize one of the young from a robin's nest. More typically, they basked on rocks and logs near meadow pools, feeding day or night from the abundance of frogs, toads, and tadpoles living in the water.[75]

The late spring cacophony of toads, treefrogs, and bullfrogs was augmented by the highly unusual call of the newly arrived American bittern. The "stakedriver" was a secretive bird. Hiding in marshes, solitary pairs hunted frogs, insects, crustaceans, fish, and even mice. In time, they constructed a platform of reeds to serve as a nest. Their call betrayed their presence: the male sounded like a pump operating—oong-KA-chunk!—discernible for a half mile. The cry was clearly audible in Concord village. People walking the streets in the spring twilight stopped to listen; almost no one knew the source of the peculiar sound. On those rare occasions when people did see a bittern flying up river, they did not associate the bird with the mysterious pumping noise. They did take the sight as a sure sign of rain.[76]

Several species of song birds returned to Concord in mid-May. Along the river, a new and joyous songster joined the avian chorus. The bubbling phrases of the bobolink soon dominated all other voices as the birds prepared to nest in the dry fields close by the banks. Within three weeks the young would fly; the profound music would cease.[77]

The full, warmer days of April and May also saw swallows return to Concord. Tree swallows and occasionally cliff swallows hurriedly passed over flooded meadows and village streets in their northward migrations. Bank swallows and barn swallows came to stay for the summer. Thousands of barn swallows flew over six hundred miles to arrive just as flying insects began to emerge on the meadows. Skimming over the rivers in great wheeling flights, constantly twittering, the barn swallows spent the daylight hours of two months feeding on insect swarms before taking to farm buildings to breed.

The bank swallows came early in May, and immediately set about digging tunnels in the sandbanks at Clamshell, Dakin's, Dennis's, the Deep Cut, and other places frequented by Thoreau. Bank swallows nested in colonies, building their nests—a grass cup—at the end of a tunnel two or three feet deep in the hillside. At Dakin's, fifty-nine holes occupied a space of thirty square feet. Pairs of bank swallows circled over the meadows and rivers in the vicinity, mingling with barn, tree, and cliff swallows to form a great, mixed, twittering flock. Young bank swallows flew early in July.[78]

Accompanying the swallows, often flying the same circuits, were nighthawks, larger birds characterized by their loud, buzzy cries and spectacular flight. In breeding season, males often rushed into long and powerful dives, pulling up suddenly to create a shrieking "boom" with their wings. Unlike the swallows, nighthawks remained in the air until very nearly dark, eating prodigious amounts of mosquitoes and flying ants. The birds nested early in June, the eggs taking roughly two weeks to hatch. Henry once found a nighthawk's eggs on a hillside shelf. He counted himself lucky; the two eggs lay on the bare ground, almost perfectly disguised by their color.[79]

At twilight, as the swallows took to roost for the night, their places in the river sky were taken by groups of little brown myotis—brown bats. As the swallows hunted the flying insects by day, the bats sought them after dark. The myotis emerged from hibernation in April, migrating some little distance to the Concord to establish nursery colonies among the cliffs and buildings near Fair Haven. The bats had mated in the fall; the females gave birth in late April, nursing one or two young constantly for the first three days of life. The nurseries lasted roughly three months, disbanding early in August in anticipation of the September migration.[80]

Both swallows and bats were subjects of human superstition, though of vastly different nature. People associated bats with the powers of evil and death, shunning them. They knew little of the brown myotis' habits, assuming them to be blind, dangerous, bloodthirsty, and prone to attack humans, especially their hair. In contrast, people held swallows in enormous awe, believing it to be bad luck to kill or injure a swallow in any fashion. Yet each occupied essentially the same ecological niche, feeding on the preponderance of insects flying over the rivers day and night.[81]

By late May and early June, insect life exploded in the Concord meadows. Hundreds of species metamorphosed and emerged as the river calmed and the weather warmed. Among the meadow plants, countless species of flies began to buzz. Perhaps handicapped by a comparative lack of useful information on insect identification, Thoreau did not devote much time or journal space to the study of these insects. Most insect notes made in the journal were mere mentions in passing, and such identifications as he made were tentative and at times confusing. In general, only the obvious—butterflies and dragonflies—or the spectacular drew his sustained attention.

He did note the appearance of the fuzzy gnats that swarmed before his face each spring, eventually identifying them as *Tipulidae* in 1859. Several notes refer to the "small black-winged flies or millers" that occasionally swarmed close over the surface of the river in late spring.[82]

Thoreau also faithfully recorded the rise of the fireflies each year. Generally their display began in early June, when he spied a few flashes as he made his way homeward along the river at dusk. Their numbers grew rapidly, and the tiny flashes continued until mid-August, when they dwindled and gradually disappeared.[83]

In a few instances, insect emergence was indeed a spectacular event. In the evening of June 2, 1854, the air over the Assabet suddenly came alive with great swarms of mayflies. Mayflies underwent a second molt after emerging from the stream, shedding their exoskeleton to assume a final adult form in which they did not eat. But they were eaten. Schools of chivin leaped madly from the water to dine on the swirling insects flying upstream: "the river was all alive with leaping fish, their heads seen continually darted above the water, and they were large fish, too. Looking up I found that the whole atmosphere over the river was full of shad flies. It was a *great flight of ephemera.* It was not so when I landed an hour and a half before. They extended as high as I could see. It was like a dense snow-storm, and all (with very few exceptions) flying as with one consent up the stream."[84]

The fish surfaced almost continually in a mad scene that lasted until dark. Two years later, the phenomenon repeated itself on the eighth of the month. Probably it occurred each year in the early days of June.[85]

Other flying insects were less sensational in their advent, but equally important to the life of the river. Dragonflies and damselflies climbed onto the stream banks in the early mornings of late May to complete their metamorphosis, attempting to escape swallows and other predatory birds. People believed incredible stories about dragonflies—they sucked blood, they sewed up ears and mouths with their long, needlelike abdomens. Actually, they ignored people. Dragonflies—blue darners, green darners, large black-bodied dragonflies—patrolled regular beats, eating vast amounts of smaller insects. The greatest enemy to the vast numbers of insects inhabiting the meadows were other insects, predators that ate many times their weight each day. Water bugs, water striders, whirligig beetles, diving beetles, and several others fed largely on other insects. Together with the birds, the bats, the spiders, the fish, the frogs, and the turtles, they held at bay the hordes of flying insects that would otherwise have overwhelmed Concord.[86]

THE APEX OF THE YEAR

By early June, lily pads filled the shallow portions of the river, a floating green mat much eaten by aquatic insects before the lilies ever came to bloom. Insects even deposited their eggs on the reddish undersides of the various pads. Fragrant water lilies grew in the quiet places along the river; yellow bullhead lilies rooted in the river shallows and also in the meadow pools. In July 1854, Thoreau rose early in the morning to time the opening and closing of the lily flowers. He discovered that opening began with the first appearance of the sun, and that the last of the blossoms was completely shut once again by 1:30 in the afternoon. Throughout the hot summer months, new blossoms opened with the dawn each morning, closed down by midday. Later in the summer, small yellow pond lilies (a separate species) bloomed in the shallows.[87]

The water lilies were just a few of the more than one hundred plants that emerged or blossomed between early June and mid-July. This was the peak of the plant season, when the greatest array of river species appeared, bloomed, and went to seed. The congregation of crowded plantlife highlighted the necessary reproductive strategies of much of the river community. Of the more than three hundred plants that comprised the community, four-fifths were perennials, growing from the same roots, stem, or rhizome year after year. In an area as dynamic as the Concord river basin, a perennial strategy offered the advantage of stability and a head start. Even in the midst of constant (though often subtle) change, a plant renewing itself from already anchored roots could overwhelm possible contenders. Thoreau's records indicate that in the lush season of June and July over one hundred of the newly emergent plants were perennial or biennial; only nineteen were annuals.

New plants popped up everywhere. On the stream margins, pickerelweed, pondweeds, blue flags, bladderworts, and mild water pepper together formed a green border to the river. On the shores, various white and yellow flowers blossomed briefly and went to seed. The larger bur-marigold dominated briefly toward the end of June. A few weeks later, the swamp rose became the prevailing flower. Small numbers of unusually colorful flowers appeared here and there; blue marsh bellflowers along the shores, orange Canada lilies along Dodge Brook. In the meadows, more than two dozen species of sedges and grasses reached their prime. The Great Meadows became a vast "sea of pipes," two and a half feet high.[88]

Much of the life in the meadows was something of a mystery to all the human residents of Concord. Not that the river held no attraction for people. By late spring, many found the Concord and its tributaries a restful and bucolic sight. The water lilies especially evoked visions of romance that affected even Henry. In 1852 he described how "the young men, having bathed, will walk soberly to church in their best clothes, each with a lily in his hand or bosom,—with as long a stem as he could get. And the young women carry their finest roses on the other hand. Roses and lilies. The floral days."[89]

A deep and many-shaded green now displaced the browns of spring, and in the stillness, the river reflected the perfect blue of cloudless days. Wispy bluish mists hung over newly growing sedges in the early morning; blue flag added splashes of color to the meadow grasses. Young rabbits were about, and skunks and woodchucks. In the evening larks sang, bees buzzed softly from flower to flower, and the song of the frogs began. Nighthawks boomed and swallows twittered overhead, gathering last insect meals before giving over to the bats. This, and one sound more, as Thoreau noted in early June of 1857. "One thing that chiefly distinguishes this season from three weeks ago is that fine serene undertone or earth-song as we go by the sunny banks and hillsides, the creak of crickets."[90]

The people of Concord used the river for recreation most extensively at this season; fishing, bathing, boating. The first two preoccupations were apparently exclusively male, but boating was more universal. All manner of boats floated the river, rowboats of various kinds, and small sailboats. The locally designed and constructed "dead-river boats" predominated.[91]

Men and women sought the river to escape the summer heat that began in earnest by the end of June. Solitary individuals, courting couples (sometimes two or three couples to a boat), whole families all savored the refreshing coolness of the river air. (Henry was in the company of his sister and mother when he observed the great "shad fly" migration.) In the Concord society of the 1850s, people dressed from head to toe even on the hottest days, though a young man might remove a jacket for strenuous rowing. At times, though not often, young people sang as they returned downriver from a row, their voices filling the late evening air, for the moment drowning out even the bullfrogs.[92]

Where there were boats, there were boat houses, and these structures jutted into the river at several points, especially near the village. Built on piles, small, square, often unfinished and a little delapitated, the boat houses spoke best of the human belief that they owned the river. "Man's boathouse is a deformity," Henry opined, "but the muskrat's cabins are an ornament to the river. The squareness of the former building, roof and all, offend. Could not the architect take a hint from the pyramidal or conical form of the muskrat's house?"[93]

A few actual houses began to appear along the river as well. In the early 1850s, villagers built a number of houses close to the river near The Island. But then, people had lived along the river and used it for one purpose or another for a very long time. As the freshets receded in the spring each year, the broken crusts of small hillocks in the meadow revealed the flakes and projectile points left by Algonkians centuries before.[94]

Not all the human uses of the river were as benign to the rest of nature as boating or living there, or even fishing, hunting, and trapping. Using bits and pieces of the world to manufacture tools and articles suited to contemporary and often very temporary tastes, human residents returned the waste by-products to the earth in corrupted form. People dumped wastes into the rivers. Barrett's sawmill operation, located on Spencer

Brook, threw their sawdust into the millstream. The Miles sawmill on Nut Meadow Brook did the same. The brooks carried the sawdust downstream to the Assabet, where Henry found that the more sluggish current deposited the debris in huge beds in the shallows. As the organic dust decayed, hydrogen gas, smelling like gunpowder, rose to the surface. If something stirred the sawdust layers, great bubbles of gas roiled the water.[95]

Near the southwest corner of Concord, the Damon Manufacturing Company constructed its textile mill on the Assabet in 1835. The mill made white wool flannels, using teasle, a plant imported from Europe, in the cloth fulling process. The company dumped the used teasle, barbs blunted and spent, directly into the river. As the waterline of the Assabet rose and fell with the seasons, the lines of teasle deposited on the shore marked the stages of the decline.[96]

Villagers generally used the meadows as refuse sites as well. In the meadow near Saw Mill Brook, a pool became a dumping ground for unwanted tins, although frogs used it yet in springtime. Several such pools existed throughout the Concord drainage, repositories for rejected ceramics, iron, slag, and other assorted trash.[97]

Still, the meadow ice created many new pools each year. Most remained free of human abuse, isolated and remote among the tall grasses. By summer, several of the smaller muddy scars left by the ice had emptied of water. Thoreau made a special effort to visit these places. "I am interested to see how Nature proceeds to heal the wounds where the turf was stripped off this meadow," he explained in 1855. He discovered that as the sun dried the exposed earth, irregular cracks appeared, roughly a foot in diameter. A new vegetation cover formed: initially a dense mosslike algae, interspersed with sedges and grasses growing from the cracks. Small growths of pineweed and low cudweed appeared here and there. By the following year, these scars had largely disappeared, reclaimed by the plant life of the meadow.[98] In his journal Thoreau noted that "Only in a very few cases can I discover where the surface has been taken up, since the water stands over and conceals the scar till it is healed, and for similar reasons it is hard to tell what is a fresh deposit and what is old growth. I should say that the largest masses, or islands, of button bushes standing in the meadows had drifted there."[99]

The hummocks left overlaying the meadows as the spring ice flows rearranged the crust assumed new covers by summer as well. In October

1855, Henry counted one every two or three rods in the lower part of the meadows. Repeated floods and weathering flattened them in a year or two. For the brief time intervening, these hummocks served as little islands in the meadow, dampish refuges where unusual plants took root. Yellow loosestrife (swamp candles) grew two feet tall on these hillocks, amid dense beds of crimson meadow beauties. Reed-meadow grass and bottle brush grass flourished, while wild mint added an aromatic scent. In the following spring, older hummocks sustained a variety of ferns, violets, swamp milkweeds, and other flowers. In a month and a half's time between late May and mid-July, an old meadow hummock supported the succession of no fewer than fifteen plant species.

Many larger pools, shallow platters seventy feet across or more, became the centers of new plant communities as well. Aquatic plants—pickerelweed and mermaid weed, ludwigia, pipes—anchored in the muddy bottom. Yellow bullhead water lilies blossomed thickly on the water's surface. On the wet shores of the pool, flowers habituated to wet soils flourished, including knotweeds, hedge hyssop, tooth cup, false pimpernel, and dwarf St. Johnswort. Cattails more than six feet tall lined the shores, marking the boundary between shallow water and marshy ground.[100]

By summer, fish and frog spawn hatched in the pools, and thousands of tiny pollywogs, pouts, and breams swam among the plant growth. Many of their parents remained as well. But trouble loomed occasionally, more trouble than that imposed by the usual relationships of predators and prey. As river waters receded in the summer heat, channels communicating with the main stream disappeared. The aquatic life resident in the pool became a closed and trapped community. Summer wore on, the sun beat down—temperatures averaged 72.35 degrees in July—and the water slowly evaporated. Vegetation leafed out, bloomed, and withered; the remains sank into the pool. Generations of tiny insects, crustaceans, and microorganic life flourished and died. The life cycle of the algae waxed. And the water level continued to fall.

By August, larger forms of life trapped in the rapidly disappearing smaller pools faced critical difficulties. Young pouts and bream an inch long swam in ever-decreasing circles, competing for diminished foods while the water grew uncomfortably warm. Pollywogs suffered also as the summer wore on. If the rains failed, many pools dried up completely, leaving thousands of fish and pollywogs stranded to die in the soft mud.[101]

Larger marsh birds found ideal hunting conditions in these evaporating pools. Thousands of prey swimming in shallow, confined platters attracted the great bitterns nesting in the meadows since May. Two species of herons also took advantage. Green herons arrived in June, raising young among the thickets in the muddy hollows close to the river. The fledglings left the nest in early August; old and young taking fish, crustaceans, and insects from the secluded and dying pools. Great blue herons came also in August, especially in dry years when shallow pools were common. The great herons did not breed in Concord, but passed through during spring migration. They returned for the good hunting of late summer, large blue forms bending over the shallows on long legs, seeking fish and frogs, or perhaps reptiles, mammals, or even small birds straying within reach. "You have not seen our weedy river," Thoreau advised, "you do not know the significance of its weedy bars, until you have seen the blue heron wading and pluming itself on it. I see that it was made for these shallows, and they for it."[102]

The turtles at least possessed the mobility to escape these death traps. Turtles lived easily on the abundant prey through much of the summer, and simply walked away when the water became too shallow and warm. Six varieties of turtles lived in Concord, five in the rivers and meadowlands. Henry found them an especially fascinating study. Each year from 1851 onward he recorded his meetings with turtles, and in 1856 devoted much of the summer to intensive study of their habits. Occasionally he brought one home for close examination in his room or in the garden.

Eastern box turtles were most rare. A favorite food of the Algonkian Indian bands, box turtles had been hunted almost to extinction. But they could live long—as much as a century—eating earthworms, slugs, mushrooms, and wild strawberries, never leaving a territory an acre in circumference. In May of 1856, Thoreau found one in a dry pasture fifteen rods from the Sudbury River—the first he had ever seen in Concord.[103]

Snap turtles were far more common. These largest of Concord's turtles spent much of their lives in the water, consuming fish, small animals, invertebrates, plants, birds, and occasional carrion. Males fought ferociously on the shores of the rivers at mating time, the clash of their shells echoing across the meadows. In June, females emerged from the water to lay already fertilized eggs in the uplands. Snapping turtles dug their nest cavities in sand banks, often walking distances of a half mile across meadows and fields to lay six dozen eggs or more. Thoreau investigated one such nest dug into the sand hills near the house of Jenny Dugan: Finding forty-three dirty white, soft-shelled eggs, he observed that "If it were not for the skunks and probably other animals, we should be overrun with them." Left buried and abandoned in the sand, these eggs incubated and hatched at the end of summer.[104]

Stinkpot turtles were perhaps even more aquatic than the snappers, mating underwater and emerging no farther than the neighboring riverbank to lay eggs under a tree stump. Females deposited between one and nine eggs in a shallow nest; the young emerged in about twelve weeks. Aggressive by nature, stinkpots secreted an evil-smelling yellow fluid that they employed to discourage enemies. On rare occasions they climbed into the willow trees along the riverbanks to bask. Uncertainty in climbing bred troubles. Now and then Thoreau found one that had slipped among the branches, caught its neck in a fork, and hanged itself.[105]

Spotted turtles and painted turtles were more adept baskers. They climbed from the river to sit in the sun at the first hint of spring, spending hours out of the water each day. Dozens shared each fallen tree trunk above the river, dropping gently into the water when a boat approached. In summer, turtles lying out flattened the grasses over large areas about meadow pools.[106]

The basking turtles also laid their eggs in the dry earth, although usually in level fields away from the meadows. Painted turtles seeking to lay eggs urinated heavily to soften the earth for digging. Excavating a hole two inches deep took five minutes. The turtle then inserted her posterior into the cavity to lay up to two dozen eggs, never moving her front legs, nor her shell. Thoreau patiently sat and watched a painted turtle depositing eggs in the sand in June 1856. She suffered openly as ants ran over her eyes, making her snap her head against her shell. After laying five eggs, the turtle began to bury them immediately, never even looking at the nest. The entire process consumed forty-five minutes.[107]

All the species of turtles lived potentially long lives, but a host of dangers and irritations plagued them, holding down their numbers. Females especially braved many perils in the effort to deposit their eggs. Each year in June, dead turtles floated on the rivers, legs and necks extended. More lay dead in the fields, bodies slowly devoured by insects. In June 1858, Henry openly wondered what killed them. Two years later he encountered the remains of a painted turtle rested on its back at Tall's Island, entrails extracted through an opening ahead of the back legs, probably by a bittern. Spine intact, the fore parts of the turtle still lived, though the hind legs were dead. Later in the same year, crows attacked a young snapping turtle in Hubbard's Meadow, pulling off its head and consuming the innards.[108]

Turtle eggs were often victims of predators. Skunks dug into many nests soon after laying, devouring this favorite article of diet on the spot. Crows too sought turtle eggs, as did some of Concord's human residents, who came with shovels. People also hunted the adults, especially snappers and stinkpot turtles. In late June 1859, Thoreau heard how a woman cooked a female snap turtle captured in the meadow, eggs and all. People considered the meat and the eggs a tasty delicacy.[109]

Turtles surviving the vicissitudes of predators had to contend with a host of annoyances. Slow-moving stinkpot turtles were a favorite target of leeches, bloodsucking aquatic worms that attached themselves to the body through the shell's tail or rear leg openings. A leech could live a year and a half from the blood of a single meal. Snap turtles also suffered the attacks of small leeches, and all the meadow turtles hosted growths of moss and algae among their scales. In the late summer and autumn, these scales curled up and fell off, to be replaced by a new, and for the moment, cleaner growth.[110]

As the elders shed their scales at summer's end, the young hatched and emerged from their subterranean nests. On reaching the surface, the baby turtles headed immediately for their parents' haunts in the rivers. They came from sandbanks in the Dugan desert, half a mile from the Sudbury Meadows. They came from tiny patches of soil in rye fields, their view of the river completely obscured by nearby vegetation. Often they walked both downhill and uphill to reach the water's edge. Predators took a heavy toll on this march, but those that made it to the river entered a food-rich aquatic world agreeable to their quiet turtle habits. Turtles were plentiful in Concord.[111]

The meadows grew very still in the unremitting heat of a Concord August. Few new plants appeared at that season; summer plants had largely blossomed and gone to seed; autumn flowers did not yet begin. By the end of July, nine-tenths of the flowers Thoreau found and noted in his journals had already bloomed. Near Fair Haven and along the damp shores of the Assabet, cardinal flowers made a brief crimson splash in late August.

In shoreline thickets elsewhere, the pink blossoms of Joe Pye weed flourished among the flowering button bushes. Fall dandelions became abundant in drier parts of the meadows. In the river, narrow-leaved bur-reeds produced an oil that filled the shallows with a bluish scum. Noonday air grew hazy as summer began to fade, casting the vegetation in bluish tints as well. Meadow odors waxed. The sun, beating on shallow pools filled with decaying fauna and vegetation, brewed a heady tea. In early mornings, dense low-lying fogs shrouded the dampish meadows as often as not. The mist disappeared shortly after the dawn, burned away by the rising sun. Seemingly, the sole respite from this "dog day" weather was the occasional burst of summer rains, and perhaps an accompanying summer flood.[112]

In some years, there was little rain at all. Droughts occurred in 1851 and 1854, each devastating to the plant life along the river. Grasses browned prematurely; shrubs on the banks and hummocks shriveled. Young willows on the cliffs overlooking Fair Haven withered and died. In the river, long-submerged rocks appeared as the water level sank precipitously.

More typically, thundershowers and occasional cloudbursts offered temporary respite from the heat. Floods could occur in any month after the spring freshet had receded. In 1850 and again in 1853, floods at the end of May inundated roads and drowned young water lilies. A flood in mid-June of 1858 destroyed the nests of thousands of birds—shorebirds and such meadow-dwelling songbirds as redwing blackbirds, bobolinks, and meadowlarks.[113]

A most spectacular flood occurred toward the end of August 1856. Several rain and thunder storms had punctuated the summer months, and on the twentieth of August, rain began once again. Already high, the river now overflowed its summer shores, invading the meadows and sending birds, mammals, and insects rushing for safety. While for the birds and mammals this meant flight away from the meadows, for insects the only safe direction was up. Water stood inches deep among the normally dry meadow grasses by August 25. Atop the vast majority of these grasses, nonflying insects had taken refuge. Springtails, beetles, grasshoppers, crickets, caterpillars—the flightless insects clung to life among the grassblades, revealing for the moment the size and extreme variation in their population. Insectivorous birds driven from their homes by the water at least had little trouble finding food for a few days. On the twenty-sixth, young swallows skimmed over the grasses, preying on the stranded grasshoppers.[114]

These summer floods greatly affected the composition of the living community of the Concord meadows. The seeds and rhizomes of trees and shrubs, scattered over the meadows in autumn and winter, lay buried in soil during the spring freshets, unaffected by the floodwaters. As the river receded, these plants took root and sprouted, threatening to displace the grasses and herbaceous plants that dominated the meadow community. As Thoreau noted, "the value of these occasional freshets in August: they steam and kill the shrubs and trees which had crept into the river meadows, and so keep them open perpetually, which, perchance, the spring floods alone might not do."[115] Periodic summer flooding dictated that Concord's meadows remain the province of the grasses.

Those grasses reached the apex of their growth late in July, just as river levels usually reached their nadir. Hard blanketing fogs began to envelop the river at night during this season, dispersing with the rise of the sun. In the trees overhead, green "alder locusts" commenced their long, dry, piercing shrills; a song that would drone on until the first frosts.[116]

RIVER HARVEST

Late July saw the beginning of the "peculiar season" of the meadow harvest, when Concord's farmers came to cut and haul away the long, rich grasses, continuing in the footsteps of the first settlers, drawn to the valley by the bounty of the meadows back in 1635. Generally, meadow-haying began sometime in the last ten days of July, soon after the farmers completed upland haying. The timing could prove quite variable however, depending on the weather and the condition of the river. Farmers told Thoreau that the condition of the grass depended on the amount of rain in June. In 1852, when too much rain fell in that month, there was virtually no crop at all. In 1853 and again in 1856, heavy rains in August severely affected the harvest. The dog days of 1856 were especially bleak. Thoreau watched farmhands "wading in overflowed meadows and pitching the black and mouldy swaths about in vain that they may dry." The wet persisted through mid-August, and in September the river flooded yet again. Most gave up completely, concluding that "the little they got since the last flood before this was good for nothing, would only poison the cattle, being covered with the dried slime and filth of the freshet."[117]

Henry took great interest in the meadow haying, noting the progress of the hayers each year, commenting on the process. In early August of 1854, he specifically undertook to describe the work of the harvest, studying the matter with the curiosity, thoroughness, and care he usually devoted to nature study. Crossing the meadows in early August, he found between sixty and one hundred men hard at work. Although property owners often worked side by side, each farmer had his team, and each carefully delineated his own meadow holdings, using twigs and leaves to mark boundaries. The harvesters worked in teams of mowers and rakers. Three or four mowers worked their way diagonally across the meadow, maintaining a straight line by aiming at a tall stake affixed with bits of newspaper set up at the far end. Occasionally they halted to sharpen their scythes. The rakers followed, gathering the fallen grass into piles, which were turned to the sun by the boys accompanying them.

After dinner, the grass was raked into long rows and loaded onto wagons standing on firm, shady ground at the edge of the meadow. One man stood in the wagon treading down the load, while the others forked up more grass or continued to rake. Henry noted that a great many other plants easily mixed with the grass in this harvest, including ferns, osiers, polygonums, and sweetgale. The main portions of the meadows were cut fairly completely. At day's end, horses or oxen hauled these great loads back to the farmers' barns, leaving the roads strewn with newly cut meadow grass.[118]

Cutting the river meadows in the heat and humidity of a Massachusetts August was brutal work, and here, far removed from the eyes of the professional classes and women generally, Victorian standards relaxed a bit. Thoreau "saw haymakers at work dressed simply in a straw hat, boots, shirt, and pantaloons, the shirt worn like a frock over their pants." Sometimes they wore no shirt at all.[119]

In Thoreau's time, many of the hands assisting in the meadow harvest were newly emigrated Irish. Sometimes this led to adventure. Water snakes abounded in the meadows, some as much as four feet long. "Irishmen," Henry recorded, "introduced into these meadows for the first time, on seeing a snake . . . lay down their scythes and run as if it were the evil one himself, and cannot be induced to return to their work."[120]

Henry recognized that the meadow harvest was hard on wildlife. In addition to the snakes, which were invariably killed, the mowers turned up the eggs of Virginia rails and great bitterns. "The bittern hardly knows where to lay its egg," Thoreau observed sadly.[121]

Typically, Henry expanded his study of the meadow harvest, speaking to farmers who harvested small fields of grass well removed from the Great Meadows, delving into the history of this toil. One farmer recalled that in the early part of the century, meadow owners from the neighboring town of Sudbury joined with those of Concord to clear weeds from the river shallows and encourage a better harvest. Another told him that formerly, once the meadow harvest was done, farmers did nothing but fish for three weeks, thinking they had nothing to do. In the 1850s, these modern and progressive farmers weeded their orchards.[122]

In 1856, George Minott provided Thoreau an unusual window on the past, explaining why there were more alders and birches in the meadows than formerly: "in olden times, when they were accustomed to taking something strong to drink, they didn't stand for such shrubs but mowed all clear as they went, but now, not feeling so much energy for want of a stimulant, when they came to a bush, though no bigger than a pipe-stem, they mowed all round it and left it standing."[123] Who would suspect that temperance had affected the vegetation patterns in Concord's meadows?

When the mowers departed in late August, the sheared meadows briefly assumed a brilliant green, "even greener than in spring." Still, Thoreau found himself pining "for the luxuriant vegetation of the riverbanks." Occasionally farmers released their cattle on the meadows to harvest this last bounteous growth of summer.[124]

The activities of star-nosed moles, present in the meadows throughout the year, became more obvious now. Throwing up heaps of meadow mould eight inches in diameter, these most subterranean of Concord's mammals tunneled through the soils day and night, preying on earthworms and insects.[125]

At the fringes stood the taller plants ignored by the farmers: barren purple grasses standing on sterile soils at the meadow boundary, sedges and grasses growing at the river's edge. Patches of wool-grass, sometimes as much as an acre, continued to occupy the soggy lowland portions of the meadow, providing cover for bitterns and rails. On the river a variety of flowers still bloomed, including mikania, polygonums, trumpet-weeds, cardinal flowers, dodder, arrowheads, and vernonia. The mikania was especially striking, woven into the branches of the button bushes overhanging the water.

These were the blossoms of late summer, a promise and a reminder that the chill and decay of autumn were not far off. Many water plants had rotted or gone to seed. Water lilies were all but gone, the flags and button bushes yellowed, the pontederias "brown and crisp." By the first of September, asters blossomed on the river banks.[126]

The avian chorus of early summer fell silent, although dense flocks of bobolinks, grackles, and redwings could be seen flying over the meadows and nearby fields. A new song of the earth arose, a steady cricket chirping inevitably associated in Henry's mind with fall. For several years Henry puzzled over this steady creaking, wondering if there was "a fall cricket distinct from the species we hear in spring and summer." By September of 1855 he had ascertained that he was indeed hearing a different song. Mole crickets, occupying the sandy ground between the meadows and the shore, were the voice of autumn.[127]

AUTUMN DECAY

Fall weather, at times arriving as soon as mid-August, dictated a thick coat and promised rain. These first fall rains cleansed the meadows and the river, removing the oily blue scum, washing away rotting debris, leaving the air clear and crisp. On the river, tiny water bugs (Gyrinas) gyrated among the lily pads in the open spaces of the river, consuming the bodies of dead devil's needles.[128]

In some years, the expected rains did not come. Ironically, 1854 was such a year. The vegetation, life cycles run out, drying in the autumn sun, became as much tinder for meadow fires. Sparks thrown by passing train locomotives or the wadding from hunters' guns provided the match, and several meadows recently mowed burned between mid-August and early September. The peaty soils of the meadows were composed of layer upon layer of partially rotted vegetation, and a fire entering into these layers was very difficult to put out. One meadow fire burned for three weeks, creating holes a foot and a half deep. Another fire penetrated three feet into the vegetation layers. Even if the surface blaze was extinguished, the peat beneath still burned until a hard rain or flood smothered the fire.[129]

In late September of 1854, Thoreau followed up his descriptions of the meadow harvest by identifying the stages of a typical autumn on the river: "First, the two varieties of yellow lily pads begin to decay and blacken (long ago); Second, the first rains come after dogdays and raise and cool the river and winds wash the decaying sparganium, etc. to the shores and clear the channel more or less; Third, when the first harder frosts come . . . , the button bushes, which before had attained only a dull mixed yellow, are suddenly bitten, wither and turn brown, all but the protected parts."[130]

Thoreau found September to be a beautiful month, with the air "wonderfully clear and all objects bright and distinct." The wild grapes hanging from the vines along the higher banks of the river emitted an enticing aroma, inspiring many townspeople, Thoreau included, to go grape-picking. The grapes—rich purple, fiery red, pure green—were as tasty as their odors promised.[131]

For many species of birds, the declining sunlight and the onset of cooler weather warned that migration time drew near. The grackles departed in late August, the bobolinks in early September, the redwings by mid-October. In the meadows, Thoreau noted in several different years the meadow larks "with their white tail-feathers" gathering into flocks. By late October they too were gone.[132]

Just as spring came earliest to the sheltered places along Concord's rivers, the autumn made its greatest initial inroads there. Henry estimated that the river vegetation decayed a full month in advance of that of the surrounding lands. And the river world grew so quiet. Mole crickets chirped more thinly, the songbirds, the frogs, and the toads were long silent. Frost had touched most river plants. The wild rice in the streams was almost entirely gone by the end of September, and the button bushes passed from yellow to crisp brown. The woolgrass left by the mowers also turned to a rich brown. In warm weather, varieties of purple asters were joined by the flowers of what Thoreau called a "second spring": violets, wild roses, lambkill, a few yellow lilies. Flocks of small yellow butterflies still fluttered among the blossoms.[133]

As autumn deepened, the landscape grew increasingly bare and bleak. The hardwood trees lining the meadows—and in places the banks—began to change color as early as mid-September. By the first of October the maples turned a vivid red, creating "memorable features in the scenery of the stream at this season." At the cliffs near Fair Haven, the ivy also reddened, as did the poison sumach near Hubbard's Meadow. The river maples and the neighboring alders shed the last of their leaves in the middle of October. The willows looked bare and faded, and even the evergreens dropped the last of their old, dry needles. The hemlock stand lining the

Assabet shed the seeds from their cones, while deeper in the nearby woods walnuts fell. The meadows assumed a sere and yellow aspect.[134]

Truly cold weather stirred a new wave of behaviors among bird and animal populations. No species of life in Concord could survive without adopting some form of defense against the cold. Only three strategies were possible. A species could simply shut down during the cold, suspending all activity until spring; it could depart, migrating to a more hospitable clime; or it could adopt measures to protect itself against the weather, try to continue on as usual. In Concord, late October saw species pursuing each of the possibilities.

Goldfinches now gathered into large straggling flocks, descended on the hemlocks to eat the seeds, passed over the meadows, sought out the roman wormwood standing in the fields. New birds flew in from the north, running ahead of arctic weather. The rusty blackbirds ("rusty grackles"), which had passed through heading to spring breeding grounds in Canada, returned once more, as did the various species of ducks and teal. Juncos and snow buntings were not long behind. Migrating hawks also became a common sight, as many as eight or ten circling the meadows in a single day.[135]

The most spectacular of the migrations was that of the Canada Geese. "It is always an exciting event," Thoreau wrote. "The children, instinctively aware of its importance, rushed into the house to tell their parents. These travelers are revealed to you by the upward gaze of men." Always the sightings were at a distance; the birds were wary, skittish of the hunters who pursued them everywhere. The flyovers began in October, lasted until the middle of December. Henry estimated that as many as fifteen hundred flew over Concord in a single day at the end of November 1857.[136]

Migrations of a smaller but equally important scale took place in the rivers. Shiners and trout, anticipating the freeze-up of the smaller streams, descended to the deeper waters of the rivers. In the rivers, freshwater mussels retreated from the shores to the deeps of midstream. Judging from Thoreau's notes, this clam migration could take place anywhere between mid-September and the end of October.[137]

Thoreau suspected that the muskrats moved out into the river to facilitate pursuit of the clams, the most important of their winter foods. Their lodges conferred no other advantage. Colder than their burrows in the riverbanks, the houses were also more prone to predation by foxes. Certainly the muskrats began work on their houses at roughly the same time that the clams descended. By the first frosts, muskrat lodges lined the river, always on the side away from human habitations. Working only at night, the muskrats began a lodge by bracing the branches of willows and button bushes against button bush stems, then piling on more and more vegetation until the lodge resembled a haystack standing in the river. Henry ventured to open one of these lodges on at least three different occasions, and was consistently amazed at the discomfort the muskrats endured. In 1853 he noted, "The nest was of course thoroughly wet and, humanly speaking, uncomfortable, though the creatures could breathe in it. But it is plain that the muskrat cannot be subject to the toothache." By mid-October evidence of the muskrats' clam diet was abundant on the river shores.[138]

For cold-blooded reptiles and amphibians, hibernation provided the only viable escape from the challenge of winter. Long before the onset of cold weather, the snakes, the frogs, the toads, and the turtles burrowed into the earth to sleep away the long months of icy weather. Thoreau did his best to track the disappearance of each species, but this was difficult as it required noting an absence, rather than a presence. He was surprised to encounter striped snakes as late as October 9, and found that frogs largely disappeared by mid-October as well. The few he found thereafter were invariably slow and torporous. Turtles held out much longer, depending on the weather. On the eleventh of November 1853, he wrote, "I have noticed no turtles since October 31st," but exactly two years later observed, "I am surprised to see quite a number of painted tortoises out on logs and stones and to hear the wood tortoise rustling down the bank."[139]

Henry was apparently unable to discover much concerning the hibernation of snakes, although he did record one suggestive story in the spring of 1860: "Moore tells me that last fall his men, digging sand in that hollow just up the hill, dug up a parcel of snakes half torpid. . . . The men killed them, and then laid them all in a line on the ground, and they measured several hundred feet. This seems to be the common practice when such collections are found."[140] Striped and black snakes were hibernating together in the sand.

THE FAILING YEAR

November ushered in a season of stillness, cold, and waiting. The leaves were completely fallen and dead, the trees presented "the aspect of waiting for winter." A lowering sun shone through the bare branches of oaks and maples, basking Concord's wild places in a suffused glow. The remaining meadow grasses were completely sere. Ferns, "almost the only things left green now," became obvious among the cliffs and boulders at Fair Haven. Even the mole crickets fell silent, crawling underground to escape the cold. Only the piercing cry of blue jays disturbed the quiet. The blue jays loved acorns above all else, and late autumn was their most joyous time. "In November," Thoreau wrote, "a man will eat his heart, if in any month."[141]

All life did not disappear from the rivers. In shallow bottoms, pollywogs and snails remained active, and caddis worms as well. Waterbugs dimpled the surface of the streams. On warmer Indian Summer days, schools of minnows leaped from the water in a flash of silver. A single torporous tree frog might creak pathetically, a last sigh of summer.[142]

Heavy rains were generally rare in the late autumn. River levels dropped, leaving a distinct line of wreckage along the shore. "The wrecks of the meadow which fill a thousand coves and tell a thousand tales to those who can read them," as Thoreau expressed it. Among the decayed vegetation, the rails, boards, and other refuse of people, cranberries began to wash up. The berries grew on creeping heath shrubs beneath the water surface in boggy areas along the river shore. A source of extra income to farmers who troubled to "bog" for them, cranberries were harvested with common garden rakes. Desperate for money in the fall of 1853, Thoreau himself attempted to derive an income from the free bounty of cranberries. As usual, profit eluded him.[143]

Henry also knew the first days of November as the "gossamer days." At Fair Haven and Clamshell, all along the river, the heavy dews revealed stream after stream of spider webbing, attached to blades of shorn grass, hanging from the willows along the shore. "It looks like a mere frolic spending and wasting of themselves," Thoreau thought, "of their vigor, now that there is no further use for it, their prey, perchance, being killed or banished by the frost." The threads were the products of tiny spiders of the genus *Erigone,* which (for reasons still unknown) spin threads that are then caught by the wind, at times carrying them a considerable distance.[144]

WINTER DESCENDS

Often snow brought an end to the gossamer days. In 1853, the first snow fell on the eighth of November; more typically the first snowstorms came toward the end of the month. Usually the fall was only an inch or two, quickly melted, but in November of 1852 and again in 1856 Concord was buried under several inches.

The snow wrought a great change along the rivers, both in aspect and in opportunity for an observer of nature such as Thoreau. He confessed himself to be "singularly interested by the sight of the shrubs which grow along rivers, rising now above the snow, with buds and catkins,—the *willows,* alders, sweetgale, etc." The meadow sedges, turned a nondescript yellow in the fall, assumed a new beauty to Thoreau in their contrast to the white snow. Equally fascinating were the acres and acres of wormwood and bluecurls rising above the shallow snows in fields adjoining the river.[145]

Thoreau was attracted by the radiance of these scenes, but his interest ran deeper than that. He recognized that these dead or dormant plants were the sole source of survival for many birds and animals facing the bitterness of the Concord winter. He often referred to the dried weeds and shrubs as the "granary of the birds," and sought to understand the full nature of their relationship. Ranging farther and farther afield in his observations, he found that the roman wormwood was critical to the visiting flocks of snow buntings, that several species depended on the hemlock seeds shed along the Assabet, that the smooth sumach berries represented meals to both partridges and meadow mice. And, in eating the seeds, the birds and animals of course assisted the plants in the propagation of their numbers, as Thoreau gradually came to understand.[146]

The snow also offered Henry the opportunity to broaden the scope of his studies of animal behavior. Much of his knowledge of mice, rabbits, hares, partridges, minks, otters, and foxes came not from observing the creatures directly, but from tracing their tracks. "Probably you can study the habits of rabbits, partridges, etc., more easily in the winter," he admitted, "their tracks being revealed by the snow." By studying the footprints, Thoreau was able to induce both the dietary and social behaviors of several species. Combining his field observations with information derived from several books, he made his most complete study of Concord's quadrupeds in the winter of 1855.[147]

On the fifteenth of January in 1857, Thoreau found the tracks of deer mice on the snow at Well Meadow, "hopping and running between bushes." He understood by then that he was observing the evidence of unusual and somewhat risky nocturnal behavior. He had determined through years of careful inquiry that mice spent much of the winter not above the snow, but in tunnels fashioned beneath the drifts.[148]

In Concord, three species of mice occupied this world beneath the snow: the white-footed mouse, the deer mouse, and the meadow vole. All were nocturnal. The meadow voles (meadow mice to Henry) subsisted largely on grasses in winter, while the two species of mice ate seeds, nuts, small fruits, and bark. Living beneath the snow assisted them in two very important ways. The small creatures could range far and wide pursuing scarce food supplies without exposing themselves to the dangers of predation. And, just as importantly, the snow provided insulation for small bodies against the cold.

The meadow voles built networks of nests and tunnels all along the edges of Concord's streams and rivers. In 1855, voles constructed a nest of dried grass among the cranberry vines imbedded in the sphagnum moss at the edge of 2nd Division Meadow. A similar nest, a dome four inches in diameter, lay in the low meadow near the Stone Bridge. Henry also discovered several nesting sites in Hubbard's Meadow. The voles preferred those portions closest to the water, where the sedges grew thick and tall. After heavy storms, ice and snow weighed down the sedge, creating arches six inches high—natural tunnels offering some protection from the owls and foxes.[149]

In drier parts of the meadows, deer mice sought out seeds, small fruits, and even occasional insects beneath the snow. These mice generally lived in underground burrows or beneath fallen trees. They ranged widely in Concord, inhabiting old pastures, woodlands, swamps, and the vicinities of kettle ponds, as well as the meadows. Rye fields, planted in the autumn and harvested in the spring, were favorite winter shelters. Winter thaws revealed long tunnels of grass crisscrossing the fields. Occasionally deer mice left their prints on the surface of the snow, but the risks were high. In February of 1855, Thoreau found a half-eaten mouse lying in the snow near the cliffs. Four days later he found another, apparently dead of exposure, which he brought home for study. The next day still another turned up.

White-footed mice also took advantage of the open space beneath the snow layers, but with a crucial difference. Although they sometimes lived on the ground, white-footed mice also inhabited trees. Usually they took over nests abandoned by other creatures, adapting them to their own purposes. In 1857, Thoreau discovered white-footed mice living in an old owl's nest, located sixteen feet up in an oak tree in Miles's Swamp. The mice cached food on the ground near such places, coming down the tree and entering the world beneath the snow when necessary.[150]

At times, normal food supplies failed the mice. In 1856, Thoreau saw reported in the newspaper that mice had girdled and killed large numbers of fruit trees, having no choice but to eat the bark after heavy snows buried other food sources. In 1860, when snow again fell unusually deep, white-footed mice gnawed the bark from pitch pines.[151]

Vegetation provided essential protection that insured the winter survival of many species. Mice relied upon the sedges, grasses, and rye for cover. Partridges, emerging from the deeper woods to bud on the orchards at Fair Haven, sheltered among snow-covered shrubs and small trees. Rabbits too depended on plant cover, especially low woods, newly sprouted scrub oak forest, overgrown pasture, and brushland.[152]

New England cottontails—Thoreau's rabbits—lived in many places throughout the town, including Pinxter Swamp, Well Meadow, and Nawshawtuct Hill, although each rabbit ranged over no more than three-quarters of an acre. The cottontails were a secretive lot, rarely leaving the vegetation coverts. They spent the winter atop the snow, huddled in the shelter of shrubs, grasses, and small trees. On his winter walks, Thoreau at times encountered hundreds of prints left by rabbits frisking together in the night. In December of 1851, he found where several left footprints as they played together near a wall at Nawshawtuct.[153]

The animals depending on vegetive sources for food ate regularly, except in the most severe weather. For predators, eating was more closely related to good fortune and day-to-day opportunity. Two preying mammals living in Concord operated by day. The marten, exceedingly rare in the town by the 1850s, spent much of its time in trees. These solitary creatures preferred to eat squirrels, but also sought mice, rabbits, and birds. Thoreau's knowledge of the marten's habits came solely from books. The only evidence that martens still passed through Concord came in 1855: one left its foot in a trap on the Concord River.[154]

River otters were slightly more common. Otters ranged over great distances from year to year. During the 1850s, two or three passed through the river valley each year, their tails leaving a track like someone had dragged a log through the snow. The otters frequented the Sudbury River near Fair

Haven, Bittern Cliff, and Clamshell Hill, and the Assabet near Assabet Spring. Each place was characterized by a high bank sloping to the river, where the otters slid down the snow into the water, as much for play as for food. But for all their playfulness, otters could be dangerous. Henry noted in his journal that an otter killed a dog in nearby Framingham in 1853.[155]

Thoreau discovered evidence of two nocturnal mammalian predators ranging the river valley during Concord's winters. Minks frequented the area's streams and rivers at periodic intervals, usually in late fall or winter. Solitary by nature and moving often, they hunted rabbits, mice, chipmunks, fish, and their favorite meal, muskrat. Thoreau found where a mink had hunted on the river ice near Clamshell Hill in 1853; another appeared on the ice at Hubbard's in December 1855. They killed by biting their victims on the neck. They in turn were hunted by foxes and owls, but only as a last resort. As Thoreau noted, "nothing will eat a mink."[156]

The most striking of the predators still living in Concord in the 1850s was the red fox, a hunter of mice, rabbits, muskrats, and birds in places not frequented by people. Thoreau had a special affinity for the foxes of Concord. Recorded observations of fox sightings at Fair Haven are among the few nature entries in his earliest journals and his fascination with these wild predators never ended. He traced their tracks into the swamps and the hollows of secluded woods, recording in his journal the locations of their dens, carefully concealing the information from the farmers for fear of hunting expeditions. Some of Thoreau's most prodigious investigative feats, combining the gleanings of inductive investigation with the conclusions of disciplined imagination, recreated episodes in the lives of foxes.

One such investigation took place in February 1854, when Henry encountered a fox track near Hubbard's Meadow. Tracing it back, he found that the fox in the previous night had crept, walked, trotted, and cantered a course of more than a mile out of a swamp, over open fields, through woods, up hillsides, across brooks and the ice on the Sudbury River, and finally into another swamp. Not merely following the trail, he reconstructed the fox's preying habits by noting how it jumped on the muskrat lodges in the river, trying to drive out the inhabitants, how it urinated on each lodge to mark its territory. He even noted where the fox briefly dragged its tail in the snow. "What expeditions they make in a night in search of food!" he concluded. "No doubt the same one crosses the river many times." Investigations such as this both heightened Thoreau's understanding of the relationships between predator and prey and encouraged his empathy with the natural world.[157]

Not all of the predators active along the Concord River were mammals. Nor were they bound to the surface of the earth. The hawks familiar to Henry migrated southward before winter, but several species of owls hunted over the snow and ice. One, the short-eared owl, was itself a migrant, retreating from even less hospitable weather to the north. Thoreau generally began seeing them late in December. They remained until early March, preying on small rodents in the meadows and open grasslands. Hunting mainly in the late afternoons, they roosted in the thick evergreens along the Assabet the rest of the day. In severe weather, these owls sheltered in hollowed tree stumps.

Concord's other species of owls were largely nocturnal in their habits. Thoreau rarely encountered them on the hunt, but in his daytime explorations of the woods and swamps he found several asleep. Most common was the barred owl, whose loud barking hoot echoed across Wheeler Wood and the Ministerial Swamp at dusk. The long-eared owl, quieter but no less dangerous to rodents (especially mice), also favored woods and swamps. Screech owls hunted rodents and small birds in woods and open forests near the streams. (Henry once caught a somnolent screech owl with his bare hands, then wrapped it in his handkerchief and carried it home in his pocket for overnight observation.) Great horned owls preferred grouse and rabbits to other prey, but in times of winter scarcity they attacked song birds, crows, minks, domestic cats, even other owls. Thoreau heard the low, booming, long-carrying hoot of the great horned owl more often in midwinter than at any other time.[158]

The bird causing Henry more anguish than any other was a migrant song bird from the north, the northern shrike. The "butcher bird" arrived in Concord early in November and ranged over open fields and meadows near the Fair Haven cliffs and The Island, hunting birds and mice. Shrikes caught small birds on the wing, then hung their captured prey by the head from the crotch of a tree or a thorn for consumption. The shrikes were solitary birds, and came to Concord in small numbers. After watching a shrike successfully kill a snowbird in December of 1850, he commented, "I find that I had not associated such actions with my idea of birds. It was not birdlike."[159]

The snow and winter cold afforded Thoreau a better opportunity to study these predator-prey relationships than at any other time of year. Winter was a special time. Forced to spend more time contemplatively indoors, the explorations he could undertake revealed nature along the rivers reduced to its most elemental qualities. The withered stalks of meadow flower and shrub spoke of all that had died, with a reappearance promised in the seed pods scattered among the drifts. Much of animal nature slept, burrowed beneath the meadows, in the beds of the rivers, high in the trees overhead. For the few creatures still awake and about, winter revealed their vulnerability and their determination to live. Food and shelter were never more important. In winter, the essentials were laid bare for Henry to see.

But even in the deepest colds of January, meadow crust was adhering to the bottoms of the ice sheets lying across the meadows. Soon the thaws would come, the ice would rise, the rivers would begin again the process of rearranging the vegetation, insuring the succession of the plants and animals dependent on the meadow. Every one of Concord's habitats lived in a constantly changing, never-ending cycle, a cycle Henry Thoreau came to recognize so intimately. Soon the flocks of crows would again be scavenging the meadows in search of torpid and unwary insects and worms.

In April 1852, confronted anew with the mystery and the majesty of nature's cycle, Thoreau attempted to summarize all he had learned in the previous year:

> Vegetation starts when the earth's axis is sufficiently inclined—i. e. it follows the sun. Insects & all the smaller (as well as many larger) follow vegetation—The fishes the small fry start probably—for this reason—worms come out of the trees—buffaloes finally seek new pastures—water-bugs appear on the water &c &c.—Next the large fish & fish hawks &c follow the small fry—fly catchers follow the insects and worms (The graniverous birds—who can depend on the supplies of dry seeds of last year—are to some extent independent of the seasons & can remain through the winter or come early in the spring—& they furnish food for a few birds of prey at that season) Indians follow the buffaloes—trout—suckers &c follow the water bugs—&c reptiles follow vegetation insects & worms—birds of prey the fly catchers &c Man follows all & all follow

> the Sun. The greater or less abundance of food determines the migrations. If ther buds are deceived & suffer from frost—then are the birds. The great necessary of life for the brute creation is food—next perhaps shelter—i.e. a suitable climate. 3dly perhaps security from foes.[160]

Too many variations of "&c" in that statement. A tremendous amount of work remained to be done.

The rhythms of the natural cycle became the beat of Thoreau's own life during the 1850s. His work was to attend and observe the natural events of the Concord year; the establishment, growth, and death of the plants, the life cycles of the reptiles, amphibians, and mammals, the nesting and migration of the birds. It was a process of observation combining new learning and knowledgeable anticipation. By the mid-1850s he understood the basic patterns of nature in Concord quite well. Repeated visits to the river enabled him to understand which plants grew where, when they would flower, when they would seed. Unraveling the mysteries of dreamy amphibian song, he could identify the mating times of each of the six species of Concord's frogs. He knew which birds would be lurking in the tall grasses, where each species would nest. He could predict when the bream would nest and spawn, when the turtles would leave the river to lay their eggs. What was more, he had performed similar investigations in each of Concord's habitats—the swamps, the bogs, the ponds, the hills and cliffs, the woods, even the village.

The goal from that point onward was to delve more deeply into the cycles he had recognized, and to fit any new gleanings into the patterns he had recognized. He had become an observer of nature without equal.

Yet this was merely a means to a larger end. For Thoreau, an intimate knowledge of Concord's natural history represented the building materials for a far more profound species of knowledge. What Henry really wanted to know was how all this confusing welter of cycles and patterns, births and deaths, growth and decay, all fit together into one grand picture. How did the life story of each plant, each animal, affect the stories of all the others? All derived life from the air, the water, the earth of Concord. What were the mechanisms, the forces, the cooperations, the dependencies, the effects, which enabled them to live together, to draw life from one another, to represent birth, death, and regeneration to one another?

Confronting those kinds of questions was a lifework indeed. As if this alone was not enough, there was one problem more facing Henry. Assuming he found at least some of the answers to his grand questions, how could he ever hope to explain them to anyone else? How could he write nature as it actually existed?

If thou art a writer write as if thy time was short—for it is indeed short at the longest.

—*Journal,* January 24, 1852

You must live in the present, launch yourself on every wave, find your eternity in each moment. Fools stand on their island opportunities and look toward another land. There is no other land; there is no life but this, or the like of this.

—*Journal,* April 24, 1859

6 INVESTIGATING NATURE

NATURE IN CONCORD fashioned a grip on Henry's soul too intimate to deny. In 1860, after more than ten years of almost continuous study of nature in his town, he still found the wind on the river more interesting to watch than any expression of human society. "I am not so ready to perceive the illusion that is in Nature," he observed. "I certainly come nearer, to say the least, to an actual and joyful intercourse with her." His daily intercourse with nature's ways derived an incomparable serenity, a sense of joy he could apprehend only in the absence of human society, even human learning. He in fact took a special interest in those plants that had no discernible economic value to humankind.[1]

The experience at times bordered on the mystical: "In my botanical rambles I find that first the idea, or image, of a plant occupies my thoughts, though it may at first seem very foreign to this locality, and for some weeks or months I go thinking of it and expecting it unconsciously, and at length

I surely see it, and it is henceforth an actual neighbor of mine. This is the history of my finding a score or more of rare plants which I could name."[2]

In the latter half of the 1850s, Henry Thoreau found himself in an unusual and almost uncomfortable position. Having achieved a minimal recognition in his own right, he earned enough money from the sale of *Walden,* his lectures, and his essays to experience a degree of financial security. His wants remained few, and the meager income was more than enough to satisfy them. Unfortunately, the experience brought with it a fear of monetary failure, and also a curious reluctance to continue on the proven path of literary success.[3]

His first publication after *Walden* was "Cape Cod," a narrative of his first journey to the Cape supplemented by materials from later travels. The essay was to have appeared in five installments in *Putnam's,* but an unusually quarrelsome Thoreau withdrew the piece after only three appeared (June to August, 1855), explaining that he had decided to enlarge the work into a book. Although he made trips to the Cape in 1855 and in 1857, he made no effort to work on such a book. He also wrote no new lectures in 1856 or 1857, nor did he deliver any. For almost three years, the journal became virtually his sole source of expression.[4]

Part of the problem was illness. Some unknown malady made him a specimen of "invalidity and worthlessness" for the entire summer of 1855, and symptoms persisted for sometime thereafter. The illness left him listless and weak, especially in the legs. The journal reflects this illness, a series of sketchy and unsatisfactory entries beginning on June twenty-second and running to the sixteenth of September. He actually wrote the entire twelve weeks of these entries in September, working from scratch notes made while fighting off the bug.[5]

Henry's father, John Thoreau Sr., also began to weaken in the mid-1850s, as the scourge of tuberculosis again exacted its due on the family. Henry found himself shouldering more and more of the responsibilities of the family pencil business; a burden he gladly accepted, although it meant a considerable investment of time in letters and accounts, leaving less opportunity for writing. As his father's illness became acute, Henry also assumed responsibility for his care, exhibiting a tenderness even his mother did not expect. John Thoreau had always accepted and encouraged his son's unusual lifework, even urging Henry to stay focused on his larger projects of observation and not be distracted by side experiments. When his father died on February 3, 1859, Thoreau found himself fully accountable for the business and his family, and in possession of one more great sorrow.[6]

Henry had friends in plenty during this period of his life, both in Concord and in other New England towns, yet he continued to feel a profound loneliness, comprised in part by his continued estrangement from Emerson and in part his long, solitary communion with nature. He and Waldo learned gradually to overlook one another's stubbornness and visit regularly, but the closeness of earlier years was gone forever.[7]

And nature beckoned Henry. "I knock on the earth for my friend. I expect to meet him at every turn, but no friend appears," he admitted. He was even tempted, in the autumn of 1855, to leave Concord, to "go off to some wilderness where I can have a better opportunity to play life."[8]

The pull of Concord's own woods and rivers was too strong to leave, but Henry did travel during the latter half of the 1850s; two trips to Cape Cod, another to the Maine Woods, four journeys to climb mountains in interior New England, a long trip to New Jersey and New York, and several visits to friends in various New England towns. Yet these were all punctuation marks to the most careful and profound of his travels, the almost daily journeys he undertook in Concord itself.[9]

For ten years, Thoreau maintained the same essential beat in life—a long walk each day to discover what nature was about, a long period spent subsequently in the quiet of his attic room, translating his rough field notes into the literary entries that filled journal after journal. Punctuated by travels to other places and more occasionally by tragedy, the journal slowly grew into one man's perceptions of nature's behavior in one geographic setting. The journal was at once a faithful record of natural phenomena and a presentation framed in prose poetry—science and art.[10]

As the journal assumed central place in Thoreau's efforts, and the project reflected in the journal became as large as nature itself, alternate avenues of expression became correspondingly difficult. Unable to present the essence of a work in progress so large, Henry fell back on two alternate vehicles to maintain a presence before the public. Late in 1854, he composed a new lecture entitled "What Shall It Profit," concentrating on themes similar to those of the first "Economy" chapter of *Walden.* And, early in 1858, he turned once more to the familiar travel essay format, writing up a lecture detailing his third expedition to the wilderness of Maine. Apart from these two efforts—only partially satisfactory in Thoreau's own mind—he wrote nothing for immediate presentation between 1855 and 1859. Instead, he peppered the journal with prickly complaints of unsympathetic audiences, lack of speaking invitations, and the like. There may have been some justice in such grumbling, but the heart of the problem lay in his refusal to be distracted from his main theme—the comprehension of nature.[11]

After 1858, he began to cast about for ideas that would enable him to typify his larger work in a limited time and space. After rejecting themes such as "November Lights," he eventually settled on two subjects that provided scope for at least a representation of his wide-ranging ideas. Each was inspired by materials entered sporadically into the journals throughout the 1850s, and each succeeded in providing audiences with at least a small glimpse of the trend of his thoughts. The first was "Autumnal Tints," completed in February 1859, and the second "Wild Apples," finished in February 1860.[12]

Thoreau conceived the idea for a book entitled "Autumnal Tints" back in November of 1853, envisioning a volume of prose celebration of the glories of autumn accompanied by a series of color plates capturing the varied beauty of New England's leaves. Nothing came of this idea, but three years later, as a consequence of examining dried oak leaves still clinging to their branches in the December cold, Henry thought of writing a lecture on those leaves, accompanied by specimens of each variety to be actually exhibited at the lecture hall. When Thoreau set to work writing a lecture on autumn leaves another two years after, he combined these two ideas, and a good deal more besides. In lecture form, "Autumnal Tints" recounted not the visions of the desiccated leaves of winter, but the full fruit of glorious, colorful fall. Henry carried with him to the lecture room pressed specimens of each of the beautiful yellow, orange, or scarlet varieties of leaf he discussed.[13]

Although the nominal subject matter of "Autumnal Tints" was indeed the breathtaking array of hues gracing the streets and countrysides of New England each autumn, Thoreau built the lecture on the foundation of an idea far more fundamental to his own work. In this particular case, he urged his audience to open their eyes and honestly observe the colors of autumn—the essay more genuinely concerns the very practice of observation. At the outset he provides the scientific explanation for the leaves' change of colors, in the same breath dismissing this account as "only a reassertion of the fact." Science is therefore imbedded in all the observations that follow, but only to serve art, the observation of beauty. After devoting several pages to this celebration, he reflects that "it requires different intentions of the eye and the mind to attend to different departments of knowledge! How differently the poet and the naturalist look at objects!" "Autumnal Tints" in effect summarizes Thoreau's long-standing argument with himself: how is the writer to use science without becoming scientific; how is nature to be expressed accurately and yet poetically?[14]

When Thoreau began work on the lecture he entitled "Wild Apples" roughly a year later, he once again reached well back into his journals for subject matter. Henry wrote the prototypical passages of this essay on the sixteenth of November 1850, foreseeing the disappearance of wild apple trees and pitying the resultingly poorer citizens of the next century. In 1860 he lifted this passage almost verbatim for his lecture, and identified late autumn passages from several subsequent years to weave into his text. "Wild Apples" again summarized one aspect of the multifaceted vision Thoreau brought to the study of nature.[15]

Generally, Thoreau celebrated the wild and spoke with eloquent concern regarding both its contribution to the national health and the danger of its disappearance. In "Wild Apples," he turned his usual point-of-view inside out, paying homage instead to a bit of domesticity gone wild. As Henry well knew, apples were not native to North America. Imported by the English immigrants to serve in orchards as a source of fruit and cider, the apples had, with the aid of various birds and animals, made their escape. Walking in the woods, Henry encountered these feral strays, and tasted apples the essence of wild and moody November. So with apples, so perhaps with people; even the most domesticated could conceivably take their places in the wild. What danger there was ran the other way: between the growing habit of grafting and the efforts of the temperance party to rid the countryside of wild sources of cider, wild apple trees were in danger of disappearing. Humankind would then be condemned "to look for our apples in a barrel," a bleak prospect to a man who valued the experience of finding wild food as much as the eating.[16]

Although these new lectures brought at least some small portion of his work to public audiences, Henry's most essential ideas—very difficult to express in a comparatively brief format—remained confined to his journals. There they shaped and guided his everyday inquiries into nature. Even after several years of minute study, he was still overwhelmed by the sheer variety in nature, and even more fascinated by the fact that this variety was annually reexpressed in a great cyclical whole.

Reveling in the profusion of nature, Thoreau noted that the "gardener with all his assiduity does not raise such a variety, nor so many successive crops on the same space, as Nature in the very roadside ditches." Yet, despite that profusion, nature maintained its equilibrium. Each disturbance corrected itself. Henry argued that such an ability gave nature a "regularity and permanence," enabling it to exist for countless years across the span of time.[17] The comparatively short life span of humanity made it difficult to recognize the patterns inherent in this permanence: "It takes us many years to find out that Nature repeats herself annually. But how perfectly regular and calculable all her phenomena must appear to a mind that has observed her for a thousand years!"[18]

While nature possessed this underlying permanence, it was also changing on a daily basis. After years of seeking to discover the events signaling a change in season, Henry had concluded by 1857 that each day was virtually a season to itself—that no two days were ever exactly alike in terms of weather, animal behavior, and plant behavior. "Each season is but an infinitesimal point. It has no duration. It simply gives a tone and hue to my thought. . . . A year is made up of a certain series and number of sensations and thoughts which have their language in nature."[19]

Nature possessed a definite rhythm, but that rhythm was dependent on far too many variables to achieve an exact understanding in one human lifetime. Even the order of the appearance of plants varied with the weather each year. Thoreau admitted in a journal entry of October of 1857, "I doubt if you can ever get Nature to repeat herself exactly."[20]

What sustained Thoreau in his patient effort to discern the complex and varying patterns of life was his ongoing belief in the presence of spirit in nature. Hearing a crow cawing across a field in January 1855, he recognized himself as "part of one great creature with him." For Thoreau, not merely animate nature but the very earth itself was organic and embodied the spirit of God. "The ultimate expression or fruit of any created thing," he wrote, "is a fine effluence which only the most ingenious worshiper perceives at a reverent distance from its surface even." Henry felt that we grew closest to the spiritual earth not in broad daylight, but on moonlit nights. Unfortunately, Henry reflected, most people never detected the spirit present in nature at any time of day.[21]

Believing that humankind might be regenerated by honestly worshiping "stocks and stones," Henry despaired of the idolatry of his neighbors, maintaining that they were afraid of ghosts. Certainly the traditional religions did nothing to encourage any recognition of spirit in nature, and science was no help either. Science books completely denied the living spirit of the animals they claimed to portray, describing only the inanimate, dead tissue of their dissections. "How much is written about Nature as somebody has portrayed her," he complained in 1857, "how little about Nature as she is, and chiefly concerns us, *i.e.,* how much prose, how little poetry."[22]

While Thoreau generally eschewed the study of human society in favor of nature study after 1850, he was very much concerned about the relationship between people and nature. Were human beings a part of nature? Or were they separate from, and superior to, the remainder of creation? Recognizing that only a portion of the earth was habitable for human beings, he wondered if people were bound to improve uninhabitable places, or rather "to live more naturally and so more safely?" Henry found himself periodically reflecting on the problem in the years after he began systematically recording his observations of nature. He never reached a genuinely satisfactory conclusion.[23]

Generally speaking, Thoreau seems to have embraced the idea that humanity was an integral part of the natural whole. This, after all, was the logical outgrowth of his belief that the same spirit infused all of creation, a conclusion supported by his ongoing studies in Oriental literature and Native American history. In 1851 and again in 1856 he firmly stated that humanity was a part of nature, labeling this "the divinest and most startling of all facts."[24]

But even if people were a part of nature, they had a unique ability to confound the fact through the exercise of their mental powers. People had deluded themselves into believing themselves separate from the rest, a belief that threw them out of harmony with the natural whole, preventing them from communicating with "the great design of the universe." By domesticating plants and animals, humankind had set itself up as "the lord of the fowl and the brute."[25] But there was a price for this domination: "Birds certainly are afraid of man. They [allow] all other creatures—cows and horses, etc.—excepting only one or two kinds, birds or beasts of prey, to come near them, but not man. What does this fact signify? Does it not signify that man too, is a beast of prey to them? Is he, then, a true lord of creation, whose subjects are afraid of him, and with reason? They know very well that he is not humane, as he pretends to be."[26]

Henry noted also that in attempting to separate themselves from nature, people diminished both themselves and the rest of the world. Coming on the cellar hole of a long-abandoned house in 1859, he remarked on the presence of vermin and the ranks of repellant weeds surrounding the site, signs of "a certain unwholesome fertility." It seemed the long residence of people in any given place cursed the locality. And the more people created artificial separations between themselves and nature—living in well-bounded towns and cities, where exposure to wild nature was carefully limited and controlled—the more sickly they became.[27]

Signs of the effort to deny the human connection with nature surrounded Thoreau. He complained of people more fascinated by Corinthian columns than trees, was amused by the fears inspired by the appearance of a great comet in 1858.[28] But far more serious was the effort by his fellow townspeople to change the very face of nature itself.

The destruction of Concord's woods, begun in the 1840s to supply the railroads, accelerated throughout the 1850s. Counting the rings on one railway tie cut from a cedar trunk, Henry found that someone in their greed had cut a tree living before the Pilgrims had set foot in New England. By 1857 people were selling even scrub oak lots for as much as six dollars per acre. In the winter of 1858 alone, Henry counted the disappearance of six separate woodlots scattered throughout the town. To the rest of Concord this may have been a process of turning standing timber into money, but to Henry it was the destruction of trees he loved, and the dwelling places of the town's wilder birds and animals as well. By October of 1860, he estimated that all of both the original and the second growth forests were gone from Concord.[29]

What was worse, as Thoreau came to recognize in the winters of 1855 and 1856, was that this destruction was part of an old and ongoing process. Reading through old descriptions of Massachusetts Bay, he saw that Concord had in times past been home to such larger animals as the wolf, the bear, the lynx, and the moose, to say nothing of the beaver and the wild turkey. Comparing the ancient lists to his own records, he bitterly complained that, "I cannot but feel as if I lived in a tamed, and, as it were, emasculated country." How different might his nature studies have proved if his fellow townspeople and their ancestors had not proven so efficient with gun and axe?[30]

To Thoreau, this uncontrolled destruction was nothing more than criminal activity. "If some are prosecuted for abusing children," he suggested, "others deserve to be prosecuted for maltreating the face of nature committed to their care." He was prepared to condemn nearly all of Concord for these sins against nature, exempting only the children, whose instinctive love of nature shamed adult humanity. "Children are attracted by the beauty of butterflies," he snarled, "but their parents and legislators deem it an idle pursuit."[31]

After taking up serious nature study early in the 1850s, Henry occasionally devoted thought to the problem of building a better relationship with nature. Like all good transcendentalists, he began this reform of humanity with himself, leaving off employing the gun to assist bird identifications. Omitting a gun suggested a greater maturity, a sentiment originally advanced in his journal in 1852 and afterward incorporated into *Walden.* Having reformed himself, he then proceeded to attack the "narrow and grovelling" economy of his neighbors, who would destroy the rare beauty of a soaring hawk to save a few egg-laying hens. From there he moved to a censure of trapping, stating that there "is a good excuse for smoking out or poisoning rats which infest the house, but when they are as far off as Hudson's Bay, I think we had better let them alone."[32]

By far the most serious problem was the destruction of forests. Private owners controlled virtually all of New England's wooded lands, leaving the fate of the patchwork forests very much at the mercy of private whim. All of Concord's primitive growth was gone, and a large primitive oak forest still existed in nearby Boxboro only because generations of eccentric owners had refused to cut it. Thoreau argued as early as 1852 for legislation to provide each town a measure of control in deciding which woods should be cut each winter, to better conserve the fuel supply. After reading works on forest management in England by John Evelyn and others, Henry dreamed of forest wardens enlisted to protect Walden Woods and other woodlots throughout the town. He dreamed also of reforestation projects, noting the custom among some cultures of planting a tree whenever a child was born. "If a forest were planted at the birth of every man," he wrote, "nations would not be likely to become effete." Fitting action to the words seven years later, he spent three days in April 1859 setting out pines on Waldo Emerson's Walden lands. By that time he had become more ardent in his desire for forest preservation, advocating in his journal that "Each town should have a park, or rather a primitive forest, of five hundred or a thousand acres, where a stick should never be cut for fuel, a common possession forever, for instruction and recreation." In January 1861, he argued further that any "natural objects of rare beauty" should be the common property of the public. Thoreau incorporated this sentiment into "The Allegash and East Branch," the third of his Maine woods travel essays. Published in book form as *The Maine Woods* in 1864, two years after Thoreau's death, the passage represented one of the first published calls for legislated wilderness preservation.[33]

Thoreau argued for the preservation of wilderness for purposes of recreation and inspiration, but his own interest in the woods was far more extensive. Each year after 1850 he broadened and deepened his studies of nature in countless ways, seeking to understand the function of the overarching spirit present in each plant and animal that made the collective community of life work together as a whole. One major component in this effort was the study of the interrelationships among plants and animals; another was the study of plant succession.

In June 1851, Henry noted the presence of a pitch pine and white pine wood where a blackberry field had stood not many years before. Less than three weeks later, he stood pondering a field of mulleins growing where millet had grown two years previously. "Who can write the history of these fields?" he wondered. In the ensuing years, Thoreau continued to contemplate a variety of examples of plant succession. In 1852 he recorded the rapid growth of huckleberry bushes after a hillside wood was cut down; in 1854 he noted the formation of a new swamp in a hollow near Fair Haven, begun a few years previously when alders took root in the springy soil by a rill.[34]

Henry also began tracking the role of animals in seed dispersion at an early date. In November 1850, he recorded in his journal the discovery of a corn kernel deep in Walden wood, secreted in a pine tree by a crow or squirrel. In the winter of 1852–53, he undertook a careful analysis of the role of squirrels and mice in planting chestnuts in leaf mould at the base of trees, comprehending for the first time the web of activities necessary to the renewal of a forest. The following autumn he came to appreciate the fall of the leaves for an entirely new reason: the decaying vegetation on the forest floor provided a perfect protection in which new seeds could root. Nothing in nature truly died. A falling leaf rose again, taken into the sap of the growing young tree it nurtured.[35]

In January 1856, Henry watched squirrels burying acorns in shallow soil and recognized them as an agent of oak reforestation as well. A month later, he deduced that the seeds of red cedar shoots growing in pastures far from any parent tree must have been carried for miles by crows or other birds. Wind, too, he recognized as an agent in seed dispersal, blowing the lightweight seeds of birch and other trees for miles and miles across the snows.[36]

Henry extended his studies of the role of animals in succession to include people and their machines. A "Query" written into his journal for September 2, 1852, called for him to investigate the distribution of seeds by the railroad between Concord and Boston. The construction of bridges and causeways over the Concord River changed the vegetation patterns there as well, providing opportunities for willow hedges to invade the meadows. He saw much of this human agency in plant dispersion as negative, arguing in 1853 that "in our localities of plants, we do not know where they would prefer to grow if unmolested by man, but rather where they best escape his vandalism."[37]

Very quickly, Thoreau came to appreciate the subtlety in the relationship between plants and animals.[38] In August 1851 he observed: "It is remarkable that animals are often obviously, manifestly, related to the plants which they feed upon or live among-as caterpillars-butterflies-tree-toads-partridges-chewinks-& this afternoon I noticed a yellow spider on a goldenrod— As if every condition might have its expression in some form of animated being."[39]

As the years passed, he multiplied his examples in countless ways, building up a vast record of interaction between plants and animals. Thoreau had no clear purpose in creating this record, but instead worked in a remarkably inductive fashion, gathering facts with breathless intensity, employing them happily to support larger ideas when some truth leapt out at him.

Such was the case in the spring of 1856, when the first ideas of the principle of forest succession occurred to him. Thoreau was surveying a pitch pine wood for his Concord neighbor George Hubbard. The farmer remarked that if he were to cut down the pines, a forest of oak would take its place. Hubbard wondered why.

The question intrigued Thoreau. He spent the next two weeks examining the forest successions in various woodlots and old pastures throughout the town. By the thirteenth of May, he was prepared to answer George Hubbard. The reason lay in the activity on the one hand of birds and animals, who carried the heavy acorns into the pine woods and often buried them, and on the other hand the wind, which broadcast the light pine seed throughout the town. On the floor of virtually every pine wood, young oaks were growing, planted by squirrels or other such agents. If the pines remained, the oak shoots were shaded out and died. But if the pines were cut. . . . Thoreau concluded that "Scarcely enough allowance has been made for the agency of squirrels and birds in dispersing seeds."[40]

In the months and years following this discovery, Henry refined and added to this basic concept, being typically dissatisfied with the pat answer advanced in his initial theory. He noted further examples of forest succession, and even extended the principle to other forms of plant behavior, recognizing (for example) the fluctuation in the cardinal flower population along the river banks from year to year. In 1858 he saw that scarlet oaks seemed to defy his basic ideas, being more or less evenly distributed across the hills. In November of that year he admitted that "We do not begin to understand the treatment of woodland yet."[41]

He enlarged his knowledge of the role of birds and animals, finding cherry-stones brought by birds to the woodland springs, examining barberry seeds voided by birds and cattle, noting the desmodium ticks he carried away from the "grape cliff" on his own jacket. He even enlisted the aid of a microscope to demonstrate that the nuts he found cached in a cliffside had been left by mice.[42]

Thoreau continued also to develop his theories of succession. In September 1857, he was pleased to find "Alternating with thin ferns and small blueberry bushes, there was, as often as every five feet, a little oak, three to twelve inches, and in one place I found a green acorn dropped by the base of a tree. I was surprised, I confess, to find my own theory so perfectly proved. These oaks, apparently, find such a locality unfavorable to their growth as long as the pines stand. I saw that some had been browsed by the cows which resort to the woods for shade."[43]

Two years later, he was examining the association of various plant groups—chiefly species of bulrush—with different points on the meanders of the river, demonstrating that the velocity of the current played a role in determining the location of each species.[44]

Henry did not carry on his studies of seed dispersion and plant succession in any single-minded fashion, but in the context of a far larger program of nature study. Intellectually, he was on largely unexplored ground, attempting to embrace and understand all of nature's behavior and to express this understanding as art. The cyclical yearly beat of his observations continued. He noted the migratory patterns of the birds, the blooming and the withering of the flowers, the reproductive calendar of the reptiles and amphibians, the pulse of the weather. Several special projects absorbed his attention from time to time. In the winter of 1856 he measured snow depths and studied old trees; in the spring he experimented with making sugar from various tree saps. April of 1858 found him deeply absorbed in the study of frogs, and in October he minutely recorded the changes in leaf color. In the summer of 1859, a study of the Concord River commissioned by several farmers preparing to sue to remove a dam flooding their meadows consumed much of his time. October brought the news of John Brown's raid and a rare involvement in politics, but he found time also to study the effects of cold weather on fruits and nuts. The odd formations of the river ice attracted his attention in the winter of 1860, along with an exacting attempt to track the fluctuations of the winter weather.[45]

So the beat continued, year after year. Thoreau understood that in studying any aspect of nature he was studying all, and this explains the seemingly scattered character of his efforts. He was searching for the keys to understand the whole thing. In the late 1850s, he began to summarize some of his observations, thoroughly reviewing all his entries since the spring of 1852, categorizing his notes on the appearance of migratory birds, the blooming of flowers, the leafing of trees, and several additional phenomena. Using large sheets of paper, he arranged these observations in a series of monthly charts in which he established the average timing of each natural event. When completed, the project would have produced a month-by-month phenological calendar of natural phenomena, a rendering of the average natural cycle in Concord. Henry produced over seven hundred manuscript pages of notes for this project, although his intended use for the calendar remains unclear.[46]

This rhythm of observation and record might have continued indefinitely, had it not been for the appearance of Charles Darwin's *On the Origin of Species* late in 1859. Thoreau first heard an accounting of the book from Charles Brace, who came to Concord on New Year's Day, 1860, to lecture on Children's Aid in New York City. At a dinner party held at the home of Franklin Sanborn, Thoreau, Brace, and Bronson Alcott discussed Darwin's work at great length. The town library soon acquired a copy that Thoreau borrowed, writing six pages of extracts into his natural history notebook in February.[47]

In *Origin of Species,* Darwin argued that species were not immutable, that each creature currently living on the earth had descended from other creatures in an immensely long and slow process in which extinction played a major role. The story of life was the story of competition for survival, with those species best adapted to the conditions of their habitat possessing the best chance of living and passing their characteristics to subsequent generations—what Darwin called natural selection. The struggle for survival was therefore very much dependent on each species' surroundings, that is, the plants and animals that comprised its community, its location, climate, and so on. Each individual species struggled on its own, but success depended to a large degree upon the interactions among all.[48]

Naturalists and clerics alike fully recognized that Darwin was advocating a theory of the evolution of species, although that specific word occurred not once in the text. Evolution was not a new idea; the possibility had been "in the wind" for at least a century. Darwin's grandfather Erasmus was one of several eighteenth-century scholars to consider the concept. As scientific research on the question of speciation intensified after 1800, discussion of the idea grew increasingly common. In 1851, Thoreau read the work of an anonymous amateur scientist entitled *Vestiges of the Natural History of Creation.* Although often inaccurate, the work was bold and arresting in its speculations, much of which centered on the obvious possibility that modern species had evolved from older forms. Reviewers, including Harvard botanist Asa Gray (whose text Thoreau relied upon for years), roundly condemned the *Vestiges* for committing a by-then familiar sin: the author had speculated without offering verifiable proof.[49]

Darwin's great achievement was to place evolutionary theory on sound scientific footing—to offer demonstrable experimental evidence for the occurence of the evolution of species. In doing so, he often cited the work of natural scientists familiar to Thoreau, especially Asa Gray. Geographical dispersion of plant species was critical to the theory of natural selection, and Darwin referred to Gray's American botanical studies at several crucial points. For example, while discussing the role of glaciation in plant distribution, Darwin noted Gray's discovery that essentially the same communities of Alpine plants inhabit the Alps and Pyrenees of Europe, the extreme latitudes of Labrador, and the White Mountains of New Hampshire. Darwin also acknowledged that Gray had assisted his studies of interbreeding by calculating the sexual distribution among various tree species in the eastern United States. Gray worked with forest species familiar to Thoreau. Now Darwin had given these trees a new importance.[50]

Darwin's theory of natural selection was a new way of looking at life in nature, one that Thoreau instantly appreciated. Yet, much of the subject matter was familiar ground to Henry. He had studied the problem of forest succession in 1856; now Darwin was using succession as a prime example of the "Struggle for Existence." "What a struggle between the several kinds of trees must have gone during the long centuries," Darwin observed, "each annually scattering its seeds by the thousand. " Henry had been out to watch those scatterings, had observed their effects several times.[51]

More importantly, *On the Origin of Species,* while a ground-breaking presentation of a seminal theory in biology, was in large measure a call to action on the part of researchers. Darwin knew he was on firm, almost unapproachable ground, but emphasized in the Introduction that "This Abstract, which I now publish, must necessarily be imperfect."[52] Throughout the *Origin,* Darwin noted and outlined myriad studies that would further confirm his ideas. While summarizing the content of two imperative chapters on the geographic distribution of species, he emphasized "how profoundly ignorant we are with respect to the many and curious means of occasional transport,—a subject which has hardly ever been properly experimentised on; if we bear in mind how often a species may have ranged continuously over a wide area, and then have become extinct in the intermediate tracts, I think the difficulties in believing that all the individuals of the same species, wherever located, have descended from the same parents, are not insuperable."[53]

Countless observations of the agency of wind, water, birds, animals, reptiles, lay buried in the almost daily journal entries Thoreau had recorded since 1850. For Henry, introduction to the theory of natural selection became a catalyst for his own research.

Not everyone was enthralled by Darwin's work, to say the least. Many clerics quickly dismissed it, of course, but the scientific community divided as well. Asa Gray's far more esteemed Harvard colleague, Louis Agassiz, openly disputed Darwin's ideas. Thoreau had long associated with Agassiz, serving as a specimen collector for the great naturalist in the late 1840s, actually meeting him at Waldo Emerson's in March 1857.[54] But Thoreau was nothing if not an independent thinker. Some minor disagreements passed between the two men at Emerson's dinner table, and Thoreau privately disagreed with Agassiz on more fundamental issues, namely speciation and spontaneous generation. Agassiz (along with Emerson, Horace Greeley, and many other intelligent people) believed that various creatures such as mice and weeds could appear in new locations spontaneously—without parents or seeds. Such an occurrence would prove a death blow to Darwin's theories.[55] Thoreau, well acquainted with the several agents of seed dispersal available in nature, did not believe this for a moment.

After publishing Thoreau's "Succession of Forest Trees," Horace Greeley challenged the essay, writing in December 1860 to describe what he thought were two instances of spontaneous generation. Henry took the time to provide a long and carefully detailed critique of Greeley's contention, which Thoreau dismissed as "*pure theory*, without a single example to support it." Noting that "there are several plants peculiarly fitted to reclothe the earth when laid bare by whatever cause," Henry argued conclusively that simple lack of observation led to belief in the magic of spontaneous generation. Plants supposedly never present in a forest before a fire were actually there all the while; seeds thought to be sprouted from scorched earth were borne to the site by the wind.[56]

Summarizing his thoughts on the question in March 1861, Thoreau observed in his journal: "If the pine seed is spontaneously generated, why is it not so produced in the Old World as well as in America? I have no doubt that it can be raised from seed in corresponding situations there, and that it will seem to spring up just as mysteriously there as it does here. Yet, if it will grow so *after* the seed has been carried thither, why should it not before, if the seed is unnecessary to its production?"[57]

Thoreau also dismissed the minute divisions of species in Agassiz's classifications of nature, commenting to Emerson that, "If Agassiz sees two thrushes so alike that they bother the ornithologist to discriminate them, he insists they are two species; but if he sees Humboldt and Fred Cogswell, he insists they come from one ancestor."[58]

Although Thoreau abhorred the idea of being thought a scientist, he quickly realized that he possessed knowledge that bore critically on the scientific debate taking shape in 1860. Suddenly, the welter of observation that had occupied him for the previous ten years assumed a definite shape in his mind. He took a renewed interest in the problems of seed dispersion and plant succession, noting in late January 1860 the presence of a pine wood "where the wind chanced to let the seed lie at last, and the grasses and blackberry vines have not yet been killed by them." Two months later he was noting the presence of English cherry trees on a hilltop overlooking Walden Pond, apparently planted by the birds. By summer he was carefully studying the windblown movement of pine pollen.[59]

The first fruit of this new and concentrated effort to understand succession was an address delivered at the Middlesex County Cattle Show in Concord on September 20, 1860. The lecture, entitled "The Succession of Forest Trees," was for Thoreau little more than an interim report, simplifying and summarizing his findings on the subject since his initial discoveries of 1856. Yet the lecture, which detailed the role of birds, animals, and wind in the rotation and succession of forests, was a fascinating revelation to his neighbors. The essay was in fact meant for the ears of the farming and landholding community, rather than the scientific audience—an important point. Although Thoreau apparently was preparing at this same time to address the scientific issues associated with succession in an appropriate medium at great length, the purpose of this particular essay was far more local and immediate. Henry was determined to bring to a halt the almost universal abuse of the forests in Concord and New England generally. Presenting the complex facts of succession in a homespun fashion, he hoped to promote both the preservation of some of the town's more vulnerable forest tracts and a wiser use of the rest. Rather than a scientific paper, "The Succession of Forest Trees" was an artfully designed polemic, a plea for conservation. He focused on the most fundamental successions—the pine to oak and the oak to pine—describing the means and the results of seed movement in a tone designed to appeal to the common farmers of Middlesex County. In his journal, Henry criticized the farmers' abuse and mismanagement of their woodlots. None of that appeared in the lecture.

Instead, he appealed to their intelligence and their own sense of economic well-being, asking only, "Would it not be well to consult with Nature at the outset? for she is the most extensive and experienced planter of us all."

The lecture was an immediate success, and was rapidly printed and reprinted in such diverse venues as *The Transactions of the Middlesex Agricultural Society,* the New York *Weekly Tribune,* the *New England Farmer,* and the *Century* magazine. Probably more people read this essay than any other of Thoreau's shorter works during his lifetime.[60]

Lying behind the descriptions of relatively simple successions included in his conservation essay was a growing wealth of material on dispersal and succession, knowledge of particular value to the scientific community in the newly dawning age of Darwinian biology. But there was much more to be done before Thoreau could present his findings in the exacting manner necessary to science. Beginning on October 6, 1860, and extending to the third of December, Henry devoted himself almost completely to the study of seed dispersion in Concord's forests and berry fields. The work became so consuming that he almost wholly neglected the general observations of seasonal phenomena that had characterized his journals over the previous ten years. Not even the John Brown episode had so completely arrested his attention.[61]

Henry quickly established a sense of order and method to the undertaking. On October 20 he committed to his journal an inventory classifying the six kinds of woods to be found in New England towns. Of these, two—primitive woods (the trees never cut) and second growth (the trees cut only once)—no longer could be found in Concord. Predominant in the town was what Henry called primitive woodland, lands where the trees had been cut time and again, but always permitted to grow back. Also to be found in Concord were woodlands cleared one or more times, new woods that grew up in abandoned croplands, and artificially planted woods. Henry appointed himself the task of determining the growth history of each of these woodland types.[62]

By early November, he completed an exacting mathematical study of the growth patterns of pitch pines, employing data on circumference and the number of rings both in old stumps and in living trees he cut himself. Armed with these measurements, he could estimate the ages of living pitch pine stands, enabling him to date the various pine forests.[63]

Also in early November, Henry compiled a list of all the forests currently standing in Concord, arranging them into three groups according to dominant species: white pine, pitch pine, and hardwood. He could now distinguish among twelve different kinds of forest in the town. For example, white pines might stand in primitive woodland, occasionally cleared woodland, former cropland, or artificially planted land; as might pitch pine or hardwood. Each of these twelve types of forest would have its own peculiar growth history, although the same essential natural laws would govern all.[64]

Thoreau quickly discovered that the *shape* of a forest very much depended on which seeds had sprouted and come to dominate the local landscape. Hardwood forests, sprouted from heavy seeds, tended to be circular, as they were primarily planted by animals. Pine woods, grown from light seed broadcast by the wind, tended to be crescent-shaped and arrayed at a distance from the parent tree. But there were variations, some dictated by seed physiology—maple seeds, for example, were also borne by the wind—and some by human interference. Thoreau readily admitted that "There are many such problems in forest geometry to be solved."[65]

Thoreau found that the largest impediment to the regeneration of the forests in Concord was human intervention. The landowners, possessing virtually no knowledge of any of the agents of forest succession, shot squirrels and birds with impunity, burned off sprouting woodland, and interfered in countless other foolish ways with the cycles of nature. Henry found that the owner was more often than not working against his or her own interests. "It is evident that in a wood that has been left alone for the largest period the greatest regularity and harmony in the disposition of the trees will be observed, while in our ordinary woods man has often interfered and favored the growth of other kinds than are best fitted to grow there naturally. To some, which he does not want, he allows no place at all."[66]

The influence of Darwinian ideas of natural selection is evident in the passage. Thoreau bore Darwin's work in mind during much of this intensive period of study. His most extensive journal comment on Darwin's theories in the context of his own work came on October 18, 1860.

> We find ourselves in a world that is already planted, but is also still being planted as at first. We say of some plants that they grow in wet places and of others that they grow in desert places. The truth is that their seeds are scattered almost everywhere, but here only do they succeed. Unless

> you can show me the pool where the lily was created, I shall believe that the oldest fossil lillies which the geologist has detected (if this is found fossil) originated in that locality in a similar manner to these of Beck Stow's. We see thus how the fossil lillies which the geologist has detected are dispersed, as well as these we carry in our hands to church.
>
> The development theory implies a greater vital force in nature, because it is more flexible and accomodating and equivalent to a sort of constant *new* creation.[67]

By extending and intensifying his own long-standing studies of seed dispersion, Thoreau could advance the cause of Darwinian biology while retaining his own focus on nature as an interactive whole.[68]

At roughly the same time that he committed these thoughts to his journal, Henry began work on the first of two sustained manuscripts intended to embody his research into seed dispersion. The first, tentatively entitled "The Dispersion of Seeds," embodied a vastly expanded version of the theories originally presented in his lecture on "The Succession of Forest Trees." The work began with a minute descriptive inventory of the different kinds of tree seeds to be found in Concord, detailing the varying ability of each seed to be planted by wind, water, or animals. A second manuscript, begun in December, was intended to present his findings on "Wild Fruits." Although this second essay again focused on the principles of dispersion and the interactions of plants and animals, Thoreau adopted a different tone for this work, one that would perhaps have been more familiar to his long-standing readers. He began this essay with a discussion of the relationship between wild fruits and people, arguing that the journey to pick a fruit or berry in the wild was a valuable and essential part of the process of eating it, a kind of indelible education in wildness. This was the mirror of the image he had employed in his lecture on "Wild Apples," which detailed domesticated nature gone wild once more. From there he launched into an inventory and discussion of the wild fruits of Concord, their uses in nature, and their significance to humankind.[69]

The two essays shared much in common, both in content and intent. Many of the agents at work in the dispersion of tree seeds also had a role to play in the growth and consumption of the wild fruits. Each essay was descriptive of the same basic principles. More importantly, Thoreau extended to each essay the same basic ideals that had governed his journals: precise description of fact derived from personal field observation and wedded to carefully chosen secondary source material garnered from pertinent books, expressed in a style at once exacting and eminently readable. Each essay was to be a model of scientific knowledge presented as literary art. And more importantly, even as he wrote each carefully detailed paragraph describing one small aspect of his subject, he bore in mind the image of a complete natural whole infused with the spirit of the universe.[70]

As he committed his ideas to paper, Henry continued to gather further information. Continually developing new theories that he quickly tested by field observations, he generally confirmed his own surmises with perfect accuracy.[71] On December 2, Henry recognized a difficulty in accounting for hickories growing seemingly alone on Smith's Hill and other localities throughout the town. The following day, he set out for the hill to investigate the mystery of hickory dispersion, determining finally that animals planted both acorns and hickory nuts in open fields beyond the edges of the established wood, but that only the more persistent hickories tended to survive.[72]

Thoreau carried with him on this expedition the beginnings of a cold, perhaps contracted from Bronson Alcott. The following day he undertook a survey in the village. That evening the first snow fell. The cold and a nagging cough confined Henry to the house for a week. When he ventured out finally to fulfill a speaking engagement in Waterbury, Connecticut, he returned home the following day far worse in health. The cold had by that time developed into bronchitis. Very soon, old tubercular lesions in his lungs would reopen. Henry Thoreau's body began to diminish.[73]

He remained in the house for much of the winter, continuing work on his dispersion manuscripts. From December through February he worked at the "Wild Fruits" essay as much as his health would allow; from March to early May he took up "The Dispersion of Seeds." Ranging back through his journals, he drew almost verbatim entries from as early as 1856, incorporating isolated instances of observation into the larger web of plant and animal relations he now so fully understood. He studied carefully the works of other botanists and incorporated their ideas into his work as well, especially the writings of Englishman John Claudius Loudon, along with Audubon, classical writers such as Pliny, and, of course, Darwin.[74]

In the spring, in an effort to bring relief to his worsening respiratory problems, Thoreau undertook a two-month journey to Minnesota with Horace Mann Jr. Departing in mid-May, 1861, the two botanized at every opportunity along the way. Yet Henry showed little of his old enthusiasm during this trip, and never bothered to write up the usual field notes upon returning home in mid-July. He had largely abandoned his journal in favor of the two dispersion manuscripts by that time, making only sporadic entries before quitting the journal altogether on November 3, 1861.[75]

His health continued to deteriorate, leaving him little energy for work of any kind. By early 1862, "The Dispersion of Seeds" amounted to 354 handwritten pages, "Wild Fruits" to 631. But each was little more than a rough-hewn first draft, confused in order, incomplete in thought. To turn either into a completed book demanded more resources than Henry had left to give.[76]

Any temptation he may have felt to struggle on with these long and complex new pieces disappeared in February 1862. The *Atlantic Monthly,* now managed by Ticknor and Fields, the publishers of *Walden,* wrote to Thoreau requesting contributions. Thoreau, fully aware that he was dying, seized this last opportunity to earn some money for his family. Abandoning his uncompleted manuscripts, he worked with his sister Sophia to produce publishable versions of his most recent lectures. In rapid succession, he submitted "Autumnal Tints," "Life without Principle" (based on his "What Shall It Profit?" address), and "Walking." He also made arrangements for new editions of both *Walden* and the book that remained to the end his personal favorite (perhaps because of the several kinds of anguish it had brought him), *A Week on the Concord and Merrimack Rivers.*[77]

By April he could no longer speak aloud. Coughing fits racked him through the spring nights, leaving him to face the following day weaker then ever. A parade of visitors paid homage to a man facing death as bravely as anyone they had ever seen. The end came on the morning of May 6, 1862.[78]

Biographers make much of the cheerful equanimity with which Thoreau faced the destruction of his own body. The numerous testimonies to his brave demise close the circle for the chronicler of a life; a death accepted in perfect harmony with the life gone before is a fitting end to a good story. Moreover, too many of Henry's biographers seem to think that 1862 was a good time for him to die; that the creative spark that brought forth *Walden* had pretty much burned out by that time anyway.[79]

Henry Thoreau deserves better. His death was a tragedy, and not merely for the obvious and usual reasons. Tuberculosis truncated a life devoted to discovering nature, killed an intelligence that had looked at living things in a way totally foreign to his time, his place, his country. In an era when virtually everyone in general and farmers and business people in particular viewed nature as so much commodity, Thoreau saw all life as equal to his own. As scientists more than ever pushed themselves into the practice of mincing and classifying a nature they viewed as dead matter, Thoreau saw all life infused with the spirit of the universe, saw the organic earth and all that lived upon it as an interrelated whole embodying the mind of God. Henry Thoreau's was a sublime vision of nature, and *Walden* was little more than a superficial summary. He had much more to say.

In 1860, Henry found a new means to express this vision. Inspired in part by Darwin, armed with a vast mountain of observations stretching back over ten years, he began two separate, yet closely related, writing projects intended to relate in part what he had discovered about nature's ways. Good health lasted only two months after he began. He struggled on for another year as his body gradually betrayed him, but it was no good. Neither manuscript came close to completion. Readers never got to hear more than a sample of what Henry Thoreau knew. "It seems an injury that he should leave in the midst his broken task which none else can finish," Emerson eulogized at his friend's funeral. Four decades later, Ellery Channing recalled that Thoreau "had lived and written as if to live forty years longer; his work was laid out for a long life."[80]

This incompleteness made Thoreau's death a genuine tragedy, and what happened in the wake of his death was also tragic. No one understood those final, incomplete manuscripts. Waldo Emerson, Sophia Thoreau, Ellery Channing, Henry's friends H. G. O. Blake and Franklin Sanborn—not one of them could understand what Henry had been getting at. The work was too far removed from the popular prejudices, the images of nature current in 1862. Left unpublished by his contemporaries, the works gradually scattered.[81] Thoreau's reputation, minimal in the nineteenth century, grew slowly with the passing of the generations, but came to rest almost wholly on the impressions to be gained from a reading of *Walden*. Thoreau's vision of nature, was, if not wholly lost, diminished in consequence.

With the publication of Henry's last manuscripts one hundred thirty-one years after he abandoned them, the world can at least capture a glimpse of his intent, share a little of his joy in the diverse expressions of the spirit to be found in nature. Both "The Dispersion of Seeds" and "Wild Fruits" exist only in rough and incomplete form, with passages undoubtedly missing, but they offer a further insight into a mind that examined the so-called desert of wild nature and found the spirit of God living there.

It is a vision we have never needed more.

What shall we do with a man who is afraid of the woods—their solitude & darkness—What salvation is there for him? God is silent and mysterious.

— *Journal,* November 16, 1850

7 A VISION OF NATURE

WHAT MAKES AN ENVIRONMENTALIST?

Confronted with the disturbing, disquieting, often horrifying barrage of information concerning the condition of the good earth today, a decision to embrace environmental values is neither surprising nor unique. To demonstrate an interest in the ways of the wild, to express a concern for the survival of forest and pond, is merely to demonstrate wisdom and good sense. But Henry Thoreau lived in an entirely different world, a world comprised of overweening pride and confidence in the ongoing triumph of material progress, shackled to an assumption that nature was limitless and existed exclusively for human benefit. "It is apparent enough to me," Thoreau wrote, "that only one or two of my townsmen or acquaintances . . . feel or at least obey any strong attraction drawing them toward the forest or nature, but all almost without exception gravitate exclusively toward men or society."[1] To speak a word for the love and protection of wild nature was to speak alone.

Henry Thoreau did not invent environmentalism and bequeath the concept to modern society—he was not even familiar with the term. As close as he ever came to such terminology was to occasionally employ the expression "nature's economy," an idiom signifying an understanding of the reciprocal relationships among all nature's parts. Thoreau employed those words sparingly and perhaps uncomfortably, comprehending that there was more at work in nature than a sort of free market behavior writ large.[2] None of the other words so familiar to the modern vocabulary—ecology, conservation, preservation—were in use in Thoreau's time at all. The need for them had not yet been recognized.

Henry Thoreau's achievement was to look America's faith in material progress squarely in the face, shake himself free of the underlying assumptions, and clearly perceive the conditions the system created, both for nature and among human beings. Henry thought for himself, and originally. Doing so, he discovered a side of nature no one else suspected, articulated a vision none of his contemporaries could truly share. He reformed himself, and in doing so, established a model for a different human relationship with nature for those who would come after him.

Thoreau's path to what modern society would label an environmental world view was in no sense an easy one. Certainly he did not set out to be a writer in 1837 with the idea in mind. Despite a reputation to the contrary, young Thoreau was not even very well acquainted with nature, nor was he much interested. Under the spell of the transcendentalists—especially Waldo Emerson—Henry sought to find the proper road to the universe of the spirit and to describe that proper path in poetry and high-flown prose. He gathered several arrows to his quiver—questions of proper virtue, political reform, history—and shot off each in turn, eager to make his own transcendental understandings heard amid the great rush of business in New England. Nature, dismissed by his friend Waldo as perhaps nonexistent, was not important enough to attract much of Henry's time.

Either Thoreau's transcendental understandings or his technical skills as a poet and essayist were unsatisfactory at this stage of his life. In seven long years he made almost no money at writing, succeeded in finding no satisfactory outlets for his work, save the Emerson-sponsored *Dial,* which folded in 1844. A lesser individual might have thrown the pen away, turned to teaching, farming, pencil-making. Henry determined instead to write a book, an elegy to his late brother. To obtain the necessary peace and quiet, he moved to a solitary cabin in the woods in 1845.

Only in the most abstract sense did nature hold attractions for Henry as he moved into the cabin at Walden Pond. He had long sought encouragement in nature, but attached little importance to the specific species greeting his senses. At Walden, the surrounding forest brought beauty, quiet, peace of mind, perhaps inspiration. It was not a subject on which to concentrate when writing. Roughing out the first draft of *A Week on the Concord and Merrimack Rivers,* he found the necessary outdoor passages extraordinarily difficult. As he wrote up the initial pages of the manuscript that became *Walden,* he neglected the woods almost completely. Nature was not Thoreau's subject in 1845 and early 1846.

Nature found Henry, more than the other way around. As he worked over his Thomas Carlyle essay in the spring of 1846, the sounds and sights of nature impressed themselves so forcefully that Thoreau began recording them—without comment, without moral—in his journals. He opened his eyes a little, wondered "what are these pines & these birds about?" That autumn, on a vacation adventure in Maine, nature unexpectedly tore the blinders from his eyes completely. Atop Ktaadn, nature, "powerful gigantic aweful and beautiful, Untamed forever," took away all his confident answers, left him only with questions: "*Who* are we? *where* are we?" If he were ever to answer such questions, he could never ignore nature again.

The next three years saw the completion of a variety of projects already in motion when the mountaintop overawed Thoreau. Committed to completion of *A Week,* hopeful of delivering *Walden* hard on the heels of this first work, he had little time to give to nature. But the lessons of the pond and the mountain were not forgotten. Even after leaving his home in the woods to live in society again, his newfound view of nature continued to inform his writing. Most importantly, his ideas took the form of a challenge to Emerson: "Is not Nature, rightly read, that of which she is taken to be the symbol merely?" Nature not only existed, it was the embodiment of the universal spirit, the equal of God and humanity.

Henry published this idea to the world in 1849, and the world ignored him. Amid a series of crushing personal blows, the failure of *A Week on the Concord and Merrimack Rivers* was the most crushing of all. Studying matters honestly, Henry was little further along in his career as a writer than he had been in 1844. Five years devoted almost exclusively to his craft, and next to nothing in funds or notoriety to show for it.

Personal growth was another matter. In learning to view the world honestly and individually, Henry Thoreau had grown enormously, grown so much that he had outstripped even Emerson and the other transcendentalists. He was looking at the world with eyes and mind wholly unique in the New England of his time. He alone perceived the unsurpassed importance of nature, the presence of the spirit in the forests, the ponds, the mountains, the animals and birds he loved. Nature was the one friend that never deserted him.

Searching through the wreckage of his career in late 1849 and 1850, Henry seized on wild nature as his proper subject. Nature alone seemed responsive to the small spark of spirit within him, seemed worthy of his time, his study, his pen. All the great variety of subjects that had captured his attention through the first twelve years of his career fell away. Nature alone remained. The time had come to discover what the pines and the birds were really about.

Having determined to study nature, Thoreau attacked the problem from a variety of angles, some obvious, others less so. He spent more time than ever walking in Concord's wilder places. Although he did not walk as far as formerly, he saw more, became bewildered, almost intoxicated with the sheer variety and complexity of his observations. Very quickly he began to organize his sightings according to the calendar, attempting to bring some cohesion to the volume of data he collected. Recognizing the need for greater technical knowledge, he undertook a voracious program of reading in the natural sciences—contemporary writers such as Darwin and Audubon, older scientific works of Bartram and Linneaus, even classical authors including Pliny. Relying heavily on the manuals of Wilson, Gray, and other naturalists, his plant and animal identifications grew more exacting. Gradually he learned to employ botany boxes, measures, telescopes, and microscopes to assist his native senses.

Despite this devotion to the technical study of nature, Thoreau never lost sight of his larger goal: to understand the whole of nature and the complex interworkings among species. Two additional reading projects assisted him: the studies of Oriental religious literature and the history of Native Americans. Neither provided him direct information regarding the exact literal workings of nature, but each rendered a universal world view that enabled him to maintain sight of his goal. Both the Hindus and the Native Americans believed explicitly in the presence of spirit in nature: that each plant, each animal was an expression of the presence of God. The Hindus especially maintained that the entire universe was one god, Vishnu, in a multiplicity of aspects. Understanding that idea, Thoreau could bear in mind as he identified each plant that he was merely naming a part of a larger whole. As his studies intensified, he could perceive that nature behaved as a vast cycle, returning always to the same sources of spiritual renewal. The human idea of progress was a sad delusion.

Armed with that knowledge, Henry could prevent himself from being wholly immersed in science. That science was a useful tool, he would not deny. But it was only a tool, a means of attaining knowledge, and not an end in itself. At bottom, the very concept of science was flawed—there was no such thing as a neutral observer—a problem Thoreau never disregarded. To understand nature, the good student needed science, but never absolutely, and never to the neglect of the lessons taught by Native American and Hindu theologies. Nor to the neglect of one's own proper moral sense. Science dictated the necessity of killing for the sake of knowledge, but what was to be learned of life by deliberately and artificially dictating death?

At the outset of his nature studies, Thoreau sought to present his ideas in an array of literary settings; advancing a radical appreciation of wild nature in lectures such as "The Wild," incorporating his vision of a cyclical world of nature into *Walden.* As his knowledge intensified, the ability to incorporate even minor aspects into smaller literary works became correspondingly difficult. For four years after the publication of *Walden,* he gave up the attempt altogether. The journal became the sole record of this vast inquiry into nature, a daily log of discovery that, despite its bulk, still captured only a tiny portion of the natural whole. Henry was wise enough to recognize that he was only one observer, and a biased one at that. He would never understand the mind of God, but perhaps he could catch a glimpse of that mind in action if he studied nature closely enough. The journal tracked his efforts.

As the years passed, Henry came to be impressed not only by nature's complexity, but also by its vulnerability. He largely concluded that humankind was part and parcel of the natural whole, but this did not prevent him from seeing that people could, through an intelligence at once superior to all other creatures and yet too limited to foresee the results of its own actions, do enormous damage. Out of his studies grew both disgust and impassioned desire to mitigate the impact of human folly. He called for preservation: the creation of forested parks within each New England town, the setting aside of original growth in the wilds of Maine. He urged also the wise use of the forests, and put his own researches at the disposal of humanity to promote more careful management of resources. Faced with the destruction of wild nature at every turn, Thoreau saw the value of both preservation and conservation.

The material he drew from his journals for the lectures of the late 1850s was chosen for this purpose. "Autumn Tints" attracted the attention of a too-acquisitive public to the beauty of nature; "Wild Apples" underscored the value of the wild; "The Succession of Forest Trees" explained the role of nature in proper forest management. Thoreau adapted portions of his carefully acquired knowledge to instruct his neighbors, attempting in the process to save the face of nature he valued most.

Beyond these utilitarian efforts lay the larger vision that informed the entirety of Thoreau's studies during the 1850s. The inner working of the natural whole, always obvious, always elusive, beckoned Henry. After several years of meticulous observation, he began to organize his data in phenological fashion, drafting charts, crafting voluminous supporting notes. The cycle of nature was plainly present, yet no two years were exactly alike. Describing the vast and minutely unpredictable cycle of nature was no simple task. The phenological calendar sputtered.

In 1860, a reading of Charles Darwin's *On the Origin of Species* both provided Thoreau an organizing principle for at least a significant portion of his vast fund of knowledge and convinced him that the world needed the information he had collected. By fall he embarked on two projects that demonstrated a profound knowledge of what our modern society would label ecological principles. In wide-ranging discussions on "The Dispersion of Seeds" and "Wild Fruits," he demonstrated an exacting knowledge of each of the many species he discussed, and more importantly, the interrelationships among them all. Squirrel and tree were mutually dependent, and the behavior of each was governed by the conditions of soil and weather, the actions of birds, insects, and other creatures. Nature was a vast circle on which everything spun inseparably together.

No sooner did the key to presenting this vast fund of knowledge fall into Thoreau's hand than he lost the ability to use it. Less than three months into his studies, tuberculosis struck him down. For another year he could still write and read, but without the fundamental ingredient of the daily walk, the work was incomplete. Book learning and personal field learning had always gone hand in hand in Henry's efforts.

With his death came an odd, incomplete, curiously truncated literary legacy. There was *Walden,* the completed masterpiece, the sole good fruit of Henry's career as far as most could see. This work offered little more than a partial impression of Thoreau's vast and important work, as well as creating an illusion regarding the time he actually spent living by the pond. There was the journal, full of seemingly "undigested" nature observation, shorn of the mastering intellect that carried the necessary keys to understanding the content, leaving other readers to intuit organization and intent. A daunting task, given that Henry's way of thinking was completely foreign to most of his contemporaries. There were the last "ecological" manuscripts; unfinished, inscrutable, untranslatable. Forgotten. The nineteenth century, and much of the twentieth, never understood just what Henry Thoreau was about.

As the conservation-preservation idea took shape and grew in the latter half of the nineteenth century, a small but influential coterie of writers came to see Thoreau as an important voice. That voice was more often than not misunderstood. John Burroughs, following lovingly in Thoreau's footsteps, revered *Walden* and wrote exquisite passages on the creatures of the forest, yet denigrated the long journals full of raw nature observations. John Muir echoed Thoreau's concern for natural preservation, but scoffed at the idea that anyone could learn of wild nature in the little streams and woods of Concord. Thoreau's legacy to the environmental movement was built on a misunderstanding.

Stripping away the misconceptions, restoring the lost manuscripts to the light of day, Thoreau's true legacy was revealed as a complex and exciting vision of nature, one composed of an abiding belief in the spirit in nature, coupled to an exacting knowledge of the ecological whole. There may have been scientists more precise in their identifications than Henry; there may have been visionaries who envisioned a natural whole as he did, but there was no one who combined the two very different intellectual achievements so powerfully. America took more than a century to evolve the same environmental concepts that Thoreau thought out in one lifetime.

What makes an environmentalist?

A love of nature, first of all, a willingness to spend long hours out of doors, learning, refining, growing closer to nature's ways. Couple to that a willingness to learn from others, a determination to read books from diverse fields, to draw especially from the sciences without becoming fully enmeshed in the scientific method. Draw also from the beliefs of other cultures; read what the Hindus had to say about the nature of creation, listen to the voices of Native Americans, who knew well the spirits present in plant and animal. Above all, refuse to be ensnared by the intellectual traps of an economic system built on greed. Know that nature is vulnerable, that every person is a part of the nature that greed destroys. Think independently, follow the path that experienced wisdom suggests.

Henry Thoreau had no models, no guidance in finding his own path.

We at least have Henry Thoreau.

Appendix

HENRY THOREAU'S WRITING PROJECTS, 1837–49

Determined to become a published author, Henry Thoreau penned a wide-ranging assortment of poems, essays, and lectures, and eventually a book, by 1849. Drawing inspiration from transcendental ideas generally and Waldo Emerson specifically, Thoreau explored several different themes in these works. His subject matter included historic and literary biography, comparative literature, issues of moral behavior, the Greek and Roman Classics, Oriental religion, travel, and personal experience. Natural history, or nature writing of any form, was a seldom explored avenue during these years. Thoreau produced fifty-four literary pieces for public consumption during the period. Only four of these might be considered descriptive nature writing, and the definition has to be stretched considerably to include one of those.

PUBLISHED OR PRESENTED WORKS

Date	*Title*	*Type of Literature (Subject)*	*Where Published or Delivered*
Nov. 25, 1837	"Death of Anna Jones"	news obituary	*Yeoman's Gazette*
Apr. 11, 1838	"Society"	lecture	Concord Lyceum
July 1840	"Sympathy"	poem	*The Dial*
July 1840	"Aulus Persius Flaccus"	translation	*The Dial*
Jan. 1841	"Stanzas"	poem	*The Dial*
July 1841	"Sic Vita"	poem	*The Dial*
Oct. 1841	"Friendship"	poem	*The Dial*

Date	Title	Type of Literature (Subject)	Where Published or Delivered
July 1842	"Natural History of Massachusetts"	review essay (nature)	*The Dial*
July 1842	"Metrical Prayer"	poem	*The Dial*
Oct. 1842	"The Black Knight"	poem	*The Dial*
Oct. 1842	"The Inward Morning"	poem	*The Dial*
Oct. 1842	"Free Love"	poem	*The Dial*
Oct. 1842	"The Poet's Delay"	poem	*The Dial*
Oct. 1842	"Rumors from an Aeolian Harp"	poem	*The Dial*
Oct. 1842	"The Moon"	poem	*The Dial*
Oct. 1842	"To the Maiden of the East"	poem	*The Dial*
Oct. 1842	"Summer Rain"	poem	*The Dial*
Jan. 1843	"The Laws of Menu"	selections from Oriental literature	*The Dial*
Jan. 1843	"The Prometheus Bound"	translation	*The Dial*
Jan. 1843	"A Walk to Wachusett"	transcendental walking essay	*Boston Miscellany*
Feb. 8, 1843	"Sir Walter Raleigh"	lecture (literary biography)	Concord Lyceum
Apr. 1843	"Anacreon"	translation	*The Dial*
Apr. 1843	"Ethnical Scriptures"	selections from Oriental literature	*The Dial*
Apr. 1843	"To a Stray Fowl"	poem	*The Dial*
Apr. 1843	"Orphics: I. Smoke; II. Haze"	poem	*The Dial*
Apr. 1843	"Dark Ages"	essay	*The Dial*
Apr. 1843	"Friendship, from Chaucer's 'Romaunt of the Rose'"	translation	*The Dial*
Oct. 1843	"Ethnical Scriptures; Chinese Four Books"	selections from Oriental literature	*The Dial*
Oct. 1843	"A Winter Walk"	transcendental walking essay	*The Dial*
Oct. 1843	"The Landlord"	essay (popular idealism)	*United States Magazine and Democratic Review*

Nov. 1843	"Paradise (to Be) Regained"	review essay (utopianism)	*United States Magazine and Democratic Review*
Nov. 29, 1843	"The Ancient Poets"	lecture (literary biography)	Concord Lyceum
Jan. 1844	"Homer, Ossian, Chaucer"	essay (literary biography)	*The Dial*
Jan. 1844	"Pindar"	translation	*The Dial*
Jan. 1844	"The Preaching of Buddha"	selections from Oriental literature	*The Dial*
Jan. 1844	"Ethnical Scriptures: Hermes Trismegistus"	selections from Hermetic philosophy	*The Dial*
Apr. 1844	"Herald of Freedom"	essay (anti-slavery)	*The Dial*
Apr. 1844	"Fragments of Pindar"	translation	*The Dial*
Mar. 25, 1845	"Concord River"	lecture (natural history)	Concord Lyceum
Mar. 28, 1845	"Wendell Phillips before the Concord Lyceum"	letter (anti-slavery)	*The Liberator*
Apr. 2, 1846	"The Writing Style of Thomas Carlyle"	lecture (literary biography)	Concord Lyceum
Jan. 19, 1847	"A History of Myself"	lecture (early *Walden* material)	Lincoln, Mass.[a]
Mar. and Apr. 1847	"Thomas Carlyle and His Works"	essay (literary biography)	*Graham's Magazine*
Jan. 1848	"The Maine Woods"	lecture (nature and travel)	Concord Lyceum
Jan. 26, 1848	"The Relationship of the Individual to the State"	lecture (moral reform)	Concord Lyceum
Feb. 16, 1848	"The Rights and Duties of the Individual in Relation to Government"	lecture (moral reform)	Concord Lyceum
July–Nov. 1848	"Ktaadn and the Maine Woods"	essay (nature and travel)	*Union Magazine*
Nov. 22, 1848	"Student Life in New England and Its Economy"	lecture (early *Walden* material)	Salem, Mass.[b]
Jan. 3, 1849	"White Beans and Walden Pond"	lecture (early *Walden* material)	Concord Lyceum[c]
Feb. 28, 1849	"Student Life, Its Aims and Employment"	lecture (early *Walden* material)	Salem, Mass.
Mar. 21, 1849	"Economy"	lecture (early *Walden* material)	Portland, Me.[d]

Date	Title	Type of Literature (Subject)	Where Published or Delivered
Apr. 27, 1849	"Life in the Woods"	lecture (early *Walden* material)	Worcester, Mass.
May 1849	"Resistance to Civil Government"	essay (moral reform)	*Aesthetic Papers*
May 30, 1849	*A Week on the Concord and Merrimac Rivers*	book (some nature description)	James Munroe & Co.

Note: All of these *Walden* lectures considered aspects of personal economy and proper moral and ethical behavior. Any nature description was incidental.

a. Repeated at Lincoln, Mass., 19 Jan. 1847.

b. Repeated at Gloucester, Mass., 20 Dec. 1848.

c. Repeated at Lincoln, Mass., 6 Mar. 1849; Worcester, Mass., 3 May 1849.

d. Repeated at Worcester, Mass., 20 Apr. 1849.

UNPUBLISHED WORKS

Date	Title	Type of Literature (Subject)	Where Refused
July 1840	"The Service"	essay (moral reform)	*The Dial,* M. Fuller, editor
Sept. 1847	"Walden"	book	not submitted
Nov. 1847	"A Week on the Concord and Merrimac Rivers"	book	Wiley and Putnam

JOURNALS

Thoreau wrote fifteen manuscript volumes of journal material between October 1837 and January 1850. Many of these exist only in part, as Thoreau often removed leaves for inclusion in lectures or essays. He regarded these volumes as raw material for other literary projects, rather than as self-contained works. The nature observations contained in these volumes may be summarized as follows:

Oct. 1837–Sept. 1841	5 vols.	Virtually all observations condensed into "Natural History of Massachusetts," *The Dial,* Jan. 1842.
Nov. 1841–Jan. 1844	4 vols.	Most observations copied into "Long Book" Journal for later inclusion in *A Week on the Concord and Merrimac Rivers.*

Fall 1842–Spring 1848	5 vols.	All volumes used during Walden stay. The "Long Book" is devoted to drafts of *A Week;* two volumes used for literary projects between July 1845 and early spring 1846 include sporadic nature observations; the "Berg" journal is devoted almost wholly to the Ktaadn adventure; a last journal kept from winter 1846 to spring 1848 was used for drafts of "Ktaadn" and *A Week.*
Summer 1848–Apr. 1850	1 vol.	Used mainly for literary projects. The character of this volume changes in the last few leaves, as Thoreau began to treat the journal as an integral work. Regular nature observation began with the next volume.

Notes

INTRODUCTION

1. Henry David Thoreau, *The Writings of Henry David Thoreau: Journal,* gen. ed. John Broderick (Princeton University Press, 1986–92), 3:69–70. Prior to 1986, the standard edition of Thoreau's journals was the fourteen-volume edition edited by Bradford Torrey and Francis H. Allen, published by Houghton Mifflin in 1906. The Princeton edition has gradually displaced these volumes. As of this writing, four volumes of the Princeton edition have been published, including all known journal material extending to April 1852. In the balance of these reference notes, the Princeton volumes will be referenced as *J*(P), while the older Houghton Mifflin volumes will be referenced simply as *J*.

2. Thoreau, *J*(P) 3:69–70.

3. Thoreau's devotion to nature study has been noted and studied ranging back at least as far as Henry S. Salt, whose *Life of Henry David Thoreau* initially appeared in 1890 (a new edition, featuring Salt's revisions through 1908, was published by the University of Illinois Press, Champaign, in 1993. See especially pp. 62–69). The first scholarly attempt to place Thoreau's role in the development of ecological science was Donald Worster's three-chapter sequence entitled "Thoreau's Romantic Ecology" in *Nature's Economy: A History of Ecological Ideas* (Cambridge: Cambridge University Press, 1977), pp. 57–111 (Cambridge University Press issued a revised edition of this work in 1995). Historians of science have severely criticized Worster, arguing that his history does not trace the origins of true scientific ecology, in which Thoreau had little actual part, but rather something Worster calls "Arcadian Ecology," apparently an intellectual predecessor to modern "Deep Ecology," which is philosophic rather than scientific (see Robert P. McIntosh, *The Background of Ecology: Concept and Theory* [Cambridge: Cambridge University Press, 1985], pp. 15–19). The current consensus seems to be that although Thoreau practiced in relative obscurity and had virtually no immediate impact on scientific thinking, the studies he undertook in the 1850s were in fact sound and orig-

inal scientific ecology. (For a bibliographic demonstration of the high scientific regard for Thoreau's work in limnology and forest succession, see Robin S. McDowell, "Thoreau in the Current Scientific Literature," *Thoreau Society Bulletin,* no. 143 [1978]:2 and no. 172 [1985]:3–4.) The most thorough study of Thoreau's place in the development of science, natural history, and nature study is Lawrence Buell, *The Environmental Imagination: Thoreau, Nature Writing, and the Formation of American Culture* (Cambridge, Mass.: Belknap Press of Harvard University Press, 1995). Buell's "Thoreau and the natural environment," in Joel Myerson, ed. *The Cambridge Guide to Thoreau* (New York: Cambridge University Press, 1995), pp. 171–93, provides an outline of the development of scholarly understanding of Thoreau's ecology, especially footnotes 19, 30, and 32.

CHAPTER I: CONCORD

1. Walter Harding, *The Days of Henry Thoreau* (New York: Dover Publications, Inc., 1982).
2. Calculated from Harding, *Days of Henry Thoreau.*
3. Ellery Channing, *Thoreau: The Poet-Naturalist* (Boston: Roberts Brothers, 1873), p. 2.
4. From Harding, *Days of Henry Thoreau.* Also useful in tracking Thoreau's day-to-day life was Raymond R. Borst, *The Thoreau Log: A Documentary Life of Henry David Thoreau, 1817–1862* (New York: G. K. Hall and Company, 1992).
5. Harding, *Days of Henry Thoreau;* Borst, *Thoreau Log.*
6. Thoreau, *J* 8:204
7. Ralph Waldo Emerson, *The Journals of Ralph Waldo Emerson,* chief ed. William H. Gilman (Cambridge, Mass.: The Belknap Press of Harvard University, 1971), 9:466; Thoreau, *J*(P) 4:317; Charles J. Woodbury, *Talks with Ralph Waldo Emerson* (New York: Baker and Taylor, 1890), pp. 76–91.
8. Thoreau, *J* 7:46.
9. Ibid., *J* 10:191; Mrs. Samuel Hoar, quoted in Franklin B. Sanborn, *Henry D. Thoreau* (Boston: Houghton Mifflin, 1882), p. 96.
10. William F. Bade, *The Life and Letters of John Muir,* 2 vols. (Boston, 1923), 2:268; Sherman Paul, *The Shores of America: Thoreau's Inward Exploration* (New York: Russell and Russell, 1958); see also F. O. Matthiessen, *The American Renaissance* (New York, 1941).
11. Jim Dodge, "Living by Life: Some Bioregional Theory and Practice," *Coevolution Quarterly* (Winter 1981):6–12; Judith Plant, "Revaluing Home: Feminism and Bioregionalism," *The New Catalyst* (January–February 1986):12.
12. Townsend Scudder, *Concord: American Town* (Boston: Little, Brown and Company, 1947).
13. Nevin M. Fenneman, *Physiography of the Eastern United States* (New York: McGraw-Hill Book Company, 1938), pp. 343–91; Neil Jorgensen, *A Guide to New England's Landscape* (Barre, Mass.: Barre Publishers, 1971); Laurence Eaton Rich-

ardson, *Concord River* (Barre: Barre Publishers, 1964), pp. 1–7; W. J. Latimer and M. O. Lanphear, *Soil Survey of Middlesex County, Massachusetts* (Washington, D.C.: United States Department of Agriculture, Bureau of Chemistry and Soils, 1929), pp. 1–56; Patrick J. Barosh, "Bedrock Geology of the Walden Woods," and Thomas Paragallo, "Soils of the Walden Ecosystem," *Thoreau's World and Ours,* ed. Edmund A. Schofield and Robert C. Baron (Golden, Colo.: North American Press, 1993), pp. 212–21, 254–59.

14. Louis Agassiz, *Geological Sketches* (Boston: J. R. Osgood and Company, 1876); Edward Lurie, *Louis Agassiz: A Life in Science* (Chicago: University of Chicago Press, 1960).

15. Stephen H. Spurr and Burton V. Barnes, *Forest Ecology,* 3d ed. (New York: John Wiley and Sons, 1980), pp. 535–56; E. Lucy Braun, *Deciduous Forests of Eastern North America* (New York: Hafner Publishing Company, 1967), pp. 443–524; W. Carter Johnson and Curtis S. Adkisson, "Airlifting the Oaks," *Natural History* 95 (October 1986):40–47; Richard Jefferson Eaton, *A Flora of Concord* (Cambridge, Mass.: Museum of Comparative Zoology, Harvard University, 1974); Mary M. Walker, "A History of Concord's Flora," *Thoreau's World,* pp. 190–95; E. C. Pielou, *After the Ice Age: The Return of Life to Glaciated North America* (Chicago: University of Chicago Press, 1991), pp. 227–50.

16. Pielou, *After the Ice Age,* pp. 251–66; Richard G. Forbis, "Eastern North America," in *North America,* ed. Shirley Gorenstein (New York: St. Martin's Press, 1975), pp. 74–101; Dean R. Snow, *The Archaeology of New England* (New York: Viking Press, 1980); Richardson, *Concord River;* Francis Jennings, *The Invasion of America: Indians, Colonialism, and the Cant of Conquest* (New York: W. W. Norton, 1978); Scudder, *Concord,* pp. 1–18.

17. Thoreau, *J* 13:186; *The Correspondence of Henry David Thoreau,* ed. Walter Harding and Carl Bode (Westport, Conn.: Greenwood Press, 1974), pp. 16–19; Robert F. Sayre, *Thoreau and the American Indians* (Princeton: Princeton University Press, 1977).

18. Sayre, *Thoreau and the American Indians,* pp. 28–58; Henry David Thoreau, "Barbarities of Civilized States," *Early Essays and Miscellanies,* ed. Joseph J. Moldenhauer and Edwin Moser, with Alexander C. Kern (Princeton: Princeton University Press, 1975), pp. 108–11; Henry David Thoreau, *A Week on the Concord and Merrimack Rivers,* ed. Carl F. Hovde (Princeton: Princeton University Press, 1980).

19. Jennings, *Invasion of America;* William Cronon, *Changes in the Land* (New York: Hill and Wang, 1983); Scudder, *Concord;* Richard Eaton, *A Flora of Concord* (Cambridge: Harvard University Press, 1974); Thoreau, *J* 10:364.

20. William Wood, *New England's Prospect,* ed. Alden T. Vaughan (Amherst: University of Massachusetts Press, 1977), pp. 33–34; Lynn White, "On Christian Arrogance toward Nature," *Environmental Decay in its Historic Context,* ed. Robert Detweiler, Jon. N. Sutherland, and Michael S. Werthman (Glen, Ill.: Scott, Foresman and Company, 1973), pp. 19–27; Roderick Nash, *Wilderness and the American Mind,* 3d ed. (New Haven, Conn.: Yale University Press, 1982), pp. 34–40.

21. Scudder, *Concord,* 1–18; Evarts B. Greene and Virginia D. Harrington, eds., *American Population before the Federal Census of 1790* (New York, 1937).

22. Thoreau, *J*(P) 4:320.

23. R. V. Reynolds, *Fuel Wood Used in the United States, 1630–1930* (Washington, D.C.: United States Department of Agriculture, Circular No. 641, 1942); A. F. Hawes, "The New England Forest in Retrospect," *Journal of Forestry* 21 (1923):209–24; Kathryn Whitford, "Thoreau and the Woodlots of Concord," *New England Quarterly* 23 (September 1950):291–306.

24. Alfred W. Crosby, *Ecological Imperialism: The Biological Expansion of Europe, 900–1900* (Cambridge, England: Cambridge University Press, 1986), pp. 145–94; Cronon, *Changes in the Land.* Information on creatures surviving in Thoreau's time was culled from the whole of his journals.

25. Douglas R. McManis, *Colonial New England: A Historical Geography* (New York: Oxford University Press, 1975), pp. 41–85; Robert A. Gross, *The Minutemen and Their World* (New York: Hill and Wang, 1976); United States Department of State, Bureau of the Census, "Census of Population," various decennial publications (Washington, D.C., 1790–1840).

26. J. B. DeBow, ed. *Abstract of the Census of the United States for 1850* (Washington, D.C., 1853); Bureau of the Census, "Schedule of Manufactures, State of Massachusetts," manuscript schedules for 1850 and 1860 (Washington, D.C.: National Archives Microfilm); Renee Garrelick, *Clothier of the Assabet: The Mill and Town of Edward Carver Damon* (Concord: Privately published by Renee Garrelick, 1988); Thoreau, *J* 4:454. See also Henry Petroski, *The Pencil: A History of Design and Circumstance* (New York: Alfred A. Knopf, 1990).

27. Thoreau, *J*(P) 4:373.

28. Ibid. 4:9; *J* 10:50; 7:497; *J*(P) 3:277–78; 4:95; *J* 5:472, 234.

29. Thoreau, *J* 6:142.

30. Thoreau, *J* 1:78; *J*(P) 3:200.

31. Thoreau, *J* 1:480–81; 12:301.

32. Bureau of the Census, "Products of Agriculture, State of Massachusetts," 1850 (Washington, D.C.: National Archives, available on microfilm); Percey Wells Bidwell and John I. Falconer, *History of Agriculture in the Northern United States, 1620–1860* (New York: Peter Smith, 1941); James Kimenker, "The Concord Farmer: An Economic History," in "Concord," Fischer, ed., unpublished papers in social history, Brandeis University, 1983; Robert A. Gross, "Culture and Cultivation: Agriculture and Society in Thoreau's Concord," *Journal of American History* 69 (1982):42–53.

33. Based on an analysis of manuscript schedules of the United States Census "Products of Agriculture," for 1850.

34. Based on extensive reading in *The New Englander Farmer* (Boston: Joel Nourse), vols. 20–40 (1842–62). Thoreau's comments on the farmer's situation may be found in *J*(P) 4:108, 294–95, 391.

35. Thoreau, *J*(P) 3:136; *Walden,* ed. J. Lyndon Shanley (Princeton: Princeton University Press, 1973), pp. 256–70; *J* 13:318; *J*(P) 4:196; Edmund A. Schofield, "The Ecology of Walden Woods," in Schofield and Baron, eds., *Thoreau's World and Ours,* pp. 155–211.

36. Thoreau, "Wild Apples," *The Natural History Essays* (Salt Lake City: Peregrine Smith, 1980), p. 191.

37. My discussion of agriculture is based on a computer analysis of the United States Census "Products of Agriculture" for 1850, undertaken in conjunction with Latimer and Lanphear, *Soil Survey of Middlesex County.* Individual farms were located on H. F. Walling's "Map of the Town of Concord, Middlesex County Massachusetts" (Boston, 1852). More than 90 percent of the farms listed in the census were located.

38. Material concerning the Concord Farmers Club, including the minute books, membership lists, and the lists of speakers and their assigned topics, is preserved at the Concord Free Library, Concord, Massachusetts.

39. Thoreau, *J* 5:225, 239–40; 9:44.

40. Ibid. 6:32; 5:15; 14:115; *J*(P) 4:227; *J* 9:296; 14:328.

41. Thoreau, *Walden,* pp. 165–66.

42. Thoreau, *J* 10:195; 2:257; 12:122; 10:174; 6:93; 6:18; 14:166

43. Among the numerous instances in which Thoreau mentions a bird being shot by one of his fellow townspeople, I count no fewer than thirty-two species. Most were varieties of ducks, geese, or pigeons, but they included also such inedible species as herons, loons, swallows, and redpolls.

44. Edward Jarvis, "Traditions and Reminiscences" (unpublished manuscript, Concord Free Library, 1878); Thoreau, *J* 5:186; 9:459.

45. Thoreau, *J*(P) 3:310.

46. J.B.R., "On Killing Robins," *New England Farmer* 36 (June 1858):259–60.

47. Thoreau, *J*(P) 2:374; *J* 12:241.

48. By far the best discussion of the relationship between people and nature in New England is Carolyn Merchant's *Ecological Revolutions: Nature, Gender, and Science in New England* (Chapel Hill: University of North Carolina Press, 1989). The reference to clams and eels is in Thoreau, *J* 10:399.

49. Worster, *Nature's Economy,* pp. 57–112; William Martin Smallwood, *Natural History and the American Mind* (New York: AMS Press, 1967), pp. 140–52; Peter A. Fritzell, *Nature Writing and America: Essays on a Cultural Type* (Ames: Iowa State University Press, 1990), pp. 153–90. Quotation from Horace R. Hosmer, "Reminiscences of Thoreau," *Concord Enterprise,* April 15, 1893.

50. Worster, *Nature's Economy,* pp. 68–70. A complete list of the published reports may be found in Thoreau, "The Natural History of Massachusetts," *Natural History Essays,* pp. 1–30.

51. D. Humphreys Storer, "A Report on the Fishes of Massachusetts," *Boston Journal of Natural History* 2 (August 1839).

52. William Jones, "A Topographical Description of the Town of Concord,

August 20th, 1792," *Collections of the Massachusetts Historical Society for the Year 1792,* vol. 1 (Boston: Munroe and Francis, reprinted 1806), pp. 237–40.

53. Lemuel Shattuck, *A History of the Town of Concord* (Boston: Russell, Odiorne and Stacy, 1835), pp. 196–203; quotation on p. 203.

54. The Minute Books of the Concord Lyceum, including listings of the program of speakers for each year from 1828 through 1859 (except for the 1841–42 season, which was mysteriously torn out) are located at the Concord Free Library. See also Harding, *Days of Henry Thoreau* p. 29.

55. Thoreau, *J* 5:453.

56. Thoreau, *J*(P) 3:186.

57. Thoreau, *J* 9:363.

58. Ibid. 11:457; 8:363.

59. Harding, *Days of Henry Thoreau,* pp. 1–20. See also "Thoreau's Inheritance," in Dr. Samuel Arthur Jones, *Thoreau amongst Friends and Philistines and Other Thoreauviana* (Columbus: University of Ohio Press, 1982), pp. 40–45.

60. George F. Hoar, *Autobiography of Seventy Years* (New York: Scribner's, 1903), pp. 70–72.

61. Ray Angelo, "Thoreau as Botanist," *Botanical Index to the Journal of Henry David Thoreau* (Salt Lake City: Peregrine Smith, 1984), pp. 15–31; Richard F. Fleck, ed. "The Bird Journal of Sophia, John, and Henry David Thoreau," *Bulletin of Research in the Humanities* 87:4 (1986–87):489–508.

62. Harding, *Days of Henry Thoreau,* p. 235.

63. Angelo, "Thoreau as Botanist," p. 25; Thoreau, *J* 5:413–14.

64. Fleck, ed., "Bird Journal," 494–508.

CHAPTER 2: WALDO AND HENRY

1. Ralph Waldo Emerson, letter to Margaret Fuller, September 13, 1841, in Ralph L. Rusk, *The Letters of Ralph Waldo Emerson,* 2 vols. (New York: Columbia University Press, 1939), 2:447.

2. For this and the biographical paragraphs on Emerson that follow, I have drawn my material from four essential secondary sources, in addition to a reading of Emerson's own journals. The secondary sources are Gay Wilson Allen, *Waldo Emerson: A Biography* (New York: Viking Press, 1981); John McAleer, *Ralph Waldo Emerson: Days of Encounter* (Boston: Little, Brown and Company, 1984); Joel Porte, *Emerson and Thoreau: Transcendentalists in Conflict* (Middletown, Conn.: Wesleyan University Press, 1965); and Stephen E. Whicher, "Introduction," *Selections from Ralph Waldo Emerson* (Boston: Houghton Mifflin, 1956). The critical journals were volumes seven through eleven of *The Journals and Miscellaneous Notebooks of Ralph Waldo Emerson,* ed. William H. Gilman, A. W. Plumstead et al (Cambridge: Belknap Press of Harvard University, 1969–75).

3. McAleer, *Emerson,* pp. 1–117; Allen, *Waldo Emerson,* pp. 1–103.

4. McAleer, *Emerson,* pp. 117–47; Allen, *Waldo Emerson,* pp. 103–219.

5. Allen, *Waldo Emerson,* pp. 220–45; McAleer, *Emerson,* pp. 170–77; Whicher, "Introduction."

6. Stuart G. Brown, "Emerson's Platonism," *New England Quarterly* 18 (September 1945):325–45; McAleer, *Emerson,* pp. 156–69.

7. Allen, *Waldo Emerson,* pp. 284, 303; Paula Blanchard, *Margaret Fuller: From Transcendentalism to Revolution* (Reading, Mass.: Addison-Wesley, 1987), pp. 123–24.

8. Matthiessen, *American Renaissance.*

9. McAleer, *Emerson,* pp. 200–216; Allen, *Waldo Emerson,* pp. 238–45.

10. McAleer, *Emerson,* pp. 316–34.

11. Ibid., pp. 228–33; Ralph Waldo Emerson, *Nature* (A Facsimile of the First Edition) (Boston: Beacon Press, 1985). I am especially indebted to McAleer for placing *Nature* and "The American Scholar" in realistice perspective.

12. McAleer, *Emerson,* pp. 234–39; Emerson, "The American Scholar," *Selections,* pp. 63–79.

13. McAller, *Emerson,* pp. 245–56; Emerson, "The Divinity School Address," *Selections,* pp. 100–115.

14. McAleer, *Emerson,* pp. 240–44.

15. Harding, *Days of Henry Thoreau,* pp. 45–47; Robert Sattelmeyer, *Thoreau's Reading: A Study in Intellectual History with Bibliographical Catalogue* (Princeton: Princeton University Press, 1988), pp. 3–24.

16. Harding, *Days of Henry Thoreau,* pp. 59–66.

17. Thoreau, *J*(P) 1:5.

18. David Greene Haskins, *Ralph Waldo Emerson: His Maternal Ancestors* (Boston: Cupples, Upham, 1887), p. 122.

19. Emerson, *Journals* 6:358.

20. Harding, *Days of Henry Thoreau,* pp. 52–157.

21. McAleer, *Emerson,* pp. 148–69, 228–33; Whicher, "Introduction."

22. Emerson, *Nature,* pp. 7, 71.

23. Ibid., pp. 59–62, 79–80; Ralph Waldo Emerson, "The Over-Soul," *Essays: First and Second Series* (New York: Vintage Books, 1990), pp. 153–70; Porte, *Emerson and Thoreau.*

24. Emerson, *Nature,* p. 76; *Essays.*

25. Jaroslav Pelikan, "Introduction" to Emerson, *Nature,* pp. 1–66; Emerson, *Nature,* pp. 12, 23–24, 30, 34.

26. Emerson, *Nature,* pp. 29–30, 33.

27. Ibid., pp. 84, 91.

28. "Notebook Naturalist," *The Topical Notebooks of Ralph Waldo Emerson,* vol. 1, ed. Susan Sutton Smith (Columbia: University of Missouri Press, 1990), pp. 27–56; quotation from p. 51.

29. "Notebook Naturalist"; Emerson, letter to William Emerson, September 28, 1853, *Letters* 4:388; Emerson, *Nature,* p. 35.

30. Emerson, "American Scholar," pp. 63–80; quotations, pp. 72, 79.

31. McAleer, *Emerson,* pp. 228–33; Emerson, "American Scholar," p. 79.

32. Emerson, "The Poet," *Essays,* pp. 215–38.

33. Ibid., p. 237.

34. Thoreau, *J*(P) 1:5, 19.

35. Ibid. 1:180–81.

36. Harding, *Days of Henry Thoreau,* pp. 3–31.

37. Ibid., pp. 33–51; Sattelmeyer, *Thoreau's Reading,* pp. 9–11.

38. George F. Hoar, *Autobiography of Seventy Years* (New York: Scribner's, 1903), p. 71.

39. Walter Harding, ed. *Thoreau as Seen by His Contemporaries* (New York: Dover Publications, 1989), p. 231.

40. Edward Emerson, *Henry Thoreau as Remembered by a Young Friend* (Boston: Houghton Mifflin, 1917), George Keyes quoted p. 24, Henry Warren, pp. 205–7; Thoreau, *J*(P) 2:10.

41. Frederick L. H. Willis, *Alcott Memoirs* (Boston: Badger Publications, 1915), pp. 91–92.

42. Harding, *Days of Henry Thoreau,* pp. 137–39; George William Curtis, *Homes of American Authors* (New York: Putnam, 1853), p. 302.

43. Nathaniel Hawthorne, *The American Notebooks,* ed. Randall Stewart (Cambridge: President and Fellows of Harvard College, 1932), p. 166.

44. Emerson, *Journals* 5:25, 480.

45. Ibid. 7:313.

46. Sattelmeyer, *Thoreau's Reading.* Sattelmeyer's book is an irreplacable source in tracing Thoreau's early intellectual growth.

47. Thoreau, *J*(P) 1:86, 353, 109; *J* 9:156–57.

48. For a discussion of the content and condition of Thoreau's early journals, see the "Historical Introduction" and "Textual Introduction" to Thoreau, *J*(P), ed. Elizabeth Hall Witherell, William L. Howarth, Robert Sattelmeyer, and Thomas Blanding, 1:592–643.

49. Thoreau, *J*(P) 1:87, 217.

50. Ibid. 1:8.

51. Fleck, ed., "Bird Journal"; Thoreau, *J*(P) 1:115; Thoreau, letter to John Thoreau, July 8, 1838, *Correspondence,* p. 27.

52. McAleer, *Emerson,* p. 336; Emerson, *Journals* 9:71.

53. Emerson, letter to Margaret Fuller, September 13, 1841, *Letters* 2:447.

54. Harding, *Days of Henry Thoreau,* pp. 52–93; Thoreau, *Early Essays,* p. 121; *J*(P) vol. 1.

55. Allen, *Waldo Emerson,* p. 357; Blanchard, *Margaret Fuller,* 139–62.

56. Raymond R. Borst, *Henry David Thoreau: A Descriptive Bibliography* (Pittsburgh: University Of Pittsburgh Press, 1982), pp. 187–89. For a full listing of Thoreau's published writings through 1849, see the Appendix.

57. Thoreau, *J*(P) 1:69.

58. Blanchard, *Margaret Fuller,* pp. 1–162.

59. Ibid.; Marie Urbanski, "Henry David Thoreau and Margaret Fuller," *Thoreau Journal Quarterly* 8 (October 1976):24–29; Harding, *Days of Henry Thoreau,* pp. 113–16; Margaret Fuller, letter to Richard Fuller, quoted in Margaret Bell, *Margaret Fuller* (New York: Albert and Charles Boni, 1930), p. 123.

60. Emerson, letter to Thomas Carlyle, May 30, 1841, *The Correspondence of Thomas Carlyle and Ralph Waldo Emerson,* 2 vols. (Boston: Osgood, 1883), 1:335; McAleer, *Emerson,* pp. 338–40; Harding *Days of Henry Thoreau,* pp. 129–31.

61. Allen, *Waldo Emerson,* p. 402; Borst, ed., *Thoreau: A Descriptive Bibliography,* pp. 189–91.

62. Thoreau, "Natural History of Massachusetts," *Natural History Essays,* pp. 1–29.

63. Frank Stewart, *A Natural History of Nature Writing* (Washington, D.C.: Island Press, 1995), p. 48.

64. Thoreau, *J*(P) 1:353, 86, 109, 240–42. For a supporting opinion, see Robert Sattelmeyer, "A Walk to More Than Wachusett," *Thoreau Society Bulletin* 202 (Winter 1992):1–4.

65. Thoreau, "Natural History of Massachusetts," p. 29.

66. Most of Thoreau's early efforts are gathered in *Early Essays.*

67. Thoreau, "A Walk to Wachusett," *Natural History Essays,* pp. 31–50; "A Winter Walk," *Natural History Essays,* pp. 51–71.

68. Thoreau, "Walk to Wachusett," p. 46.

69. Thoreau, "Winter Walk."

70. Harding, *Days of Henry Thoreau,* pp. 132–33; Steven Fink, "Thoreau and his audience," *Cambridge Companion to Thoreau,* pp. 71–91.

71. McAleer, *Emerson,* p. 364; Douglas Crase, "Chronology," in Emerson, *Essays,* p. 385.

72. Emerson, *J* 6:304; Harding, *Days of Henry Thoreau,* pp. 116–17; 145–56.

73. Harding, *Days of Henry Thoreau,* pp. 140–42; Thoreau, "The Landlord," *United States Magazine and Democratic Review* 13 (October 1843):427–30; "Paradise (To Be) Regained," *United States Magazine* 13 (November 1843):451–63.

74. Harding, *Days of Henry Thoreau,* pp. 152–56.

75. Ibid., pp. 170–78. Impressions of the increasingly prickly relationship between Thoreau and Emerson may be gleaned from the latter's journals. See, for example, Emerson, *Journals* 9:45, 71.

76. Thoreau, *J*(P) 3:75–78.

77. Ibid. 3:78; Mary Hosmer Brown, *Memories of Concord* (Boston: Four Seas Books, 1926), p. 103.

78. Linck C. Johnson, *Thoreau's Complex Weave: The Writing of A Week on the Concord and Merrimack Rivers* (Charlottesville: University Press of Virginia, 1986), pp. 3–84.

79. Robert Sattelmeyer, "Historical Introduction," *J*(P) 2:449–54. The "Long Book" itself appears in *J*(P) 3:1–152.

CHAPTER 3: THE POND AND THE MOUNTAIN

1. Ralph Waldo Emerson, "Henry D. Thoreau: Emerson's Obituary," reprinted in Dr. Samuel Arthur Jones, *Thoreau amongst Friends and Philistines and Other Thoreauviana* (Columbus: University of Ohio Press, 1982), pp. 67–72; and "Thoreau," *Atlantic Monthly* 10 (August 1862):239–49; James Russell Lowell, "Thoreau," in *My Study Windows* (Boston: Houghton, Mifflin and Company, 1884), pp. 193–209; quotation, p. 208. Henry S. Salt noted that it was "a mistake to suppose that Thoreau was isolated from society during his seclusion at Walden" (*Life of Thoreau,* p. 46), a sentiment echoed in such early twentieth-century biographies as Joseph Wood Krutch, *Henry David Thoreau* (New York: William Sloane Associates, 1948) and Henry Seidel Canby, *Thoreau* (Boston: Houghton Mifflin Company, 1939). The interpretation is standard today. As much as anything, this demonstrates the enormous gap between scholarly understanding and popular perception.

2. J. Lyndon Shanley, *The Making of Walden* (Chicago: University of Chicago Press, 1957); Thoreau, *Walden.* On the creation of myths and misrepresentations growing from Thoreau's Walden experience, I cite the creative powers of my own students. Armed with misapprehensions derived from previous readings at high school and junior college levels, they have presented me with an astonishing array of novel interpretations. Of course, this is nothing new. See Bradley P. Dean and Gary Scharnhorst, "The Contemporary Reception of Walden," *Studies of the American Renaissance,* ed. Joel Myerson (Charlottesville: University Press of Virginia, 1990).

3. Thoreau, *J*(P) 2:156.

4. Thoreau, "The First Version of Walden," in Shanley, ed., *Making of Walden,* pp. 105–208. The quotation is on p. 141.

5. Harding, *Days of Henry Thoreau,* pp. 123, 179–80.

6. Ellery Channing, letter to Thoreau, March 5, 1845, Thoreau, *Correspondence,* p. 161.

7. Harding, *Days of Henry Thoreau,* p. 181; Thoreau, *Walden,* pp. 40–45.

8. The primary source for the physical descriptions of Walden Woods and Thoreau's cabin is *Walden* itself. Also of critical importance are Thomas Blanding and Edmund A. Schofield, "Walden Woods," unpublished manuscript (Concord, Mass.: Thoreau Country Conservation Alliance, 1989); Brian Donahue, "Henry David Thoreau and the Environment of Concord," in Schofield and Baron, eds., *Thoreau's World and Ours,* pp. 181–89; and Philip Van Doren Stern, "The Cabin and Walden Pond," *The Annotated Walden* (New York: Clarkson N. Potter, 1970), pp. 45–52. Copies of Sophia Thoreau's drawing of the Walden cabin are available at the Concord Free Library, Concord, Massachusetts.

9. Thoreau, *Walden,* pp. 3–80.

10. Ibid., pp. 256–64.

11. Thoreau, *J*(P) 2:153–229.

12. Thoreau, *Walden,* pp. 167–72, 263–70. For a discussion of the physical and

spiritual distances between Thoreau and the rest of Concord's inhabitants, see Lawrence Buell, "Thoreau and the natural environment," *Cambridge Companion to Thoreau,* pp. 171–93.

13. Roughly half of the first and second Walden journals are missing, presumably used in various literary projects, while nineteen of the seventy-two leaves of the "Berg Journal" are gone. For a complete discussion of the condition of the journals remaining from the period 1844 to 1848, see the "Textual Introduction" to Thoreau, *J*(P), ed. Robert Sattelmeyer, 2:467–83.

14. Harding, *Days of Henry Thoreau,* pp. 179–80; Johnson, *Thoreau's Complex Weave,* pp. 220–22.

15. Thoreau, *J*(P) 2:1–152.

16. Harding, *Days of Henry Thoreau,* pp. 211–12; Thoreau, "Thomas Carlyle and His Works," *Early Essays,* pp. 219–67.

17. "Historical Introduction," *J*(P) 2:454–59.

18. Thoreau, *J*(P) 2:1–152.

19. Johnson, *Thoreau's Complex Weave,* pp. 3–201.

20. Thoreau, *J*(P) vol. 1.

21. The original notes of the journey appear in Thoreau, *J*(P) 1:134–37.

22. Nature entries copied from earlier journals are interspersed throughout the "Long Book." See Thoreau, *J*(P) 2:1–152. Thoreau, "Text of the First Draft of A Week on the Concord and Merrimack Rivers," ed. Linck Johnson, *Thoreau's Complex Weave,* pp. 289–393. The quotation appears in the first draft of *A Week* on p. 310, and in slightly different form in the "Long Book" on 2:11.

23. The purple finch appears in the draft on p. 90; in the "Long Book" on 2:50; while the witch hazel appears on pages 383 and 2:54 respectively. The song sparrow appears in the "Long Book" on 2:20, the fox on 2:89.

24. Thoreau, "Natural History of Massachusetts"; Storer, *Fishes of Massachusetts;* Thoreau, *J*(P) 2:103–12.

25. Thoreau, "First Draft of A Week."

26. Thoreau, *J*(P) 2:55.

27. Ibid. 2:76, 91.

28. Ibid. 2:171, 188, 229.

29. Ibid. 2:191–93.

30. Ibid. 2:242.

31. Ibid. 2:243–45.

32. Ibid. 2:249–51.

33. Harding, *Days of Henry Thoreau,* pp. 208–10; Thoreau "Ktaadn and the Maine Woods," *The Union Magazine* 3, five installments (July–November 1848):29–33, 73–79, 132–37, 177–82, 216–20.

34. Thoreau, "Ktaadn"; J. Parker Huber, *The Wildest Country: A Guide to Thoreau's Maine* (Boston: Appalachian Mountain Club, 1981).

35. Thoreau, "Ktaadn," pp. 31, 76–77, 219.

36. Ibid., pp. 21–58; Huber, *Wildest Country,* 123–58.

37. The view seems to have originated with an article by John G. Blair and Augustus Trowbridge, "Thoreau on Katahdin," *American Quarterly* 12 (1960). The most important elaborations came from the pens of James McIntosh, *Thoreau as Romantic Naturalist: His Shifting Stance toward Nature* (Ithaca, N.Y.: Cornell University Press, 1974), pp. 179–215; and Roderick Nash, *Wilderness and the American Mind,* 3d ed. (New Haven, Conn.: Yale University Press, 1982), pp. 84–95, 122–40. Both authors attempt to force Thoreau into a larger history of nature writing as a kind of transitional figure between earlier wilderness-hating pilgrims and later celebrants of nature such as John Muir. See also John Frederick Jaques, "The Discovery of 'Ktaadn': A Study of Thoreau's *The Maine Woods*" (Columbia University, Ph.D. diss., 1971). Ronald Wesley Hoag, in "The Mark of the Wilderness: Thoreau's Contact with Katahdiin," *Texas Studies in Literature and Language* 24 (1982), alternatively argues that Thoreau was attempting to convey a transcendental experience of the sublime. The best summary of these analyses is Joseph J. Moldenhauer, "The Maine Woods," *Cambridge Companion to Thoreau,* pp. 124–41.

38. Thoreau, *J*(P) 2:270–349. In the journal entry for August 30, 1856, Thoreau noted, "I have found my account in travelling in having prepared beforehand a list of questions which I would get answered, not trusting to my interest at the moment, and can then travel with the most profit" (*J* 9:38–39).

39. Thoreau, *J*(P) 2:270–349.

40. Ibid. 2:275

41. Ibid.

42. For a supporting argument regarding this theme, see Joan Berbick, *Thoreau's Alternative History* (Philadelphia: University of Pennsylvania Press, 1987), pp. 84–86.

43. Thoreau, *J*(P) 2:278.

44. Harding, *Days of Henry Thoreau,* pp. 187–88; Thoreau, "First Version of Walden," pp. 105–6.

45. Shanley, *Making of Walden,* pp. 18–19.

46. Emerson, *Letters* 3:377–78; Shanley, *Making of Walden,* pp. 17–22.

47. Thoreau, "First Version of Walden," pp. 105–77. J. Lyndon Shanley's pioneering work in retrieving the original draft from the mass of Walden manuscripts was an incomparable contribution to Thoreau scholarship.

48. Shanley, *Making of Walden,* pp. 17–22, 93–103.

49. Thoreau, "First Version of Walden," pp. 105–77.

50. Ibid., pp. 123–24, 137, 157, 161–63.

51. Shanley, *Making of Walden,* pp. 22, 99–101.

52. Thoreau, "First Version of Walden," pp. 177–208.

53. Ibid., p. 190.

54. Ibid., pp. 202–7.

55. Ibid., p. 207.

56. Ibid.

57. Thoreau, *J*(P) 2:339–40.

58. Thoreau, letter to Horatio R. Storer, February 15, 1847, *Correspondence,* pp. 175–76.

59. Lurie, *Louis Agassiz;* Harding, *Days of Henry Thoreau,* p. 195.

60. The correspondence between James Elliot Cabot and Thoreau, which occurred from March through May of 1847, is reproduced in Thoreau, *Correspondence,* pp. 177–83. Kenneth Walter Cameron, "Emerson, Thoreau, and the Society of Natural History," *American Literature* 24 (1952):23; Thoreau, *J* 11:346–50.

61. Shanley, *Making of Walden,* p. 24; Harding, *Days of Henry Thoreau,* pp. 197–98.

62. Johnson, *Thoreau's Complex Weave,* pp. 226–47; McAleer, *Emerson,* pp. 344–45.

63. Harding, *Days of Henry Thoreau,* pp. 228–30.

64. Thoreau, "Ktaadn," p. 136.

65. Thoreau, "First Draft of A Week," p. 15.

66. Thoreau, "Ktaadn," pp. 180–81.

67. Ibid.

68. Ibid., pp. 216–17.

69. Ibid., p. 217

70. Harding, *Days of Henry Thoreau,* p. 229.

71. Johnson, *Thoreau's Complex Weave,* pp. 240–43.

72. McAleer, *Emerson,* pp. 345–46; Thoreau, letter to Emerson, February 23, 1848, *Correspondence,* p. 207.

73. Emerson, *Journals* 10:343–44.

74. Ibid. 10:15–16.

75. Ibid. p. 20; Sophia Peabody Hawthorne, letter of February 28, 1849, quoted in Rose Hawthorne Lathrop, *Memories of Hawthorne* (Boston: Houghton Mifflin, 1897), pp. 92–93; Borst, *Thoreau Log,* pp. 133–75.

76. James Elliott Cabot, *A Memoir of Ralph Waldo Emerson,* 2 vols. (Boston: Houghton Mifflin, 1887), 2:497.

77. Thoreau, *Correspondence,* pp. 237–38.

78. Johnson, *Thoreau's Complex Weave,* pp. 202–47; Thoreau, *A Week.*

79. Thoreau, *A Week,* pp. 382.

CHAPTER 4: ABSORBING NATURE

1. James Russell Lowell, *A Fable for Critics* (New York: Putnam, 1848), p. 21. (If Thoreau's story needed a villainous counterpoint, Lowell would be an excellent candidate for the position.)

2. Harding, *Days of Henry Thoreau,* pp. 256–59.

3. Anonymous, "Reminiscences of Thoreau," *Outlook* 63 (December 2, 1899):820; Mrs. Minot Pratt, quoted in Edward Emerson, *Thoreau as Remembered by a Young Friend* (Boston: Houghton Mifflin, 1917), p. 80.

4. Harding, *Days of Henry Thoreau,* pp. 256–59; Ellery Channing, *Thoreau: The*

Poet-Naturalist (Boston: Roberts Brothers, 1873), p. 11. I suspect that the journal passages devoted to "A Sister" also were written with Helen in mind, although many scholars perversely contend that they were inspired by Lidian Emerson. See Thoreau, *J*(P) 3:17–18.

5. Johnson, *Thoreau's Complex Weave,* pp. 257–59.

6. Borst, *Thoreau Log,* pp. 148–62.

7. Johnson, *Thoreau's Complex Weave,* pp. 202–60.

8. Thoreau, *J* 5:459.

9. Thoreau, *J*(P) 3:26.

10. Shanley, *Making of Walden,* pp. 29–30.

11. Thoreau, *Cape Cod,* ed. Joseph J. Moldenhauer (Princeton: Princeton University Press, 1988), p. 3. For reasons I cannot explain even to myself, this is my favorite of Thoreau's books.

12. Ibid., pp. 3–13.

13. Shanley, *Making of Walden,* pp. 29–31; Thoreau, *J*(P) 3:20–116.

14. Thoreau, *J*(P) 3:43–44.

15. Ibid. 3:97, 313.

16. Ibid. 3:106, 135, 190; *J* 8:314; 10:237; Marcia Moss, ed. *A Catalog of Thoreau's Surveys in the Concord Free Public Library* (Geneseo, N.Y.: Thoreau Society, 1976).

17. Thoreau, *J*(P) 3:13, 23; Sattelmeyer, *Thoreau's Reading,* pp. 66–77; Jones, "Topographical Description."

18. Thoreau, *J*(P) 3:49, 72, 74.

19. Harding, *Days of Henry Thoreau,* pp. 277–79; Blanchard, *Margaret Fuller,* pp. 264–337.

20. Thoreau, *J*(P) 3:95. Joan Berbick argues that Thoreau's response to the Margaret Fuller death horror was "untranscendental" in that it destroyed the transcendental link between nature and the spirit. I agree with the assessment regarding nature and the spirit, but find the passage to be a momentary lapse into a more Emersonian point of view. See Berbick, *Thoreau's Alternative History,* pp. 88–90.

21. Thoreau, *J*(P) 3:108–9, 111, 115–16. Sensitive to the relationship between Thoreau and the community of Concord, Lawrence Buell argues that Henry turned to nature study as "partly an accomodation to and partly a dissent from nineteenth-century norms of thinking." See "Thoreau and the natural environment," *Cambridge Companion to Thoreau,* p. 185. For the full scope of this argument and an evaluation of Thoreau's place in the development of environmental understanding in the nineteenth-century, see Buell, *The Environmental Imagination.*

22. Thoreau, *J*(P) 3:146.

23. Ibid. 3:166.

24. Thoreau, "Walking," *Natural History Essays,* p. 107. Consider also:

> "*Wilderness, wilderness. . .* We scarcely know what we mean by the term, though the sound of it draws all whose nerves and emotions have not yet been

irreparably stunned, deadened, numbed by the caterwauling of commerce, the sweating scramble for profit and domination.

"Why such allure in the very word? What does it really mean?"

In Edward Abbey, *Desert Solitaire: A Season in the Wilderness* (New York: Simon and Schuster, 1990), p. 166.

25. Thoreau, "Walking," *Natural History Essays,* p. 119.

26. Thoreau, *J*(P) 3:27, 141, 179; 4:473; *J* 4:104.

27. Robert D. Richardson Jr., *Henry Thoreau: A Life of the Mind* (Berkeley: University of California Press, 1986), pp. 224–33.

28. Thoreau, "Walking," *Natural History Essays,* p. 93.

29. James Kendall Hosmer, *The Last Leaf* (New York: Putnam, 1912), pp. 235–36.

30. Thoreau, "Walking," pp. 98, 112–14.

31. Ibid., 130, 132, 133–36.

32. Thoreau, letter to Jared Sparks, September 17, 1849, *Correspondence,* pp. 476–77.

33. Sattelmeyer, *Thoreau's Reading,* pp. 29, 67–68; Thoreau, *J*(P) 3:10. Thoreau's edition of the *Bhagvat-geeta* was translated by Charles Wilkins (London: C. Nourse, Opposite Catherine Street, in the Strand [by Bradstreet Press], 1785). Modern readers should seek a more recent and sympathetic translation. Several scholars have addressed Thoreau's interest in Oriental literature, including Arthur Christie, *The Orient in American Transcendentalism* (New York: Columbia University Press, 1932); F. I. Carpenter, *Emerson and Asia* (Cambridge: Harvard University Press, 1930); Beongcheon Yu, *The Great Circle: American Writers and the Orient* (Detroit: Wayne State University Press, 1983); Roger C. Mueller, "Thoreau's Selections from *Chinese Four Books* for *The Dial,*" *Thoreau Journal Quarterly* 4 (October 1972):1–8; Frank MacShane, "Walden and Yoga," *New England Quarterly* 37 (1964):322–42; William Bysshe Stein, "Walden and the Bhagavad Gita," *Topic* 3 (1963):38–55; Stephen D. Strachner, "Thoreau's Orientalism: A Preliminary Reconsidration," *Thoreau Journal Quarterly* 6 (1974):14–17; Strachner, "Walden: Thoreau's Vanaprasthya," *Thoreau Society Quarterly* 5 (January 1973):8–12. For an excellent overview of Hindu religious belief, see Arthur L. Herman, *A Brief Introduction to Hinduism* (Boulder, Colo.: Westview Press, 1991).

34. Thoreau, *J*(P) 3:21–22, 29; *Mahabharata, Harivansa, ou Histoire de la Famille de Hari,* 2 vols. (Paris: Printed for the Oriental Translation Fund of Great Britain and Ireland, 1834–35); Thoreau, "The Transmigration of the Seven Brahmins," *Translations,* ed. K. P. Van Anglen (Princeton: Princeton University Press, 1986), pp. 135–44.

35. *Puranas. Vishnupurana. The Vishnu Purana, a System of Hindu Mythology and Tradition* (London: J. Murray, 1840); Isvarakrsna, *The Sankhya Karika,* trans. Henry Thomas Colebrooke (Oxford: Oriental Translation Fund, 1837); *Vedas. Samaveda. Translation of the Sanhita of the Sama Veda,* trans. Rev. J. Stevenson (London: Oriental Translation Fund, 1842); Kalidasa, *Sakoontala; or The Lost Ring,*

trans. Sir William Jones (London: Rivingtons and Cochrane, 1825); Asiatic Society of Bengal, *Bibliotheca Indica: A Collection of Oriental Works,* vol. 14 (Calcutta: East India Company, 1853); David Collie, *The Chinese Classical Work, Commonly Called The Four Books* (Malacca: Mission Press, 1828); Confucius, *The Works of Confucius,* vol. 1, trans. J. Marshman (Serampore: Mission Press, 1809); Thoreau, *J*(P) 3:61.

36. *Sankhya Karika;* Thoreau, *J*(P) 3:216–17.

37. Thoreau, "Transmigration of the Seven Brahmans."

38. Manu, *Institutes of Hindu Law,* trans. Sir William Jones (London: Rivingtons and Cochrane, 1825), chapter 1, verses 10–50; Thoreau, "Literary Notebook," extracts published by Kenneth Walter Cameron, *Transcendental Apprenticeship: Notes on Young Henry Thoreau's Reading* (Transcendental Books, 1976), pp. 189–90.

39. *Vishnu Purana,* chapters one, two, and five.

40. *Mahabharata. Harivansa;* Thoreau, *J*(P) 3:215.

41. *Bhagvat-Geeta,* trans. Charles Wilkins, pp. 37, 52–54, 62–64, 75.

42. Thoreau, "Walking," p. 122; Shanley, *Making of Walden,* p. 29; Thoreau, *Walden,* pp. 57, 85, 96, 106–7, 270, 298. Both Walter Harding and Robert Richardson argue that Thoreau's interest in Oriental scripture waned by 1855, but I am not convinced this was so. Certainly Thoreau spoke on the subject with enough spirit to inspire the English visitor Thomas Cholmondeley to send him a gift of forty-four books of Oriental literature in 1855, and he continued thereafter to discuss the works with friends and to refer to them in his journals between 1856 and 1859. See, for example, Thoreau, *J* 8:134–35; 9:55; 10:46, 54; 11:154–55, 424.

43. For discussions of the place of nature in traditional Western thought, see Merchant, *Ecological Revolutions,* and also *The Death of Nature: Women, Ecology, and the Scientific Revolution* (San Francisco: Harper and Row, 1980); Clarence Glacken, *Traces on the Rhodian Shore: Nature and Culture in Western Thought to the End of the Eighteenth Century* (Berkeley: University of California Press, 1967); Worster, *Nature's Economy;* William Leiss, *The Domination of Nature* (New York: G. Braziller, 1972); and Nash, *Wilderness and the American Mind.*

44. Loren Eiseley, "Thoreau's Vision of the Natural World," *The Star Thrower* (New York: Harcourt, Brace, Jovanovich, 1978), p. 229; see also H. Daniel Peck, "Better Mythology: Perception and Emergence in Thoreau's Journal," in Schofield and Baron, eds., *Thoreau's World and Ours,* pp. 304–15.

45. Thoreau, *A Week; J* 6:45, 50; "Indian Notebooks," 11 vols., unpublished, Pierpont Morgan Library, New York City; *The Maine Woods,* ed. Joseph J. Moldenhauer (Princeton: Princeton University Press, 1972); Sayre, *Thoreau and the American Indians.*

46. Thoreau, "Indian Notebooks." Extracts from the notebooks may be found in *The Indians of Thoreau: Selections from the Indian Notebooks,* ed. Richard F. Fleck (Albuquerque: Hummingbird Press, 1974).

47. Thoreau, "Cape Cod," *Putnam's Monthly Magazine* 5–6, published in three

installments, (June–August 1855):5:632–40, 6:59–66, 157–64; "Chesuncook," *Atlantic Monthly* 2, published in three installments, (June–August 1858):1–12, 224–33, 305–17; *Maine Woods.*

48. Thoreau, *J* 4:400.

49. Fleck, ed. *Indians of Thoreau,* pp. 27–54.

50. See, for example, Thoreau, *J* 4:136.

51. Thoreau, letter to James Russell Lowell, June 22, 1858, *Correspondence,* pp. 515–16. William Howarth attempts to cast doubt on whether Lowell purposely omitted the line, but in the end is unable to convince even himself. See Howarth, *The Book of Concord: Thoreau's Life as a Writer* (New York: Penguin Books, 1983), pp. 148–49, 157. Martin Duberman, Lowell's most thorough biographer, has no doubt that Lowell was responsible. Duberman, *James Russell Lowell* (Boston: Houghton Mifflin Company, 1966), pp. 169–71.

52. Laura Dassow Walls, "Seeing New Worlds: Thoreau and Humboldtian Science," in Schofield and Baron, eds., *Thoreau's World and Ours,* pp. 55–63. For an elaboration of Walls's contention that Thoreau was heavily influenced by Humboldt, see her book, *Seeing New Worlds: Henry David Thoreau and Nineteenth-Century Natural Science* (Madison: University of Wisconsin Press, 1995).

53. Sattelmeyer, *Thoreau's Reading,* pp. 58–60; Walls, "Seeing New Worlds"; Thoreau, *J*(P) 3:121, 177, 224–27, 238–41, 253–59; 4:187, 305–6, 386; *J* 5:46, 65, 83; "Commonplace Book," Unpublished Notebook, 1853–60, Berg Collection, New York Public Library. Walls maintains that Humboldt was a primary influence on the development of Thoreau's ideas; Donald Worster (*Nature's Economy*) is among those maintaining that Thoreau intended to model himself on White.

54. William Bartram, *Travels Through North and South Carolina, Georgia, East and West Florida* (Philadelphia: Jones and Johnson, 1791).

55. A. Hunter Dupree, "Thoreau as Scientist: American Science in the 1850s," and William Rossi, "Thoreau as a Philosophical Naturalist-Writer," in Schofield and Baron, eds., *Thoreau's World and Ours,* pp. 42–54, 64–73; Ronald Wesley Hoag, "Thoreau's later natural history writings," *Cambridge Companion to Thoreau,* pp. 152–70; Walls, *Seeing New Worlds,* pp. 54–55; Richardson, *Henry Thoreau,* pp. 362–68.

56. Richardson, *Henry Thoreau,* pp. 260–65; Thoreau, *J*(P) 4:406; *J* 4:339; 6:53, 55–59; Nuttal quotation, 6:625; Gilpin quotation, 4:83.

57. See, for example, Thoreau, *J* 4:259, 490–91; 5:109, 114; 6:250.

58. Thoreau, *J*(P) 3:131–33.

59. Ibid. 3:143.

60. Ibid. 3:148.

61. Ibid. 3:178, 185, 253; 4:10, 28, 47.

62. Ibid. 4:174.

63. Ibid. 4:223. The development of the journal as a vehicle for accurately representing nature is traced by Sharon Cameron, *Writing Nature* (New York: Oxford University Press, 1985). She is primarily interested in Thoreau's approach to

the problem of developing a system of expression to reproduce nature on the written page. Tellingly, she sees this as an effort to compose a total picture "which at any given moment evades him" (p. 129).

The underlying purpose of Thoreau's later journals has been long debated. At one extreme, scholars including Henry S. Canby and Sherman Paul saw the massive content as raw material for a book or long prose poem about Concord, while at the other, Perry Miller saw the journal itself as a completed "work of art" (Miller, *Consciousness in Concord* [Boston: Houghton Mifflin and Company, 1958], p. 4.). Scholars began to take increasing interest in the journals after the Princeton edition began publication in 1981. In addition to Cameron, important analyses of the journal include William Howarth, who saw the journal as "a mirror" reflecting Thoreau and Concord, "a place where life and art merged at the highest level" (*The Book of Concord,* p. 10); H. Daniel Peck, who makes a careful study of the relationship between the journal's structure and its themes (*Thoreau's Morning Work: Memory and Perception in "A Week on the Concord and Merrimack Rivers," the Journal, and "Walden"* [New Haven: Yale University Press, 1990]); and Leonard N. Neufeldt, who relates the shifting nature of the journal to the changing goals and perceptions of its author ("Praetextus as Text: Editor-Critic Responses to Thoreau's Journal," *Arizona Quarterly* 46 [1990]:27–72). For a solid introduction to studies of the journal, see Leonard S. Neufeldt, "Thoreau in his Journal," *Cambridge Companion to Thoreau,* pp. 107–123. Howarth's introduction to *The Book of Concord* also treats the history of journal analysis.

64. Thoreau, *J*(P) 4:296.

65. Ibid. 4:336.

66. Ibid. 3:245; *J* 4:15, 40, 66, 99, 409, 471.

67. Thoreau, *J*(P) 4:169, 238–39.

68. Ibid. 3:228; *J* 5:119. Thoreau made other mistakes that he did not catch. See, for example, where Thoreau mis-identifies a species of owl in June 1857 (*J* 9:457).

69. Robert Sattelmeyer, ed. "Historical Introduction," *J*(P) 4:21, 631–44; *J* 5:235; 6:192; 9:150–58.

70. Thoreau, *J* 5:478.

71. Thoreau, *J*(P) 3:282–85, 366–67; *J* 4:49–52, 112–13, 257–58, 360, 414–15, 477; 5:160, 175, 351, 405, 412; 6:229–30, 235, 255, 297–302.

72. Thoreau, *J* 5:60; 6:389–90.

73. Ibid. 6:228. Although Thoreau clearly intended to comprehend the full range of plant and animal species in Concord, he was never able to achieve the goal. A few species, discovered by later naturalists, eluded him, and more importantly, he made some mistakes in identification. This is not surprising, considering that he was almost wholly self-taught and aided only by voluminous texts containing either poor illustrations or none at all. The amazing thing was that he was able to come as close to full comprehensiveness as he did. See Ray Angelo, "Thoreau as Botanist," for a discussion of his plant identification ability.

74. Thoreau, *J*(P) 3:150; 4:60, 435; *J* 5:267.
75. Thoreau, *J* 4:258.
76. Ibid. 6:439.
77. Thoreau, *J*(P) 4:137, 274, 426, 434.
78. Thoreau, *J* 5:188.
79. Ibid. 5:365.
80. Emerson, *Journals* 8:122.
81. Thoreau, *J*(P) 3:202–9; *J* 6:329, 358. The quotation appears in *J*(P) 3:274.
82. Thoreau, *J* 5:135.
83. Thoreau, *J*(P) 3:380; 4:107, 416.
84. Ibid. 4:6, 310; *J* 4:144, 174, 320; 5:45, 183.
85. Thoreau, *J*(P) 3:244; *J* 5:4.
86. Thoreau, *J* 4:410.
87. Thoreau, *J*(P) 4:156.
88. Ibid. 4:144
89. Ibid. 4:357.
90. Thoreau, *J* 5:37.
91. Thoreau, *J*(P) 3:44, 4:329; *J* 4:163, 5:135, 6:237.
92. John Shepard Keyes, letter to Francis H. Underwood, November 15, 1886, *Thoreau Society Bulletin* 103 (Spring 1968):2–3.
93. Thoreau, *J* 10:294.
94. Quoted in Edward Waldo Emerson, "A Different Drummer," in Walter Harding, ed., *Henry David Thoreau: A Profile* (New York: Hill and Wang, 1971), p. 86.
95. Thoreau, *J*(P) 3:298; *J* 6:236.
96. Thoreau, *Walden,* p. 212; *J* 6:310–11.
97. Thoreau, *J* 6:452.
98. Thoreau, *J*(P) 3:174, 306; 4:221–22; *J* 4:156–58.
99. Thoreau, *J*(P) 3:184, 354–55; *J* 4:495; 5:4, 42; 6:236–38. Henry's criticisms of science continued through the remainder of his journals. See, for example, *J* 12:28, 171; 13:141, 168–69.
100. Thoreau, *J* 4:126; 6:293–95. See also 10:239 for an anti-nature sentiment expressed in January 1858.
101. Thoreau, *J*(P) 4:483.
102. Ibid., *J*(P) 3:217; 4:159, 220; *J* 4:166; 5:517.
103. Thoreau, *J*(P) 3:263, 368; 4:55, 390, 433; *J* 4:289, 445; 5:225.
104. Thoreau, *J*(P) 4:6.
105. Ibid. 4:468.
106. Thoreau continued to remove leaves from his journal as a common practice until July 8, 1850. He began a new volume on that date, which survives virtually intact. Each volume thereafter is virtually whole. For discussion of the condition of journal volumes dated between 1848 and August 1851, see the "Textual Introduction" to Thoreau, *J*(P), ed. Robert Sattelmeyer, Mark R. Patterson, and

William Rossi, 3:499–508. Conditions of journal volumes from that date through April 1852 are in the "Textual Introduction" to Thoreau, *J*(P), ed. Leonard N. Neufeldt and Nancy Craig Simmons, 4:645–58.

107. *J*(P) 4:275; Shanley, *Making of Walden,* pp. 18–91.

108. Thoreau, *J*(P) 4:283; *J* 4:379–81.

109. Thoreau, *Walden,* pp. 3–98.

110. Ibid., p. 249. For a close examination of the evolution of Henry's ideas as expressed in the succeeding drafts of *Walden,* see Robert Milder, *Reimagining Thoreau* (Cambridge: Cambridge University Press, 1995). For reasons that frankly escape me, Milder contends (p. 164) that Thoreau saw nature and spirit as "disjunctive and separate" by the time he completed *Walden.*

111. Thoreau, *Walden,* pp. 129, 137–38, 206, 258, 272.

112. Ibid., pp. 299–319.

113. Thoreau, *J*(P) 2:382; 4:230, 302, 384, 388–89; *J* 6:99, 109, 147, 148–49.

114. Thoreau, *Walden,* pp. 308–9. Gordon V. Boudreau also sees the sand foliage as the synthesizing image of *Walden.* See Boudreau, *The Roots of Walden and the Tree of Life* (Nashville: Vanderbilt University Press, 1990).

115. Thoreau, *Walden,* pp. 290–91. To genuinely understand *Walden,* the reader must also read (and sincerely attempt to understand) the *Bhagvat Geeta.*

116. Thoreau, *J* 6:176; Borst, *Thoreau Log,* pp. 297–334; Dean and Scharnhorst, "Contemporary Reception of Walden."

CHAPTER 5: THE RIVER

1. William Howarth has done the most thorough work endeavoring to portray Thoreau's journal as a single large literary text, rather than the record of an intellectual task in progress. Even Howarth, however, chose to illustrate his interpretation by concentrating on such unusual but dramatic incidents as the great azalea hunt of 1853 and the pig chase of 1856. See Howarth, *Book of Concord,* especially pp. 84–85, 124–25.

2. Walter Harding, "Introduction," Thoreau, *J* 13:v. There is no substitute for reading the whole of Thoreau's journals to entertain any idea of the sheer volume of his observations.

3. In organizing the material for this chapter, I have in some ways mirrored approaches undertaken by Thoreau himself. Working with the whole of the journals, I have abstracted his nature observations and organized them according to geographic location, particular habitat, species classifications, time of year, and so forth. The result was a series of phenological tables describing the typical behaviors of nature in the various Concord habitats as Thoreau found them. This material is far too voluminous to recreate in these pages, or even to reference. The pages of this chapter are a narrative presentation of the essence of this material; the reference notes reflect major (but not all) sources in the journals where information was derived.

4. Richardson, *Concord River.*
5. Thoreau, *J* 4:238; Marie Morisawa, *Streams: Their Dynamics and Morphology* (New York: McGraw-Hill, 1968).
6. Morisawa, *Streams,* pp. 1–7; Thoreau, *J* 12:221.
7. Richardson, *Concord River;* Moss, ed., *Catalog of Thoreau's Surveys,* pp. 10–11; State of Massachusetts, *House Document 1* (1862), p. 216.
8. Garrelick, *Clothier of the Assabet,* pp. 1–18; Richardson, *Concord River.*
9. Thoreau, *J* 12:238.
10. Ibid. 7:315.
11. Ibid. 9:165–67; *J*(P) 4:373.
12. Thoreau, *J* 6:68; 7:216, 224; 8:368; 11:441; 13:133.
13. Ibid. 13:58–59; *J*(P) 4:206.
14. Thoreau, *J* 5:46–47, 491; 7:156, 202; *J*(P) 3:183.
15. Thoreau, *J* 5:82; 6:181; 7:190–91.
16. Ibid. 9:212; 12:41.
17. Ibid. 11:433.
18. Thoreau, *J*(P) 3:188, 197.
19. Ibid. 3:199; *J* 6:345.
20. Thoreau, *J* 7:223.
21. Ibid. 7:211, 221, 241, 253.
22. Ibid. 6:183, 257; 12:132.
23. Ibid. 12:135, 228; *J*(P) 3:198.
24. Thoreau, *J* 8:171.
25. Ibid. 12:139.
26. Ibid. 5:101; 7:262, 272; 8:232; 9:276, 278, 303, 306; 10:259; 11:418; 12:45; *J*(P) 3:208.
27. Thoreau, *J* 5:8.
28. Ibid. 7:263; 8:56; 9:281; 11:407; 12:78; 3:175, 179, 376.
29. Ibid. 5:65; 9:287; 10:334; 12:94, 101, 147; 13:164, 214; *J*(P) 4:461.
30. Thoreau, *J*(P) 4:398; *J* 7:299; 10:320, 335.
31. Thoreau, *J* 5:59; 6:187; 7:271, 315–16; 9:456; 13:207.
32. Ibid. 8:304.
33. Ibid. 6:233; 7:130, 159, 248, 286, 296; 8:248, 256–57, 259, 283, 297; 9:265; 11:69, 422, 431, 456; 12:53; 13:53, 161, 181; *J*(P) 4:364, 410, 477.
34. Thoreau, *J*(P) 3:196–97; 4:365–66, 391; *J* 5:62, 79, 102; 6:141; 7:189, 229, 330; 13:107, 133.
35. Thoreau, *J*(P) 4:349, 420, 456, 459, 469, 476, 481–82, 484; *J* 4:6.
36. Thoreau, *J* 5:27; 6:153; 9:463.
37. Ibid. 8:180; 9:20; 12:138, 260.
38. Ibid. 6:197; 9:334; 12:33; James H. Emerton, *Common Spiders of the United States* (New York: Dover, 1961), pp. 91–106.
39. Thoreau, *J*(P) 4:429; *J* 3:483; 6:187.
40. Thoreau, *J*(P) 3:316–17; *J* 4:78; 5:46; 13:274.

41. Thoreau, *J*(P) 4:491; *J* 7:311; 8:273; 10:373; 12:133.

42. Thoreau, *J*(P) 3:264; *J* 4:234; 10:319; 13:245.

43. Thoreau, *J* 6:390; 7:342, 421; 10:395; 13:291. References to grackles and blackbirds are especially confusing in the journal, as present nomenclature seems almost the opposite of that used by Thoreau. Essential to discerning this and all other mysteries of Thoreau's bird identifications was Edward Howe Forbush, *Birds of Massachusetts and Other New England States,* 2 vols. (Boston: Massachusetts Department of Agriculture, 1925), which listed the Linnaen identifications, the current English names, and all names previously applied to each bird.

44. Thoreau, *J* 5:514, 6:174, 181; 7:256; 8:303; 12:53, 54, 57; *J*(P) 3:187–88.

45. Thoreau, *J*(P) 3:66; *J* 5:123, 152; 6:307; 7:295; 9:5; 13:296.

46. Thoreau, *J*(P) 3:240–41.

47. Ibid. 3:281; *J* 5:147; 13:278, 401.

48. Thoreau, *J*(P) 3:55.

49. Thorerau, *J* 6:318, 345, 406; 7:345; 8:214; 10:408; 12:274; 13:277.

50. Thoreau, *J* 12:108.

51. Ibid. 6:192; 7:282; 8:294, 309–10; 10:363.

52. Ibid. 8:399; 9:183, 10:195; *J*(P) 3:81.

53. Thoreau, *J* 7:458; 8:431.

54. Ibid. *J* 4:24; 10:374; *J*(P) 4:397.

55. Thoreau, *J*(P) 4:491, 494–95; *J* 4:17; 5:36; 9:313, 393, 10:346–48, 355, 360, 391.

56. Thoreau, *J* 6:219; 8:268; 10:382.

57. Thoreau, *J* 8:249, 260.

58. Ibid. 6:189, 190, 214, 215; 7:308–9; 10:397; 11:117, 118, 131; *J*(P) 4:445.

59. Thoreau, *J* 4:193; 5:76, 99, 202, 307; 10:390; 12:127; 13:243.

60. Ibid. 4:214; 5:132; 6:373; 10:484; 12:202, 232.

61. Ibid. 4:165; 5:325; 6:355; 10:486; 13:323.

62. Ibid. 10:314.

63. Thoreau, *J*(P) 3:249; *A Week,* pp. 33–34, 88–89.

64. Thoreau, *J* 9:327.

65. Ibid. 10:378, 399, 406, 407, 417; Storer, *Fishes of Massachusetts,* pp. 548–52; Elsie B. Klots, *Freshwater Life* (New York: Putnam's, 1966), pp. 285–88.

66. Thoreau, *J* 7:170; 8:327, 328, 96; 10:114.

67. Ibid. 4:23; 8:303.

68. Ibid. 5:30.

69. Ibid. 4:78, 104–5, 223; 5:313; 6:260, 283; 8:285, 308, 353; 9:349, 354; 10:415, 482, 485; *J*(P) 3:228.

70. Thoreau, *J* 5:106; 8:424; 10:388; 13:335.

71. Thoreau, *J*(P) 3:261–62

72. Thoreau, *J* 5:222, 285; 7:318; 8:413, 424; 10:397, 401.

73. Ibid. 9:342.

74. Ibid. 4:396; 11:142; 12:114; *J*(P) 4:135.

75. Thoreau, *J* 5:209; 8:402; 10:416.

76. Thoreau, *J*(P) 3:304; 4:73, 85; *J* 4:237; 11:148.
77. Thoreau, *J* 4:229; 5:133, 136, 137, 282; 9:413; 10:503, 507.
78. Ibid. 4:35, 93; 5:162; 6:228, 240, 295, 384; 8:324, 330, 333, 404; 10:432.
79. Ibid. 4:72; 5:209–15, 268; 8:360.
80. Ibid. 5:132; 7:10, 58; 8:5; 9:383; 13:332; *J*(P) 4:16.
81. Thoreau, *J* 8:433.
82. Ibid. 5:66; 7:327, 408; 10:326; 12:106, 174, 183, 196.
83. Ibid. 4:79, 111, 313, 341; 5:277, 321; 10:485; *J*(P) 3:260.
84. Thoreau, *J* 6:324.
85. Ibid. 5:219, 232, 312, 338; 8:324; 9:404; 11:233.
86. Ibid. 4:83; 5:296; 6:286; 8:316, 373, 441; 9:407; 12:190; 13:194, 321, 325, 327, 360.
87. Thoreau, *J*(P) 3:281, 309; 4:26; *J* 4:182–83, 233; 6:398.
88. Thoreau, *J* 4:168, 300; 6:391; 8:431; 10:6; 12:205, 231.
89. Ibid. 4:148.
90. Ibid. 5:283; 9:403.
91. Thoreau, *J*(P) 4:149.
92. Ibid. 4:56.
93. Thoreau, *J* 4:422.
94. Ibid. 5:259; 12:57.
95. Ibid. 6:169, 180, 203; 8:348; 9:358, 474; *J*(P) 4:439.
96. Thoreau, *J* 5:85; 8:275; 14:251.
97. Ibid. 8:288.
98. Ibid. 7:407.
99. Ibid. 12:209.
100. Ibid. 6:472, 488; 7:492; 8:440.
101. Ibid. 5:478; 6:464, 471, 479–80; Latimer and Lanphear, *Soil Survey of Middlesex County.*
102. Thoreau, *J*(P) 4:472; *J* 8:4; 11:113; 12:286, 288.
103. Thoreau, *J* 8:338; John L. Behler, *Audubon Society Field Guide to North American Reptiles and Amphibians* (New York: Alfred A. Knopf, 1979), pp. 468–69.
104. Thoreau, *J* 6:270, 276, 368; 7:66.
105. Ibid. 4:222; 6:271, 349, 388; 7:451; 8:399; 10:340; 11:80–81.
106. Ibid. 5:122; 6:249, 397; 7:268, 393; 8:407; 10:329, 380; *J*(P) 4:431.
107. Thoreau, *J* 5:250; 6:330; 7:357, 425–28; 8:374.
108. Ibid. 6:341; 10:500; 13:345; 14:296.
109. Ibid. 10:489, 507; *J*(P) 4:466.
110. Thoreau, *J* 7:452, 455, 485; 8:350; 12:282.
111. Ibid. 6:358; 7:29, 43, 454.
112. Ibid. 4:243; 6:406; 12:229.
113. Ibid. 10:495.
114. Ibid. 9:13, 18, 19, 22.

115. Ibid. 9:19.

116. Ibid. 4:294; 14:64; *J*(P) 3:313.

117. Thoreau, *J*(P) 4:9; *J* 4:188, 202, 246, 276; 5:318, 353, 362; 6:415, 420, 464; 7:452; 8:406, 426, 438; 9:17, 90, 94; 11:75, 120; 12:249; 14:5. It is surprising that agricultural historians have not explored Thoreau's journals more thoroughly, as he regularly recorded the activities of his farming neighbors, thus conveying an excellent picture of the cycle of the farmer's year. He was also quite often very detailed in his descriptions of farming activity.

118. Thoreau, *J* 5:339; 6:422; 8:443; 12:265.

119. Ibid. 8:434; 12:278.

120. Ibid. 5:354.

121. Ibid. 10:444; 11:151.

122. Ibid. 6:378, 424, 449.

123. Ibid. 9:95.

124. Thoreau, *J*(P) 4:32, 191; *J* 4:329.

125. Thoreau, *J* 8:173, 367, 368.

126. Ibid. 5:388, 402; 6:421, 485; 9:3, 5, 13; 11:96, 117, 125, 152; 14:73.

127. Ibid. 4:129, 141, 246, 296; 5:367; 6:432; 9:14, 91, 104, 461; 10:9; 11:95, 138; *J*(P) 3:288, 359; 4:55.

128. Thoreau, *J*(P) 3:115, 372; *J* 4:182; 7:54, 71; 12:294, 302.

129. Thoreau, *J* 6:439, 466, 485, 490; 7:7.

130. Ibid. 7:54.

131. Ibid. 7:24; *J*(P) 3:120; 4:70, 85, 99.

132. Thoreau, *J*(P) 4:124; *J* 4:364; 7:456, 487; 11:190, 223.

133. Thoreau, *J*(P) 4:58, 73, 91; *J* 4:354, 363, 367; 5:373; 10:59, 71; 11:198; 12:360.

134. Thoreau, *J*(P) 3:120; 4:85, 104, 141, 143; *J* 4:389; 5:450; 7:517.

135. Thoreau, *J*(P) 4:86, 121, 198; *J* 4:352, 360, 393; 9:115; 10:48, 127; 11:215; 12:202, 446.

136. Thoreau, *J* 4:430; 8:22; 10:169, 216; 11:243, 319.

137. Ibid. 5:376; 6:461; 7:55, 68, 113, 463; 10:126; 11:252.

138. Ibid. 4:378, 389, 413; 5:479, 499; 6:5, 67; 7:26, 54, 70, 72, 454, 488; 8:20; 11:155, 213, 293, 329; 12:391; *J*(P) 3:151; 4:86, 129, 147.

139. Thoreau, *J* 4:378, 399; 5:495; 8:13, 21; 9:114, 129.

140. Ibid. 13:254.

141. Ibid. 4:386, 405; 5:486; 10:123, 189; 11:272, 279, 297, 308; *J*(P) 3:131–32, 137, 170; 4:100, 190, 175–76.

142. Thoreau, *J* 4:408; 5:510; 8:3.

143. Ibid. 4:269; 5:39, 512; 7:72.

144. Ibid. 5:465; 8:13; 11:58; *J*(P) 4:159; Emerton, *Common Spiders,* 148–53.

145. Thoreau, *J* 7:83; 13:122.

146. Ibid. 5:463; 8:102, 155; 13:32, 67.

147. Ibid. 6:37, 144; 7:98, 141; 9:219; *J*(P) 4:361–62.

148. Thoreau, *J* 9:223–24.

149. Thoreau, *J* 6:20; 7:231, 246, 262; 9:223–24; 10:270; 13:98. For an excellent

discussion of winter ecology, see Peter J. Marchand, *Life in the Cold: An Introduction to Winter Ecology,* 2d ed. (Hanover: University Press of New England, 1991).

150. Thoreau, *J* 7:187–89, 197–99, 239–41, 246; 13:325.

151. Thoreau, *J* 8:291; 13:325.

152. Ibid. 6:50; 14:265; *J*(P) 4:356.

153. Thoreau, *J*(P) 4:218.

154. Thoreau, *J* 7:239.

155. Ibid. 4:474; 5:71, 353; 8:183; 9:162, 247; *J*(P) 4:379.

156. Thoreau, *J* 4:420; 6:270; 7:270; 8:22, 27, 36.

157. Ibid. 6:97–98; 7:174; 9:228; 10:129, 220; 11:387, 408; 13:123

158. Ibid. 4:5, 30, 31; 5:85; 6:14; 7:457, 521–25; 11:373; 13:421, 422.

159. Ibid. 13:66; *J*(P) 3:168. Contrast this observation to the poem Thoreau recorded in his journal on February 25, 1839:

The Shrike

Hark-hark-from out the thickest fog
Warbles with might and main
The fearless shrike, as all agog
To find in fog his gain.

His steady sails he never furls
At any time o' year,
And perched now on winter's curls,
He whistles in his ear.

160. Thoreau, *J*(P) 4:485.

CHAPTER 6: INVESTIGATING NATURE

1. Thoreau, *J* 9:209–10; 10:198; 11:282; 12:371; 13:174.

2. Ibid. 11:285. See also 10:188. Thomas Blanding intends to thoroughly explore this mystical side of Thoreau in his forthcoming work. Personal communication, Concord, Mass., 1989.

3. Thoreau, *J* 8:120–21.

4. Thoreau, "Cape Cod"; Borst, *Thoreau Log,* pp. 338–508.

5. Thoreau, *J* 7:417.

6. Ibid. 8:217; 11:435; Harding, *Days of Henry Thoreau,* pp. 408–9.

7. McAleer, *Emerson,* pp. 348–51; Thoreau, *J* 7:416.

8. Thoreau, *J* 7:519.

9. Accounts of each journey are scattered through Thoreau's journals. For exact dates of each trip, see Borst, *Thoreau Log.*

10. Thoreau, *J* 7:10, 8:134; 9:306.

11. Borst, *Thoreau Log,* 338, 340; Harding, *Days of Henry Thoreau,* 342–43; Thoreau, *J* 7:197; 11:324–25.

12. Thoreau, *J* 9:121, 11:331.

13. Ibid. 5:516; 9:191; Joseph Slater, "Caroline Dall in Concord," *Thoreau Society Bulletin* 62 (Winter 1958):1.

14. Thoreau, "Autumnal Tints," *Natural History Essays,* pp. 137–77.

15. Thoreau, *J*(P) 3:143; *J* 7:520; 8:7; 10:136–37.

16. Thoreau, "Wild Apples," *Natural History Essays,* pp. 178–210.

17. Thoreau, *J* 9:174; 13:38.

18. Ibid. 13:279. See also 9:33.

19. Ibid. 9:406–7. For a discussion of this point, see Robert D. Richardson's Introduction to Henry Thoreau, *Faith in a Seed: The Dispersion of Seeds and Other Late Natural History Writings,* ed. Bradley P. Dean (Washington, D.C.: Island Press, 1993), pp. 10–11.

20. Thoreau, *J* 8:241; 9:82; 10:97, 127, 403–4; 11:296.

21. Ibid. 7:28, 50, 112–13; 12:23.

22. Ibid. 7:53; 9:45; 10:69; 13:154.

23. Ibid. 8:330; 12:367.

24. Thoreau, *J*(P) 3:229; *J* 8:341.

25. Thoreau, *J*(P) 4:407; *J* 4:405.

26. Thoreau, *J* 7:510.

27. Ibid. *J* 8:448; 12:340–41.

28. Ibid. 10:80; 11:191, 199.

29. Ibid. 9:210; 10:288; 11:299; 12:447; 13:232; 14:141, 265; Kathryn Whitford, "Thoreau and the Woodlots of Concord," *New England Quarterly* 23 (September 1950):291–306; Gordon G. Whitney and William C. Davis, "Thoreau and the Forest History of Concord, Massachusetts," *Journal of Forest History* (April 1986):70–81.

30. Thoreau, *J* 7:132, 200–201; 8:150, 220–21. William Cronon makes excellent use of these observations in the Introduction to *Changes in the Land.*

31. Thoreau, *J* 6:333; 7:514; 10:51; 12:170.

32. Ibid. 4:11; 5:245; 12:121; Thoreau, *Walden,* p. 194.

33. Thoreau, *J*(P) 4:276, 441; *J* 4:87; 12:152, 387; 14:228, 305; *Maine Woods;* John Evelyn, *Sylva, or a Discourse of Forest Trees* (London: Jo. Martyn and Ja. Allestry, 1679); *Terra: A Philosophical Discourse of the Earth* (York: J. Dodsley, 1778).

34. Thoreau, *J*(P) 3:275, 295; *J* 4:176; 5:330; 6:116.

35. Thoreau, *J*(P) 3:146; 4:434; *J* 5:9, 442, 443.

36. Thoreau, *J* 8:81, 166, 198.

37. Ibid. 5:338–39; 8:180–81; *J*(P) 4:32.

38. Thoreau, *J*(P) 4:6; *J* 5:329; 7:318.

39. Thoreau, *J*(P) 4:6.

40. Thoreau, *J* 8:315–16, 329, 335.

41. Ibid. 9:373–74; 11:108, 248, 347.

42. Ibid. 8:411; 9:92; 10:39, 158, 178–80, 448, 510; 12:160.

43. Ibid. 10:40.

44. Ibid. 12:231–32.

45. Ibid. 8:38–195, 207–26; 10:338–88; 11:189–360; 12:3–196, 216–89, 400–457; 13:3–15, 71–236.

46. A listing of the scattered locations of the unpublished phenological tables and accompanying notes may be found in William L. Howarth, *The Literary Manuscripts of Henry David Thoreau* (Columbus: Ohio State University Press, 1974), pp. 306–22. The calendar is discussed most thoroughly by Peck, *Thoreau's Morning Work* (see n.63, chapter 4). See also Richardson, *Henry Thoreau,* pp. 379–83, and Leo Stoller, "A Note on Thoreau's Place in the History of Phenology," *Isis* 47 (June 1956):172–81. A portion of one of the tables is reproduced in Thoreau, *Faith in a Seed,* p. 222.

47. Charles Darwin, *On the Origin of Species* (London: John Murray, Albemarle Street, 1859); Harding *Days of Henry Thoreau,* p. 429; Sattelmeyer, *Thoreau's Reading,* pp. 89–90; Thoreau, "Natural History Commonplace Book," Berg Collection, New York Public Library.

48. Darwin, *Origin of Species.* For a discussion of the ecological impact of Darwin's ideas, see Worster, *Nature's Economy,* 113–87.

49. Robert Chambers, *Vestiges of the Natural History of Creation* (London: John Churchill, Princes Street, Soho, 1844; reprint New York: Humanities Press, 1969). Gavin de Beer's Introduction to the reprint edition discusses Erasmus Darwin's ideas concerning evolution. Chambers was not revealed as the author of *Vestiges* until 1884, when he was safely dead. Asa Gray's comments appeared in "Explanations of the Vestiges," *North American Review* 62 (April 1846).

50. Darwin, *Origin of Species,* pp. 100, 365.

51. Ibid., pp. 74–75.

52. Ibid., p. 2.

53. Ibid., p. 407.

54. Lurie, *Louis Agassiz;* Thoreau, *J* 9:298–99.

55. Lurie, *Louis Agassiz,* pp. 83, 87, 151–52; Berbick, *Thoreau's Alternative History,* p. 126.

56. Bradley P. Dean, "Henry D. Thoreau and Horace Greeley Exchange Letters on the Spontaneous Generation of Plants," *New England Quarterly* 66 (December 1993):630–38.

57. Thoreau, *J* 14:333; see also 14:311.

58. Emerson, *Journals* 9:270.

59. Thoreau, *J* 13:114, 191, 364–67.

60. Thoreau, "The Succession of Forest Trees," *Natural History Essays,* pp. 72–92; quotation, p. 86. Harding, *Days of Henry Thoreau,* 439–40. Lawrence Buell contends that Thoreau's interest in conservation was in no way imperative. See Buell, "Thoreau and the natural environment," *Cambridge Companion to Thoreau,* pp. 186–87.

61. Thoreau, *J* 14:101–292.

62. Ibid. 14:158–60.

63. Ibid. 14:203–5, 232–33.
64. Ibid. 14:207–8.
65. Ibid. 14:124–27, 290.
66. Ibid. 14:243. See also 14:130–31.
67. Ibid. 14:146.
68. Darwin, *Origin of Species;* Richardson, *Henry Thoreau,* pp. 383–84.
69. "A Thoreau Chronology," in Thoreau, *Faith in a Seed,* pp. 214–15; Thoreau, "The Dispersion of Seeds," "Wild Fruits," *Faith in a Seed,* pp. 23–203. The preponderance of "Wild Fruits" remains unpublished, the majority of the manuscript resting in the Berg Collection, New York Public Library. The most extensive portion, intended by Thoreau to be delivered as a public lecture, was extracted, edited, and published by Leo Stoller as "Huckleberries," *Natural History Essays,* pp. 211–62. Robert Milder refers to this project as "the encyclopedic, uncompleted, and probably uncompletable 'Dispersion of Seeds.'" Milder, *Reimagining Thoreau,* p. 182.
70. Thoreau, "Dispersion of Seeds"; "Wild Fruits."
71. Thoreau, *J* 14:196.
72. Ibid. 14:287–92.
73. Edmund A. Schofield, "The Origin of Thoreau's Fatal Illness," *Thoreau Society Bulletin* (Spring 1985):171; Harding, *Days of Henry Thoreau,* pp. 491–92.
74. Thoreau, *Faith in a Seed; J* 14:297–302, 323, 326. Thoreau incorporated most of the observations on seed dispersion previously referenced in this chapter into his final text.
75. Walter Harding, *Thoreau's Minnesota Journey* (Geneseo, N.Y.: 1962); Thoreau, *J* 14:342–46.
76. Thoreau, "Dispersion of Seeds"; "Wild Fruits"; Richardson, "Introduction," *Faith in a Seed,* p. 3.
77. Thoreau, *Correspondence,* pp. 641, 643; Harding, *Days of Henry Thoreau,* pp. 457–59. "Walking" appeared in the *Atlantic Monthly* in June 1862; "Autumnal Tints" in October; "Wild Apples" in November, and "Life Without Principle" the following October.
78. Harding, *Days of Henry Thoreau,* pp. 459–68; Borst, *Thoreau Log,* pp. 600–606.
79. See, for example, Odell Shepard's Introduction to *The Heart of Thoreau's Journals* (Boston: Houghton Mifflin, 1927).
80. Emerson, "Thoreau," *Atlantic Monthly,* p. 249. Ellery Channing quoted in Franklin B. Sanborn, *The Personality of Thoreau* (Boston: Goodspeed, 1901), p. 66.
81. Howarth, *Book of Concord,* pp. 3–11; Walter Harding and Michael Meyer, *The New Thoreau Handbook* (New York: New York University Press, 1980), pp. 75–76; Fritz Oehlschlager and George Hendrick, *Toward the Making of Thoreau's Modern Reputation* (Urbana: University of Illinois Press, 1979); Bradley P. Dean, "Afterword," *Faith in a Seed,* 271–72. All due thanks to Mr. Dean, whose accomplishment in

bringing "The Dispersion of Seeds" to print has restored some much-needed poetry to the literature of science. The publication has also, incidentally, made the task of writing this chapter far less onerous and more enjoyable. There is perhaps no challenge quite so intimidating as attempting to decipher Thoreau's handwriting (with original corrections in pencil, of course) from microfilm copies.

CHAPTER 7: A VISION OF NATURE

1. Thoreau, *J*(P) 3:186.
2. Thoreau, *J* 8:109–10; 9:20; 12:24; Worster, *Nature's Economy.*

Index

ROBERT KUHN McGREGOR, an easterner by birth and inclination, is an associate professor of history at the University of Illinois at Springfield, where he teaches early American and environmental history. His interest in Thoreau's view of nature emanated from research for an article entitled "Deriving a Biocentric History," which appeared in the *Environmental Review* (Summer 1988).